ROUGH DIAMOND

First Published in Great Britain in 2023 by
LOVE AFRICA PRESS
103 Reaver House, 12 East Street, Epsom KT17 1HX
www.loveafricapress.com

Available as eBook and paperback

YADILI SERIES

<u>Duke: Prince of Hearts</u>
<u>Xandra: Killer of Kings</u>
<u>Osagie: Bad Santa</u>
<u>Rough Diamond</u>
<u>Tough Alliance</u>

DEDICATION

To Oluwakemi, Queenie and Ngozi, for riding this creative roller-coaster with me. Ladies, you rock!

AUTHOR'S NOTE

Rough Diamond is a second chance, dark, romantic suspense presented in two parts. Part One: The Origin is set a decade before Part Two: Deal & Close, which is set in the present. This is a complete story with a happy ever after.

I hope you enjoy Mason's and Sophie's journey as much as I loved writing it.

ROUGH DIAMOND

THE ORIGIN

This is the becoming of an antihero and his undoing.
Before Mason became the Yadili fixer and acquired the Mace nickname, he learned to navigate loss, grief, and treachery. Then he meets Sophie and briefly experiences respite with a woman who matches his wildness. But can he hang on to her?

ONE

Ten years ago

A week after his father was buried, Mason Maduka was on the hunt for pussy.

Not the animal.

But the part of the female anatomy designed to take a pounding.

Because it was what he needed. Rough, rugged, bed-quaking sex to make him forget, if only for a little while, that he'd buried his most favourite person in the world seven goddamned days ago.

Hence he sat on a leather couch in this dimly lit lounge while thumping Afrobeat music rattled the graffiti-covered walls and water-stained ceiling.

Women in little more than lingerie lined up in front of him. They varied in size—slender and plump, short and tall, young and not-so-young.

Prostitutes, one and all.

Or sex workers, as they were termed these days.

He liked the newer phrase. An apt label—clear and concise. No danger of mistaking it for something else.

No way to mistake what these ladies of the night were offering. They fluttered lashes coquettishly, plumped up boobs, jiggled arses, and pouted their lips, all vying for his attention.

They were preaching to the converted.

Mason hadn't experienced sexual pleasure since receiving news of his father's death six months ago. So, he was raring to go. Excitement flushed his skin, and he darted out his tongue, licking his lips.

The atmosphere of danger and dingy darkness spiked his heart rate and sent blood rushing to his dick. The prospect of trouble thrilled him as much as the nearly naked women did. He'd driven over an hour to the city slum for these exact reasons—peril and pussy.

He could get pussy closer to home, but tonight he needed extra, some recklessness to tip him over the brink.

These women were up for anything. Would accept anything for a monetary price.

This suited him perfectly because all sex was transactional. The people who didn't demand cash for sex still taxed their partners in other ways, mainly in the form of relationships. Relationships sucked time and energy, which amounted to money. So, every sexual encounter had a financial implication. He would rather pay it up front and walk away at the end.

He'd fucked a few of his neighbourhood girls. Nevertheless, navigating the respectability involved in courting middle-class brats whose parents would show up at his doorstep because he stole their daughter's cherry and broke her heart was a nightmare. Or worse, the ones who wanted to snap photos together and post them online, claiming they were in a relationship with him. Never mind that he could never fully express his deviant desires with those local women. In other words, messing with them proved unfulfilling.

So, it had been revelatory when for his eighteenth birthday, his older brother Rocha gifted him a Runs Girl, a woman willing to get with him purely for the financial rewards. A terrific alternative. From then on, his sexual interactions changed, and he always negotiated the fee upfront before he fucked anyone.

Hence his ease around hookers. He loved the transactional nature of the encounters because they were clear and concise. Requirements laid out, there lay no room for misunderstandings. Satisfaction for the control freak in him.

So, yes, he was in his element, right here and now.

A deep inhalation drew stale air, cigarette smoke, and weed aroma into his nostrils. He could light up, too, but he didn't like being stoned. He hated having his senses dulled or being out of control. He wanted to feel everything, pain and pleasure.

Otherwise, what was the point?

Indeed, why was he procrastinating, delaying his selection? Any one of these women should do the job. Then again, he had specific requirements.

He eyed the woman with locs and nipple rings showing through her white crop top. A tattoo snaked down her belly, disappearing into her black lace knickers. It would have been excruciatingly uncomfortable when it was inked. Anyone who purposely punctured their genitalia region with needles would like pain, undoubtedly, which suited his needs.

"Her. Tattoo girl." He indicated with his index finger. She was heavily made-up, which wasn't his cup of tea. But he didn't care as long as the rest of her assets were functional.

The beefy man standing in the shadows nodded at the woman who sauntered over. The rest disappeared into the corridor, barely masking their disappointments.

Mason patted the cushion beside him.

With a smile, Tattoo Girl lowered her slender body on the sofa and placed a hand on his lap. "You want to go to the room?"

He grabbed her wrist and twisted her arm. Not enough to injure her but hurting sufficiently to cause discomfort.

Her face twisted in a grimace as she gasped. She slipped off the sofa and landed on her knees to relieve the pressure. She looked up, pupils dilated, mouth slackened.

Oh, she enjoyed pain. The sadist in him cheered, and his dick hardened.

"What's your name?" he asked in a firm tone, not releasing her arm, keeping her on her knees.

"Jet, sir," she replied, puffing out a heavy breath.

A sizzle went down his spine, the sensation weird and yet pleasing.

He would be twenty-six years old in a few months, and she should be in her late thirties, if not forties. So, her addressing him as 'sir' should make him feel old.

Instead, it gave him a hard-on.

In a country where old age was exalted over youth and old people without wisdom or maturity frequently cruelly lorded over the young, this was his way of flipping the tables.

To have someone who would otherwise demand to be addressed with reverence on her knees about to service him?

Yes! He felt powerful. Respected.

"Respect is earned by action alone," his late father's words played in his mind.

Without thought, his hand clenched tightly around the woman's arm, and her breath hitched. He loosened his grip and leaned back in the leather seat. His father's words, while helpful, were not suitable for this moment. He shoved it aside and focused on the reason he was there.

"Jet," he said. "I ask the questions. If I need you to do anything, I'll tell you. Understood?"

"Yes, sir." She nodded but didn't move from the floor.

He gestured for the man in the shadows to draw the wooden partition, secluding their section. He didn't want to go to a room since there was a high likelihood of a camera being set up there. Not that he had a problem exhibiting himself. But he would rather it wasn't recorded without his permission.

Then again, there was his family's reputation to consider if the photos went public. He'd travelled this distance to an environment outside his circles and family's influence, partially for anonymity.

"Think about your family," his mother's words played in his mind.

What the fuck? Now, he needed to remember something his brother said, and he would require a stint in a psychiatric hospital.

He was seriously screwed up if he couldn't concentrate on the woman and get lost in pussy like he intended.

"Strip off your clothes and suck my dick," he said in a growly voice.

The woman's mouth and naked body should distract him from his unwelcome thoughts.

She shuffled forward, pulling her top off and exposing her breasts. Then she shoved her panties and manoeuvred to pull them from her legs.

He widened his legs, undoing his belt buckle. Then he leaned forward, pulled the string of flavoured condom packs from his back pocket, and placed them beside him.

Next, he reached into his boxer briefs, tugged his semi out, and pumped it a few times until it filled out and hardened before rolling a condom on.

She watched him, licking her lips as if she couldn't wait to taste his erection.

He grabbed her head roughly and shoved it down onto his dick. She choked as the breath left her lungs, and he pulled her up and repeated the action until she got used to the rhythm he wanted. Then, he loosened his grip and allowed her to do her job.

He reached down and tugged at her nipple rings repeatedly, causing her to moan and writhe each time. The blowjob was okay, but she enjoyed it more than he did. Minutes ticked by, and he couldn't reach release or shake the lingering grief constricting his chest.

On the verge of deflating, he pulled out of her mouth and flipped her onto her stomach. Hand on her nape, he shoved her face to the carpet. Then he lined up his dick and slammed into her. Gripping her neck tightly and roughly, he rammed into her repeatedly, his belt buckle digging into her skin with each slam.

She didn't complain, loving the pain. Instead, her moans filled the space, and her body soon quaked with multiple orgasms.

Still, no luck for him, release proving elusive.

Frustrated, he pulled out and sank heavily into the sofa.

"Make I finish am." She reached for him.

"Don't touch me," he growled, smacking her hand away and standing instead.

He rolled the condom off, wiped himself with some tissues and stuffed his partially erect dick away, tidying himself up.

He pulled an envelope out of his wallet. Although he'd already paid upfront before he made his selection, there was no reason he shouldn't tip the woman. She'd done her job. The problem was in his head.

"For you." He dropped the cash on the sofa and headed towards the exit.

"Thank you," she called out behind him.

He didn't turn, ignoring her as he entered the dark corridor with oily blue walls lit by fluorescent bulbs. A man stood by the door, smoking weed. One of the gangsters who ran the brothel. He'd been in that exact position when Mason went in about an hour ago. He nodded at Mason as he exited the dingy building.

"Ashawo, give me my money!"

Mason heard the racket as soon as he stepped outside, away from the thumping music.

The sense of danger returned, sending a thrill through him. Like the flick of a switch, his pulse rate accelerated, and adrenaline rushed through him.

He'd witnessed street fights before and had never butted in. If someone was going to pick a fight, they better be ready to defend themselves or take what was coming to them.

It had been a week since his dead father was buried, and he was hurting. Hurting to unleash the ball of rage in his gut. Hurting to be used as a punching bag. Hurting to inflict pain and to receive enough physical pain to mask the emotional ones. He'd attempted sex, but it hadn't worked. He was still a keg of dynamite waiting to explode.

Why had his father gone so soon? His old man had been diagnosed with bowel cancer, and within a month, he was dead. Mason had been away at Law School. His family hadn't informed him until it was too late. He hadn't had time to say goodbye. To tell his father he loved him. To listen to the man tell him stories of his youthful exploits one last time.

The second of two sons, Mason had been closest to his father, his favourite person in the world, until his death. The old man had been strict but fair, a hands-on father. Sure, he'd worked long hours, but he'd shown up whenever Mason had needed him.

"Why should I give you all my money? I do the fucking work."

The defiance in the woman's angry voice roused Mason from his melancholy, and he surveyed the scene before him.

The sun had set, and the area was poorly lit with broken streetlights. Lamps were attached to the outside walls of some of the dilapidated single-storey buildings. The only multi-level structure was the one he had recently exited. The road was in such a state of disrepair the tarmac had utterly broken down, leaving jagged edges and crater-sized potholes. No demarcated pavements existed between the residences and the road, only open gutters covered with metal or concrete slabs at building entrances to provide walkways or driveways.

Several wooden stalls lit with kerosene lamps stood outside the houses, selling wares from basic groceries to cooked meals.

However, no one was purchasing anything. Instead, a crowd had gathered in the middle of the street, their attention focusing on the quarrelling couple. Enthralled and silent as if they were watching an outdoor theatre performance.

A huge, balding man in a black shirt and a pair of green trousers held a girl's throat. Petite in height, she wore a fitted black blouse stretching over her bountiful boobs and tapering at the waist. The undone buttons of her top revealed her flat stomach. White hotpants hugged her wide hips and barely concealed her ass, while smooth legs led to the white fake-leather wedge sandals on her feet. Loose, straight black braids partially obscured her face, making her appear wild as she glared at the man strangling her. But she seemed no older than Mason from this distance.

Her boldness and bravery ensnared him. Intrigued him.

For the first time in months, he forgot his loss, his grief. His despair. Instead of heading home, he stayed rooted, watching as if he'd joined the theatre audience, wondering how she would extricate herself from the situation. Taller than most in the crowd, he could see proceedings above their heads as if he were in an amphitheatre.

"Give me my fucking money!"

Mr Green Trousers smacked the girl across the face, the sharp sound of flesh against flesh unmistakable.

Mason flinched, shocked by the violent reminder. This wasn't a fictional street performance. This was reality.

It was one thing for a couple to shout at each other publicly. Quite another when it turned physical, especially when they were unevenly matched.

However, no one intervened to protect the girl. Like this was a regular occurrence. Just another piece of morbid entertainment. Just another means of escaping their miserable lives for a few minutes.

Disgust and anger rolled through him. His hands clenched and unclenched.

How could these people stand by and watch a man beat up a woman? How could they do nothing when the disparate power dynamic was so evident?

They reminded him of a similar crowd from long ago. A group who'd punished a victim by doing nothing.

Evil prevails when good people do nothing.

Not that Mason considered himself a good person. Yet, he couldn't be a bystander any longer. There was a pounding in his ears, and his throat dried out as he rushed his breaths.

Shoving men aside, he marched through the gathering, his mind set on a new purpose. He'd come to this slum for rough sex to ease his grief. Now, it seemed he would bloody his knuckles.

Adrenaline tingled through his veins as he yanked Mr Green Trousers' shoulder. "Leave her alone."

The man turned, snarling. "Small boy, waka pass. You know who I be?"

He was beefy, older, and in his forties. Eyes cold and deadly. He could beat Mason to a pulp.

However, with zero concerns, Mason felt reckless.

Desperate to feel something other than overwhelming grief, he was prepared to take a beating if it happened. Prepared to dish out some pain too. He flexed his muscles in preparation for a fight. "I don't care who you are. Just leave her the fuck alone."

"You dey mad?" The man swivelled, shoving the girl aside.

Mason didn't wait for the man to charge. Instead, he allowed six months of rage to flow through him. Taking a quick half-step backwards, he fluidly raised his left leg and landed a front kick into the man's groin.

The man grunted and grabbed his crotch, eyes bulging in unexpected pain.

Mason followed up with a jab and a hook, fists connecting with flesh and bone. The man toppled, face-planting on the road. Out cold.

The emotional constriction in Mason's chest eased. The man deserved a dose of his own medicine.

Wincing, the young woman pushed off the ground and stomped on the man's back. "Bastard!"

She turned to Mason with the most ridiculous smile he'd ever seen, blood dripping from her nose. Not exactly what he expected to see from someone being choked to death only minutes earlier.

"Thank you," she said, still smiling and wincing. "You for leave me, make I beat am, well well. I just dey prepare myself."

Surprisingly, he chuckled for the first time in months because she claimed she would've beaten up Mr Green Trousers any minute. Brave that she could find humour in her situation.

"No need to thank me. It was the only way I could get to where I was going. You guys were in my path." He spoke wryly as he stepped over the prone man and continued his journey.

The crowd seemed stunned into inaction, frozen to the spot as they gaped at the Mason. They hadn't expected him to survive the encounter. Best to keep moving.

The adrenaline in his veins ebbed, his rage de-escalating, allowing him to reason. He was far from home without friends or backup. Not that he liked an entourage, but they were sometimes necessary.

"In your path, eh. So where exactly are you going?" The girl grabbed her handbag from the ground and followed him, half laughing and half coughing.

He shrugged and continued walking but stopped when she kept shadowing him. "You should go to a hospital. You're injured."

"Hospital?" She laughed-coughed again, wiping her bloody nose with the seam of her top. "So, some quack doctor can take my hard-earned money. I don't think so. It's nothing that won't heal with time."

He could only imagine why she would have an aversion to medical doctors. Perhaps the ones in the slums were no good. He had news for her—some of the medics in the posh areas were bad too.

"Go home and rest, then," he said instead. She must be exhausted and in pain.

"Home? Are you kidding me? The place I stayed belongs to Bomba over there. Can you imagine what he will do to me when he wakes up? No. I'm not staying to find out. Everything I own is in this bag." She lifted the fake leather tote slung over her shoulder.

Confusion warred with disbelief. How could all her belongings fit in one bag? Sure, she was a hooker who lived in the slums. But she would have clothes, shoes, and personal effects, wouldn't she?

He frowned as his chest tightened. "Don't you have friends or relatives you can stay with?"

She rolled her eyes heavenwards as if the concept was ridiculous.

"You think if I had friends or family nearby, I would live with a pimp? I go find hotel. Somewhere wey cheap, sha. But not in this neighbourhood because Bomba and his friends will find me. So, I am following you. No one else around here was brave enough to stand against him. So right now, you're my security."

She flashed her pearly white teeth at him again with bravado. Yet, a longing in her tone echoed the intense ache suddenly welling inside his chest. He understood what it felt like to be isolated even when surrounded by people, a sensation hovering around him for the past six months.

"Oh." Mason rubbed his shaved chin, suppressing the unwanted emotion. He hadn't come here to play the Good Samaritan or pick up strays. Yet, he couldn't abandon her. "What's your name?"

She tilted her head to the side, and her voice softened. "People call me Sophie. And you?"

"I'm Mason. I'll get you to a hotel." He would get her somewhere safe tonight and leave her to sort herself out thereafter. Unfortunately, he lacked the emotional capacity to handle her problems. He had his own demons to wrangle.

"Then we better hurry because Bomba's boys are coming," she replied, jogging ahead.

He glanced back to find a group of men about fifty metres away, heading in his direction. Heart racing, he started running. The men gave chase, footsteps pounding on the road.

TWO

Once upon a time, Sophie Ojo considered Bomba her knight in shining armour.

Not anymore.

These days, she hated him. Kinda.

Bomba had found her sleeping on a bench under a wooden market stall. She'd been drenched and shivering from the night's downpour. She'd already been living on the streets for a few days after running away from the house where she'd worked as a maid. The madam had nearly killed her, accusing Sophie of stealing her money. She'd threatened to lock her up in police custody.

Sophie had no option but to run. But she'd left with nothing. No personal effects. No money. Just the clothes on her back and the tattered sandals on her feet.

She'd had no way of contacting her family in the village. No money to pay for the transport fare home.

Not that she'd wanted to go home in disgrace. Her mother had sent her to work for a wealthy family to earn income. Going home empty-handed with the risk of being sent to prison terrified her. Sleeping in the market stall had seemed a better option.

Then she'd woken to a harsh prodding to find Bomba standing over her. She'd been scared. But instead of shooing her away like other people who discovered her sleeping rough, he'd taken her to his digs, a studio in a compound in the slum with similar apartments and communal bathrooms. He'd fed her the first proper meal she'd eaten in about a week. He'd promised he would help her. She'd had water to bathe, and he'd gotten new clothes for her. He'd left her to sleep that night.

The next day she'd made herself useful, cleaning up his house. That night he'd taken her to a club. She'd had her first smoke of weed. Loaded with alcohol, he'd fucked her that night and claimed her virginity.

She hadn't minded. She'd been infatuated with him. He'd been nice to her. And her virginity was one more thing hanging over her head. And she would have been happy fucking Bomba and playing his woman. But things degenerated because he started passing her off to others. She resisted at first. But he said she should earn some money for them to build a life. Moreover, she already owed him since he'd given her money to send to her family.

But he said she was special. So instead of making her line up like the other girls in front of the clients, he sent her on unique errands—parties or rich men's homes. She got used to it, discovered she was good at sex, and most of her clients became regulars.

The only problem became Bomba and his greed. He kept most of her income, making her ask him for money whenever she needed it for something significant like her sister's school fees or when her mother was in the hospital. So, it seemed like he was generously giving her money when it was actually earned from her sweat.

But enough was enough.

And here she was, running away again.

Just like she'd run away from her former madam.

But this time, she was prepared. She wouldn't leave all her belongings behind. She'd started carrying all her essentials in her shoulder bag—toiletries, sex toys, change of clothes, money, documents. Bomba had never bothered to search the bag. He'd glanced into it once. She'd explained that it was so she could clean up at the clients' if necessary, and he'd accepted it. He had no reason to believe she would ever run away. She'd kept her head down and obeyed him for so long—like a starved, neglected pet whose cruel owner forgot could bite.

Well, she was biting back today.

First, she had to escape Bomba's tight grip around her throat. If he didn't choke the life out of her first. Her vision blurred. She struggled to breathe, clawing at his arm to tear it away from her neck.

"Ashawo, give me my money," he demanded, loosening his grip enough to allow her to breathe.

"Why I go give you all my money? Na me do the fucking work." She spat in his face, glaring at him.

She'd worked damned hard for that tip from a party two days ago, participating in an orgy involving several people. He'd been paid already for it, and the money he was now demanding was the tips she'd earned directly from the clients.

Anyway, she no longer had the money as she'd sent it to her family in the village.

Bomba smacked her across the face, making her head spin and struggling to catch her breath.

"Leave her alone," a deep husky voice cut through the ruckus, making her heart rate accelerate.

Not recognising the voice, she blinked several times, trying to clear her vision to see who'd spoken.

Bomba turned, warning the person to go away. But it seemed the person had a death wish and refused to walk away.

Blood rushed in her ears, and her skin tingled. No one she knew ever stood up to Bomba around here.

Bomba was violent. She'd seen him in action several times against the other prostitutes.

One minute, he shoved her aside, making her stumble on the potholed road. The next thing, Bomba groaned in pain and ended up on his arse, out cold. She stared at his prone body for a few seconds, not believing her eyes.

Then she looked up at the stranger with amazement sending adrenaline through her.

There stood her hero. Wow. He was young, definitely younger than her. Fresh-faced and in double denim with a white T underneath, he looked like those campus boys who came to the neighbourhood to party or score drugs.

But there was a confidence about him, a swagger that hinted at a dark maturity.

The man started walking away, and she followed him. It was purely a survival mechanism. Staying would have meant death or serious injuries because Bomba would be angry and take it out on her when he woke. No one had ever disrespected him in his territory. So, she would stick to her new saviour until she got as far away from here as possible.

He had to be better than the alternative.

Still, that's what she'd thought once about Bomba and look where she'd ended up. She would make her own way once she was out of here.

The boy introduced himself—Mason. She rolled it around on her tongue. First time she'd said the name.

Then Bomba's boys started chasing them

And she ran.

Mason followed her, running down the street.

They turned into another road, and suddenly the lights of a car flashed, and the lock beeped.

"Get in!" Mason ordered as he opened the door and hopped into the driver's seat.

She didn't need another prompt and ran across to the passenger side, yanking the door and diving in as Mason pressed the ignition. She slammed the door, and the car kicked to life. He accelerated just as Bomba's boys reached the car, leaving them in a cloud of dust.

"Oh my god! Oh my god!" She clutched her chest, trying to calm the rapid thumping of her heart. She leaned forward, holding her head and rocking back and forth as the adrenaline ran its course in her body.

"Put your seatbelt on," the order was calm without inflection.

She lifted her head and stared at him. He appeared so composed, almost serene. As if he hadn't just raced through the streets of the slum with her to avoid being beaten up or killed by the gang. As if he got comfort from inflicting pain on Bomba.

She was in awe of him, of his composure. Of his entire vibe. "I swear. I fear your face. Na you be Eleniyan."

"What does that mean?" He glanced at her quickly.

Even the way he spoke indicated he was not from around here, of a different class. Yet he had still bossed Bomba, taken him unawares.

"It means you're the boss of all bosses," she laughed with relief.

He turned to her, grinning, his eyes gleaming with something wickedly delicious and dark. "I like that."

Her heart skipped a beat, and heat flushed on her skin. Damn. He was handsome, and his eyes held her captive for the brief seconds they bore into her before he gave his attention back to the road. Something niggled about him like she knew him. Then again, she would never forget a face like his. Not if he'd ever been her client.

Nah. There could be a simple explanation. He could be among the many celebrities who grace social media and TV.

Her gaze trawled up his body. She might not be wealthy, but she'd learned to read a client's wealth by the cut and style of clothes they wore.

And the car aside, this young man was on the loaded end. His shoes were Italian leather loafers, not Aba-made like her sandals. He smelled of expensive cologne. The jeans were designer and not Okirika like her hot pants. He shifted in the seat and drew her gaze to the way the trouser fabric stretched tightly over his crotch, straining against the weight of his manhood.

Her heart rate spiked, and her mouth watered. What would he be like during sex?

What the hell? Why was her mind going there?

Maybe because every time she'd been alone with a man in a car, she'd either been on her way to have sex or had just had sex.

Still, she forced her mind away from her job. Mason hadn't mentioned sex, and for now, she would not broach the topic, although she expected it to come up at some point. It always did.

Her gaze tracked to his torso. His button-down shirt was undone, showing a white tee over a broad chest. The shirt sleeves were rolled up to the elbows, revealing dark-toned arms, and the gold watch on his wrist sparkled in the fading light.

She looked up at his face again. He looked like a model-slash-celebrity with his jutting jawline, sharp cheekbones, and fade cut. He was a proper fine boy. But with a dark edge.

She would fuck him. No question. Even if he didn't pay her.

Huh? What was she thinking?

Since when did she start considering fucking men for free? Sex would always be transactional. She'd learned that hard lesson by caring about Bomba, who'd only used her. She wasn't going to make that mistake again.

In fact, she needed to get out of his car, so she wouldn't be considering such stupidity.

"I think you can drop me off somewhere here," she said, waving at the roadside through the windscreen.

He glanced at her. "Do you know where you're going to stay?"

"Not yet." She shook her head. "But no need to worry. I'll find somewhere."

"Then, in that case, you're coming with me."

"Coming with you? Where are you going?"

"It's not far," he said, turning off the main road into a residential street.

"But I don't know where you're going."

"Trust me. You'll be safe there."

She had no reason to doubt him when he said to trust him. He'd saved her from Bomba and his boys without prompting. He'd been a knight in shining SUV with kickass moves. And these streets looked more affluent than the slums they'd escaped. So maybe there was no reason to worry. The worst thing he could do was ask for sex, right? And she already wanted to do him. So, a roof over her head for sex wasn't bad. Of course, it was temporary because she would eventually need to find her own way. But at least for tonight, she could stay with him.

After a few more turns into a tree-lined street, he stopped outside what looked like a detached house surrounded by a high brick fence and wrought iron gates. He beeped the car horn, and a security man appeared through the side entrance. He went back inside, and then the gates were pulled apart.

Mason drove in, parked under a carport, and killed the engine.

Hibiscus hedges and a gravel driveway led up to the two-level cream-coloured brick house.

"Is this your house?" Sophie asked before he reached for the door.

"Yes," he said and stepped out. "Come on."

"Wait." She followed him out and rushed to his side, lowering her voice. "Are you sure it's a good idea to bring me here? What about your parents?"

"How do you know I don't own this house?" he asked in a severe tone.

She laughed nervously. "Look, I might not look like much to you. But I'm good at reading people, especially when it comes to money. I can smell a spoilt rich kid from a mile, and you were oozing it tonight. Someone else is paying for you to live a finesse life. You don't own this house any more than you own me."

His demeanour changed immediately. He growled and stepped towards her.

Her breath caught, and she swallowed the lump in her throat. Why did she challenge and taunt him, considering he'd just helped her? Still, she wanted to get a rise out of him. To see what the man was made of since he hadn't spoken much in the drive over.

"Do you think you know me? Because I saved you? Do you think I'm a Good Samaritan?" His voice was a baritone edged with steel that pulled at something deep inside Sophie, something dark and wickedly delicious.

"You know shit about me. You don't know if I own this house," he gritted out, his demanding gaze sweeping over her tight shirt and skimpy hotpants. The muscles in his neck tensed, and he moved closer. "You don't know where you are or what I can do to you."

"What?" She gasped, stumbling until her back hit the vehicle, and she had nowhere else to run. He was right. She had no clue what part of town they were in, although it looked like the GRA or one of the affluent estates. Maybe coming here had been a terrible idea.

His dark eyes glinted dangerously as he placed his palms flat on the car's roof, caging her in.

"Didn't your mother warn you not to enter the cars of strangers?" he purred in her ear, his breath feathering her skin, sending tingles through her.

She swallowed as her whole body melted under his heated scrutiny.

"I—" she swallowed again and shook her head. This had to be a first for her, lost for words. No man had ever taken her breath and speech in this manner before.

Her pulse raced, and her clit throbbed, her body primed. If they had any kind of physical contact, she would combust from the sexual energy coiling inside her.

She definitely wanted to fuck him.

Before she could do anything about it, he stepped away. "You are free to go. The gateman will let you out. But if you stay, if you step into my house, I own you for however long I wish to keep you. Leave or stay. It's your choice."

He swivelled and headed towards the house.

Shit. Was he serious? She glanced at the gate keeper who stood by the entrance and back at Mason, who didn't pause until he reached the portico.

"Aboki, open the foot gate. My guest wants to go home," Mason shouted.

Damn it. He was serious. He would let her go after bringing her all this way. But she'd looked for trouble by taunting him. She should have kept her big mouth shut.

Because what home did she have to go to? She couldn't go back to Bomba. And she couldn't travel to the village tonight, even if she wanted to. She would have to find a hotel locally which would eat up the little savings she had.

Then again, what other option did she have?

THREE

Mason stood on the portico, watching the prostitute. Sophie.

She appeared unsettled, uncertain and hesitated as she glanced from him to the gates.

She was fucking beautiful, no doubt, and with endless curves. Yet, there was more to her. Her hair was braided long and fell around her shoulders. He pictured wrapping it around his fist, tugging it back, arching her neck. Making her bend for him. How far could he push her without breaking her?

His dick throbbed painfully, a constant state since he'd sat in the car with her.

He had little interest in physical beauty or painted dolls. Partly the reason the neighbourhood girls or university students did little for him. He wanted more— a wildness and darkness to match his.

He'd seen both in Sophie's brown eyes. She was brimming with rebellion and arrogance too. She'd run away from her pimp, showing she was brave. She thought she could make it out in the world by herself. Time would tell.

He kept his hands in his pocket, legs apart in an intimidating stance, and face devoid of expression. He enjoyed seeing her rattled and didn't care if she stayed or left.

She'd thought he was her saviour. Her hero. Laughable. If only she realised saving people was not his modus operandi. He had nothing to do with the spineless. They never survived in his world.

Yet, he'd saved her. Perhaps because he'd seen her fighting back, defending herself, even if her pimp would have hurt her. She wasn't afraid of being hurt. Partly the reason he'd allowed her to come with him. She wasn't scared of being hurt. Oh, how he could hurt her.

Still, she'd had the nerve to be disrespectful toward him. Even after he'd saved her.

Okay, his intention hadn't been to save her. He'd just needed an outlet for the rage boiling inside him. And Mr Green Trousers had been there, right on cue.

And letting her get into his car had seemed like the right thing to do at the time.

Perhaps he should've left her there for the gang to handle.

"Son, actions have consequences, and it's the consequences that will bite you in the ass if you're not prepared for them," his father would say in this situation.

Bringing Sophie here had been a consequence of knocking her pimp out. She wouldn't have the opportunity to mouth off at him if he hadn't intervened in their quarrel. He should have 'waka-ed pass' like the Bomba guy had warned him.

Then again, when had he ever heeded a warning from a low-life. The pimp had those punches coming. He wouldn't let a pimp disrespect him. Neither would he allow a prostitute to do the same.

Sophie shifted, lifted her chin, and sashayed towards him slowly, swinging her hips provocatively.

The corner of his mouth curved up. He was a gambler and made decisions at the toss of a coin.

Punching the pimp had been a toss of a coin. Letting Sophie come with him had been a toss of a coin. Giving her the choice to stay or leave had been a toss of a coin.

Life could flip on a coin. He'd learned that lesson quick and hard.

So, he'd gambled that she would cave in and come to him. Even after he'd threatened to own her and keep her until he was done and would discard her afterwards. And he'd won.

She stopped in front of him, a step down from the portico. He towered over her, yet she kept her chin up and held his gaze with icy determination. She was no goddamned meek little lamb. No, she was feral. She would fight him, tooth and claw. He could see it in her eyes gleaming with insolence.

The idea made his dick pulse, ache, and leak precum. He resisted the urge to adjust himself.

Yet, he wanted to punish her for it. Why not? He was a sadist, after all. He would enjoy seeing her squirm in discomfort.

"What is it going to be, Sophie? Leave or stay?" he asked just so there were no misunderstandings.

She stood there defiantly. "You forget, Mr Mason, that I'm one of those women your mother warned you to stay away from. I follow strangers in their cars for a living. So, I'm staying."

Freaking brave, she was. And a little foolish too.

"Strip," he commanded.

"Before we get to that, how much are you going to pay me?" She swallowed, lifting her chin higher.

Irritation prickled through him, and the urge to punish her increased. He had to bring her arrogance down a notch. So, he opened with a meagre number. "Five thousand naira a day."

Her mouth dropped open. She turned away, muttering, "Which kind Wenger be dis one."

He heard and understood the Pidgin this time. She was calling him a stingy motherfucker. He'd been demoted from her hero-knight Eleniyan.

He said nothing. If she wanted his reaction, she would have to address him directly.

"That's too low," she sounded annoyed. "I earn more a night working for Bomba."

He shrugged. "Last time I checked, you ran away from your pimp. So those gigs are gone. I'm guaranteeing a roof over your head and food in your stomach for a few days instead of being homeless."

Her shoulders fell, and she swallowed, showing fear for the first time tonight.

"But you can afford to pay me more. You know I need it." She waved at the house, her voice faltering.

"Yes, I can afford to pay you more. But you've done nothing to earn it except give me attitude." He raised his brow.

Her eyes widened in realisation, and she dropped her gaze and arms in despondency. Then after a few seconds, she lifted her head, met his gaze, and started unbuttoning her shirt.

At the same time, a car horn beeped outside the gates. The gate keeper, whom Mason had briefly forgotten, was watching them stirred to life, going to the pedestrian entrance to check the new arrival.

He wasn't expecting a visitor at this time of night. Then again, it had never stopped his friends before. Still, no one knew he was here. So, who was it?

"Wait," Mason ordered, and Sophie's hands froze on the second button.

The gateman came back in.

"Na Oga Rocha," he said before going to open the main gates.

Damn. Mason's back muscles stiffened. This was not going to be good.

"Who is it?" Sophie asked, seemingly reading his response as troubling.

Annoyed with himself for letting that slip, he blanked his expression, ignoring her question. "Tidy yourself up. And do not speak unless you're asked a direct question."

She opened her mouth. He raised his brow, and she shut it.

The car drove in and parked next to his under the carport. A man exited the front passenger seat and opened the back door. Interesting. His older brother now travelled with an entourage.

Rocha Maduka stepped out of the back passenger seat wearing a navy-blue linen tunic and trouser set. He strode across the gravel driveway, his shoes crunching against the stones with a confident swagger.

He had every reason to be confident. He was the firstborn son of late Barrister and SAN Alfred Maduka, the adviser to prominent Yadili godfather Chief Sylvester Odili. As he approached, the bronze ring on his pinkie finger indicated that he had ascended from recruit to associate in the Yadili network, which meant he'd taken the oath and had been inducted into the secret organisation. At the rate he was going, there was no doubt he would become a captain soon, in charge of one of the business operations overseen by the chief.

"I knew you'd be here," Rocha said as he walked past Sophie as if she was invisible and stepped onto the portico beside Mason. Typical Rocha. He kept things close to his chest. But he noticed Sophie and would mention her eventually.

"What are you doing here?" Mason asked the obvious question.

"I should ask you the same thing," Rocha replied. "You left the villa without telling anyone where you were going. And you're not answering your phone."

He'd gone silent for a reason. He hadn't wanted contact from anyone, especially his family. They hadn't deemed it necessary to contact him when it had been important. When his father was on his dying bed. For one fucking month.

No one had said it. But he'd known Mother had been trying to punish him, using his father's illness to control him. A power play. Why else did she transport his sick father abroad without his knowledge? Meanwhile, Rocha had been there.

His father was buried, and he didn't have to hang around the rest of his family. And he would not concede defeat by admitting they'd hurt him.

"I couldn't stay there any longer. I had to get away," he said instead.

Rocha nodded. "I can understand that. Those meetings with Umunna are endless sometimes."

"You're the firstborn son." Mason shrugged. "It all falls on your shoulders. I don't have to be there."

"But you can stand with family. You can show your support."

Mason huffed. Stand with family, indeed. He should sympathise with Rocha because their father's passing meant he was now the new head of the family with all the irksome responsibilities.

Rocha liked to think he was the new head of the family. But their mother was the matriarch, and Rocha had to go through her first.

"How is Mother?" he asked.

"She's not happy with you."

"There's nothing new there, then." Their mother had never given Mason a break because he'd never been easy to control.

Rocha indulged her frequently, so they got on like a house on fire. They'd always been inseparable.

"You could try not doing things to annoy her. Anyway, you'll see her when you get back to the villa."

"I didn't say I was going back there."

"You don't have a choice. Chief wants to see you tomorrow."

Mason stiffened. This was not good. "Chief? Why does he want to see me?"

If Chief Odili summoned him, he'd have to go to see him. No one disobeyed the godfather, not even him. Not if he liked his life.

"You're asking me? I'm just the messenger." Rocha replied. "We'll go and see him tomorrow. In the meantime, I see you brought a toy."

Here we go. Mason had been expecting the words. Still, they unexpectedly punched him in the gut, and he responded without thinking. "She's not ..."

He realised what he was saying too late and shut his mouth. What the fuck was wrong with him? Why did he fall for that trap? Why hadn't he planned for his brother's arrival?

Rocha's eyes glinted with mischief. Mason had given him an opening by taking the bait. *Toy* was code between the brothers for a plaything, someone to be used and tossed. Someone to be shared.

"She's not what, brother? You know the house rules. You must share your toys." Rocha spoke to Mason, but his lascivious gaze stayed on Sophie, undressing her with his eyes. He stepped down from the portico and circled her, running his fingers along her shoulder and through her braids.

For the first time in Mason's life, a ball of jealous rage pulled in his gut. He took a step towards his brother, intending to break his arm for touching Sophie. But he stopped before he got off the portico, shocked at the strength of the strange emotion. What the fuck was wrong with him? Why would he care if his brother touched the woman? She was a prostitute, after all. Free to fuck anyone who paid her.

And his brother was right. They'd shared women in the past. So, it wasn't a big deal.

Yet, he knew one thing beyond all else. Sophie was his—his property for the near future—and he would not share her with anyone. Not even his blood brother.

"Toy, what is your name?" Rocha asked Sophie, drawing Mason's attention again.

"I'm not a toy," Sophie said defiantly, eyeballing his brother.

Warmth bloomed through Mason's chest, another weird emotion he hadn't experienced—joy at Sophie's defiance.

"Watch your mouth, toy." His brother grabbed Sophie's hair and yanked it back. She gasped, her neck tilted, her eyes shimmering with tears.

Without thought, a growl ripped through Mason's chest as his muscles curled tight in preparation for a fight. "Let her go!"

Rocha jerked back and turned towards him. He must have seen Mason's murderous expression because he released Sophie's hair and stepped back.

"You need to teach her some manners," Rocha muttered, heading towards the front door.

It meant the matter was only parked briefly, and he acknowledged Mason's ownership of Sophie. She was his to play with or break. However, once they were inside the house alone with Sophie, his brother would want his turn with Sophie eventually.

Not happening. His hand clenched into fists.

"Sophie, go sit in the back seat of the car." He pressed the fob, and the light flashed, unlocking the doors.

Sophie eyed him with a frown but obeyed, walking towards his car.

"What are you doing?" Rocha turned towards him, looking irritated.

"We're going back to the villa tonight, and I'm taking her with me," Mason said. It was the only way to ensure Sophie's safety and not commit murder.

FOUR

Sophie pulled the back door of Mason's car and glanced at him.

The brothers argued, Rocha gesticulating, Mason ramrod straight. Although she couldn't hear them, it didn't take a genius to figure out they were arguing about her.

What the hell was that about? How had her evening degenerated so much?

Sure, it hadn't been going great when Bomba tried to strangle her. But she'd thought Mason's intervention would improve her life. She'd dared to hope it even when she'd been haggling with him about the price of her staying. She could see that he was playing a game with her. A game she'd intended to win.

Then his brother arrived, and his entire demeanour had changed.

And the man's actions, daring to call her a toy and painfully pulling her hair when she'd challenged him, had proven his maliciousness.

However, she hadn't expected Mason to order his brother to leave her alone. Instead, he'd defended her the second time tonight. First with Bomba and now with his brother. Both were formidable opponents.

Saving her from Bomba had been understandable if surprising. They'd been strangers, and so was Bomba. He'd been saving someone in distress.

However, this time it was his brother. His family. And from his brother's words, she'd inferred that they behaved appallingly towards women anyway. So why defend her, considering she was a prostitute and their encounter was transactional—sex for money and a roof over her head for a few days.

Still, it looked like that plan was changing again.

For the first time this evening, Sophie wished she had Bomba here or at least one of his men as protection.

She couldn't trust either of these brothers—Mason or Rocha. They were dangerous men, and she didn't want to be caught in the middle of whatever was going on between them.

She had to get out of here. She would have to spend her money on a hotel room. Instead of getting in the car, she stood by the door, waiting for Mason.

He swivelled away from his brother and strode towards the vehicle.

"Benji, you're driving my car," he said to one of the two men who'd arrived with Rocha.

"Okay, sir," the man replied, walking around the parked automobiles.

Mason reached his and stood outside the other back door. "Sophie, I thought I told you to sit in the car."

"You did, but I'm not going with you to wherever you're going. I want to leave," she said, crossing her arms over her chest.

He kissed his teeth and rolled his eyes heavenwards. "You can't leave. You chose to stay."

"I've changed my mind."

"Tough. You can't leave."

"You can't make me stay." She backed away from his car, her heart racing.

Behind her, Rocha laughed like a hyena, making the hairs on Sophie's neck stand straight.

"You can come with me, Sophie," Rocha said, walking down from the portico. "I will take you wherever you want to go."

"Really?" She glanced at him and returned her gaze to Mason, who just stared at her with his expressionless face. Why did he always have that poker face on? It had only slipped once tonight when Rocha arrived, and she'd seen the worry cross his features. He stood on one side, alone, while the other men stood together. It was as if they were all against Mason.

"Of course," Rocha replied as he reached her. He lowered his voice, "First, I'm going to fuck you real good. Then my boys will have their turn. Then the driver will drop you home. I'll pay you double whatever my brother was offering for each of us and an extra one hundred grand bonus."

"How many men?" she couldn't help asking. That offer was good. Better than Mason offered. She needed to maximise her income since she didn't know how soon she would start earning again. At least she needed to make enough money to get out of town.

"Five," Rocha said. "You can handle us, can't you?"

"Yes." Sophie swallowed. She'd handled that number before. "So, you're going to pay me one-fifty grand?"

"Sure. I can even double it to three hundred grand. What do you say?"

She gasped. Three hundred grand all to herself. With no Bomba to take a massive chunk of it. It was so tempting.

Yet something felt terribly wrong. And it was oozing off Mason. His silence was disconcerting. She'd expected him to pitch in and bid for her. He'd been fighting his brother for her. Yet, he stood there like a tree. Silent and with an air of foreboding about him.

What was going on with him? Why had he suddenly gone quiet?

"Mason, are you not going to say anything?" she asked in annoyance.

"What is there to say? Your options have been laid out for you. You can either come with me or stay with my brother."

"Are you going to increase your offer?"

"No. I will not enter a bidding war with my brother for you. I believe what I offered you was better—"

"Better for who?" She cut him off. He'd offered her peanuts. She needed money. Hard cash.

"For you, damn it. Better for you." He slammed his palm on the roof of his car. "But if you don't see it, then stay with him and good luck to you."

He yanked the car door open. "Benji, come and drive this fucking car!"

Shit. He was angry. The second time tonight, he'd lost his temper. It had to do with his brother and her. She didn't want to annoy him. He had helped her. Her reward shouldn't be pissing him off.

Why was this so hard? The choice was to stay and earn enough money to get her out of town and away from Bomba's clutches. And in the process, annoy the man who had helped her get this far.

Or lose three hundred grand for ten or twenty grand, depending on how many days Mason meant to keep her.

"Let him go. Come inside the house," Rocha said with triumph in his voice.

A cold finger travelled down her spine, and dread filled her. It was that same voice of triumph Rocha had used when he'd first called her a toy.

Without responding, she rushed to the car door closest to her and yanked it open as Benji started the engine. She slid into the back seat, shutting it before anyone could react.

Mason turned in the seat to glare at her. "What are you doing?"

"I'm coming with you. I've survived the night so far by sticking with you. I'm not going to jinx it by going with your brother."

He huffed and turned to the driver. "Let's go."

The man reversed the car as the gate keeper opened the gates.

What was Mason's problem?

"You're not even going to say thank you because I chose you instead of your brother," she bit out.

Mason ignored her, fuelling her annoyance.

"I swear to god, this better be worth it or—"

"Or what?" His hand shot out and gripped her neck tightly, his eyes blazing with fury. "You'll fuck my brother instead?"

"Mason—" she clawed at his hand and wheezed, fear rippling through her "—you're choking me."

He released her, and she collapsed against the leather seat, gasping for air.

He puffed out a heavy breath and scrubbed his head. Then he deflated against the car seat. "I should drop you off somewhere. Are you sure there's no place you can go? No one who will protect you?"

"What are you saying?" Her eyes fluttered open, and her heart raced. Even after he'd been angry at her, he was still trying to save her. What was really going on with him? The composure he'd had when he'd handled

Bomba seemed to have fizzled out with his brother's arrival.

He met her gaze. "I'm saying that you're not safe with me or my family."

Shock rippled through her. Why was he saying this? He was admitting to being dangerous. Yet, somehow she felt obliged to defend him. "But … but you saved me at least twice today."

"I'm going to hurt you too. Hurt you and humiliate you. And I'm going to enjoy doing it."

"Hurt me. You mean like you just did by choking me?"

"No. There was no pleasure in doing that. It was pure anger, and I shouldn't have done it."

Huh? "Are you apologising?"

He puffed out a sigh. "Yes, my brother's arrival riled me. I thought I would spend a few days with you, just the two of us. And at the end of it, I would pay you, and you would leave without any of my family ever finding out. Now, my brother is in town, and he wants you too. And to top it off I must return to my hometown where you will meet my mother. Ordinarily, I would not have reacted to your threat about fucking my brother. However, everything together is making me a little crazy. So, my apologies. You didn't deserve my anger."

His self-awareness undid her, and her fear fizzled away. It was apparent the situation with his brother was messy. This was sibling rivalry on a dysfunctional level. "Apology accepted, but I didn't say I would sleep with your brother."

"You implied it. It's the same thing."

She swallowed. He was kind which was weird considering how dangerous he was. Truthfully she'd provoked him. "I'm sorry for threatening to fuck your brother."

"Okay. But as I said, is there anywhere else you can go? I'm giving you a second chance to escape from me and my family."

She scratched her neck as her stomach pitched. She didn't want to be separated from him yet for some reason. "I can go to a hotel."

"That's not going to be safe for you. My brother will find you there."

"Your brother? How?"

"He'll be told where you are." He tilted his head in the direction of the driver without saying anything.

She frowned at first, then she understood. Benji worked for Rocha and would tell his brother where he dropped her.

"Oh," she nodded in understanding. "Then let me stay. I need the money anyway."

"Of course. The money trumps everything else. Don't say I didn't warn you," he said in a clipped tone, his lips pursed in a hard line.

She realised she'd annoyed him again and sighed.

He leaned forward, reached into a compartment between seats and pulled out a bundle of cash. He reeled some out and tossed them at her, the notes fluttering around her onto the foot mat.

"Go ahead. Pick them off the floor. You will get to earn them soon enough. Strip." There was a sneer of disgust on his face.

A chill of dread went through her like she'd been locked in an ice-cold dungeon waiting to be fed to the monster. "What?"

"Why the fuck do I need to repeat myself with you every time? Strip. Now!"

FIVE

Sophie pressed her lips into a grimace fighting the pull of opposing emotions.

Mason's order to strip wasn't a big deal. After all, she made a living by taking her clothes off.

However, the way he'd spoken to her rankled, and the rebellious part of her wanted to fight back and tell him to go and eat shit.

Bristling, she sat there, clutching her bag to her lap and glared at him. She expected him to lash out like he'd done earlier.

Instead, he sat perfectly still, his face shadowed and devoid of expression in the dimly lit back seat. He stared at her in an unnerving manner with those dark profound midnight eyes.

The silence sat heavily between them, not even interrupted by the engine humming or the aircon. It was as if those things were far removed, and she sat in a vacuum with him.

Her lungs constricted, and she struggled to breathe. What was it about him? Darkness surrounded him like a crushing blanket. She seemed entangled in it when she only wanted to do her job and get paid.

Look at her. She sat in a staring match with him while clutching her bag, which contained all the items she owned in the world, as if she were some innocent girl who'd never been with a man. It was ridiculous. What was happening to her?

It was Mason and his ridiculous mind games. They were connected somehow. Perhaps because he'd saved her from Bomba and his men. Maybe because beneath the danger shrouding him, he needed her, right here and now.

He could make her strip. Force her. Tear her clothes off. Even get the man driving—Benji—to do it for him.

She'd been with rich men who thought they could get whatever they wanted from women.

And she knew Mason was dangerous. He'd proven it several times tonight. So, what was he waiting for?

She couldn't relax, couldn't take her eyes off him.

Sighing, she dumped her bag on the seat beside her and unbuttoned her shirt. She'd undone the top one earlier before Rocha arrived at the house. So, she picked up from where she'd left off. She shifted to tug it off, yet he didn't move.

Then she undid the clasp for her hot pants. Finally, she lifted her hips and pushed them off with her thongs, letting them drop onto the foot mat.

"What now?" she muttered, rolling all the clothing into her bag. She might be a prostitute, but she liked to keep things neat.

The overhead lamp flicked on, illuminating the back seat and revealing her bare body to him.

Her eyes widened as her breath hitched. She'd thought she would have the shadows concealing her in the car. But it looked like he wouldn't even give her that leeway.

"Is the light a good idea?" she glanced towards the driver. Nigerian roads were dangerous in the daytime, let alone at night. Travellers battled potholes, drunk or reckless drivers, malfunctioning vehicles, extortionate police checkpoints and bandits plying the highways.

"It is. I want to see you." Mason didn't seem troubled by any of that. Instead, he undid his seatbelt and shifted closer. Then he glanced into the rear-view mirror and caught the driver looking at her. Then his tone was filled with menace again. "Benji, keep your eyes on the fucking road. If you crash this car and I survive. I will kill you."

"Yes, sir." The man stiffened and cleared his throat, facing forward.

She wanted to ask if the threat would be enough. But somehow, she realised that Mason would keep his word. He would kill the man if he crashed the car. And the driver-slash-bodyguard knew it too.

"Look at me," Mason commanded, drawing her attention again.

She lifted her gaze and met his compelling one. The intensity of his scrutiny made her breath catch. No one else looked at her the way he did. Like he saw her, saw beyond flesh and bones into her soul.

Once more, she was back in that cocoon. In another dimension where the driver and the car speeding down the expressway didn't exist. A world encompassing the two of them.

Mason and Sophie.

For a moment, she couldn't help sinking into the insane attraction she felt towards him. The urge to feel him against her skin. Inside her already dripping, contracting channel. Fierce and forceful.

It was insane because she didn't usually feel this way towards clients. Yes, some made an effort to arouse her, but she always carried lubricant around for a reason.

But here, she wanted a client, an alarming prospect.

His eyes swept over her body as if he was registering everything—her skin colour, size, the swell of her breasts, the dip of her belly, the width of her hips, the mound of her pussy and the length of her legs.

He shifted closer, fingers lifting her braids off her shoulder and tucking it behind her ear.

"Do you wear your hair like this often?" his voice was soft.

More than the question itself, the gentleness in his husky voice startled her, making her eyes widen. The way he switched from hot to cold in the blink of an eye was scary and uncanny. A moment ago, he threatened to kill a man. Now he spoke as if he cared about her appearance. About her.

She swallowed. "Yes. Sometimes I use wigs."

"No wigs," he said vehemently. "I want to feel your scalp and tug your hair without it coming loose in my hands." At the mention of tugging her hair, her clit throbbed, more of her juices smearing the seat. He wasn't touching her yet, and she was coming apart.

He spread his legs and patted the leather seat between them. "Come and sit here."

She moved, eager to get closer to him, yet reluctant to reveal the wet patch on the seat. Hopefully, he wouldn't notice.

She settled between his legs, caged by his thighs and arms.

He trailed his palms over her arms from shoulder to fingertips, spreading goosebumps over her skin. He lifted her arms, placing her hands on the back of the headrest in front, making her lean forward. Then he gathered the mass of hair and put it over the left shoulder, giving an unimpeded view of her back. He traced his palms across her back, over every inch of skin, sending more tingles through her. Then like he was playing each piano key, he pressed every vertebra along her spine all the way to her sacrum.

She never wanted to bend over and welcome a client into her body so much. Never had a client pay this much attention to her, study her body the way Mason was doing. Most of them did the bare minimum required to reach release. If anything, she did most of the work.

But it proved the opposite for Mason.

Why was it vital for him to know her body? To trace every part of her skin? Did he get pleasure from it?

Curiosity mingled with desire. She wanted to know him. Know what brought him pleasure. Know what his body looked like beneath the clothes.

When he finished examining her back, his fingers tangled in her scalp, tugging her hair back.

A moan bubbled in her throat, and she bit her lip to stifle it.

He leaned close, his breath feathering her neck. "When I bring you pleasure, you should show gratitude. Let me hear you."

He yanked her hair harder.

Her eyes watered, and she couldn't hide the moan that ripped out of her even if she wanted to.

"That's better."

She heard the grin in his voice and glanced at the rear-view mirror where their gazes collided. His eyes sparkled in a wicked grin.

She bristled, which was becoming a constant state around him if she ignored the burning desire. He seemed to enjoy annoying her.

"Why the hell did you get angry with your brother earlier when he yanked my hair if you were going to that?" she goaded him, knowing he was tetchy about his brother touching her.

"No one else is allowed to hurt you without my permission," he said ominously. He placed his hand around her neck like earlier, reminding her how easily he could hurt her.

She lifted her hands, ready to claw at his arm in case he was going for a repeat of the choking.

But he didn't. He tenderly traced the sore skin, which would have shown bruises immediately had her skin been fairer. There was an acknowledgement and ownership of the pain he'd caused, yet reverence in the caress.

How can one person be so contradictory, so black and white, so gentle and vicious?

He continued the featherlight massage down her collar to the valley of her breasts.

Her fight or flight responses dissipated as her nipples puckered in anticipation, her boobs becoming heavier. A thousand butterflies took flight in her belly.

He cupped her breasts with both hands, weighing and squeezing, then pinching the nipples hard.

She squirmed, rolling her hips, squeezing her thighs together. His hard erection strained his trouser, prodding her hip. Great. She wanted to make him come fast, just like every other man who'd been inside her. At least she could wipe the smug smile off his face and score a point since he seemed to like playing games.

He released her breasts, and she thought he wanted to open his fly. Excited to feel him inside her, she reached for her bag for the pack of condoms.

But his hand clamped hard around her neck, the other sliding between her legs. He tilted her chin up, making her look in the rear-view mirror, meeting his fiery black stare, his face next to her, his warm breath on her skin.

The sound of her shallow breathing filled the air as his fingers delved into her wet folds. Yet his fingers on her bruised neck stayed painful. Not as much as earlier, but it hurt.

She licked her lips, trying to control herself. To hold back. Because the pleasure of his hand in her pussy mixed with the pain of his grip on her neck, confusing her brain.

She shouldn't like it, should feel uncomfortable. Yet she writhed against him, tilting against him and arching her back and neck into him involuntarily.

He noticed because his grin in the mirror only became fiercer. He was driving her insane on purpose.

Fuck him. She pushed against his thighs, trying to break free from him, but he didn't let go. Instead, his hand worked her clit and pussy, driving her closer to release, his fingers around her throat getting tighter, holding her in place.

"You're hurting me." She didn't want to cum, not like this. Not while he was sending mixed signals to her brain. So, she dug her fingernails viciously into his thighs, enough to cause pain.

"And you're hurting me in return," he whispered in a husky voice before biting her earlobe as his fingers dug into her pussy, cupping her hard. "I warned you, and you chose to stay. Did you think I would give you my dick without you working for it? I own you now, Sophie. And I will do whatever I wish to your body."

Sure, he'd warned her, and he was paying for her. But she had thought she could control the interaction like she did with other men. But Mason wasn't letting her win this tug of war. He didn't seem phased by the pain of her nails digging into his skin. He would have bruises too.

"I hate you," she bit out, suddenly realizing she was fighting a failing battle.

"Good. You can join the growing list of haters," he said in a surprisingly calm voice, and then he pressed his lips to the sensitive spot behind her ear just as his fingers gentled on her skin. He tangled fingers in her scalp, tugging her head back. At the same time, his thumb pressed down on her clit, digits pumping into her pussy.

The overload of sensation—tingling pain, intense pleasure, and gentle caresses—all collided and sent her hurtling over the edge before she could even form a coherent thought to halt it. Then she gasped for breath with "Oh … oh … oh" out of her mouth. The intensity of the orgasm made tears flow down her cheeks.

Exhausted, she sagged against him, closing her eyes. She couldn't meet his gaze after she'd come apart so readily like an amateur. That humiliation was enough. She didn't need to see his smug smile.

Still, he didn't say anything for a long while, thankfully. Neither did he release her from her position. Instead, his arms stayed around her, not tight, anchoring her to him.

She should move and get dressed again. But she didn't want to. There was comfort in his embrace as if he was making up for the humiliation and forced orgasm.

And she liked it.

Liked that he was giving cuddles after torturing her.

Perhaps she was as insane as he was.

SIX

Mason sat in the car with a subdued Sophie on his lap. After the intensity of her orgasms, she'd slumped against him, and he'd closed his spread thighs, allowing her to settle on top of him.

Her quietness and acquiescence, temporary for sure, allowed him time to control his raging libido. His erection sat like a brick and throbbed like a motherfucker. The fight to control her with the duality and dichotomy of pain and pleasure had been exhilarating and incredible. He'd nearly cum in his jeans. Mostly because she'd grappled him and had inflicted pain in return, consequently heightening his pleasure. An adrenaline and dopamine cocktail, hell yeah.

He'd needed the fight to bring him relief, especially after this excruciating period of his life.

That had been what was missing earlier when he'd visited the brothel. The prostitute—Jet or whatever her name was—had been too compliant, too meek. She didn't have the edge or defiance that Sophie seemed to have.

Sophie was precisely what he needed and more reason why he couldn't share her with his brother. Fuck, no! He wasn't going to let his brother get his hands on her. Rocha can go find his own.

Involuntarily, his arms tightened around her, and she shifted as if to get comfortable, her head lolling against his shoulder. Was she asleep?

He'd flicked off the overhead light, and the car interior was dark, backlit by the bright headlamps. There were no streetlights on this stretch of the expressway, and they were approaching the exit to his hometown.

He glanced down at her face. Sure enough, her eyes were closed, and her breathing had evened out.

Her shadowed features appeared serene and relaxed. She had an oval face with high cheekbones and a regal button nose. Her full, heart-shaped lips were provocative, and his dick stirred when he pictured ways of making use of them.

Instead of letting her snooze, he really should put her to work. Get her on her knees, her face on his crotch. He had no doubts he would come within minutes of jamming his dick down her throat.

Then again, he didn't want to give Benji a reason to crash this car. The driver barely controlled himself while Sophie had been in the throes of climax. The man probably ejaculated in his pants.

Mason grinned, the sadist in him pleased about torturing Benji as well. Sophie's naked body was a glance away, but the man couldn't look or touch her, although he'd heard her cries of pleasure. Probably even felt her pushing against the back of his seat as she'd struggled with Mason.

"I'm cold. Can I get dressed?" Sophie muttered against his chest, stirring.

"Fair enough." She was naked in an air-conditioned car. They were approaching his home, and people would be around the premises, although it was late.

He released her, and she moved onto the seat beside him, slipping on her skimpy clothes in silence. He couldn't see how the clothes could keep her warm, but he supposed it was better than nothing. She snuggled into the corner, ignoring him, eyes closed again.

He sighed, tugged off his jeans shirt and draped it over her. "Put this on."

Her eyes fluttered open, and she frowned. "You're giving me your shirt?"

"You're cold, and your skimpy clothes will not keep you warm."

"But you can tell the driver to switch off the AC."

"No. I like the AC. Take the shirt."

She grabbed it, putting her arms through the sleeves and buttoning it up.

Warm sensation fluttered in his chest. He reached for the back seat vents and flicked off the one directed at Sophie, preventing the cold air from blowing at her.

"That's better. Thank you." She sounded relieved and smiled.

He grinned. "You look cute in my shirt."

Her eyes sparkled with humour. "I'm going to keep it then so I can keep being cute."

He chuckled. He liked her. This camaraderie between them developed when he'd taken down her pimp, and they'd run away from the chasing gang. Under different circumstances, they would get along. If he wasn't who he was, she wasn't what she was.

Actually, what she was didn't matter to him.

Except when she was offering her services to his brother.

His humour died.

If Rocha had gotten his hands on Sophie, they wouldn't be sitting and chatting. He wouldn't give her a break to recover until he was thoroughly satisfied.

Are you so different from your brother? The voice in his head nudged.

Perhaps he wasn't different from his brother. They were raised together and shared DNA, after all.

However, his brother had done things he would never have considered doing to him. Things that a brother should never have done to his brother.

"Why do you flip like a switch? One minute you're laughing. The next, you're frowning," her query cut through his thoughts like a knife through butter.

A valid question. One his father would ask him too after his behaviour tonight.

"You must master your emotions. Don't let others control you through them," his father had reiterated many times.

Members of their family were prone to violent outbursts, more so with Mason, who would go batshit crazy at the drop of a hat. But over the years, he'd learned to control his temper.

However, the past six months had taken its toll on him, and he was beginning to fray at the edges.

Wanting to spend a few days with Sophie alone and then having his brother show up had triggered him. He was close to losing the plot. There was no way he could have stayed in the house in the city tonight with Rocha touching Sophie without burning shit down.

Hence the midnight trip to the villa, where he hoped a semblance of sanity would descend on him and daresay his brother due to the proximity to their recently buried father.

Or, at the very least, his mother would act as a referee, although sometimes she was a fuel to fire more than a calming influence.

And there were others, family members and kinsfolk. Although none of them could exert as much influence on them as Chief Odili.

"Do you have family?" he asked, aware of her continued scrutiny and curiosity. He didn't have a simple answer to her question, so best to turn the attention to her. And although he liked her, he wasn't sure he could trust her.

"Yes, I do. My mother and my sister," she replied, unfazed by his changing the topic. "What about you? I met Rocha, and he talked about your mother. What about your father?"

Just like that, the anguish of losing his father returned. He clenched his jaw and rubbed the back of his neck. His throat hurt, and he had difficulty swallowing to clear the lump before he could speak. "We buried him a week ago."

"Oh no. I'm so sorry," she sounded sincere for an acquaintance and reached for his arm, placing her palm on it, soothing him.

"Thank you," he muttered, closing his eyes, biting back the swell of emotions.

No member of his blood family had offered him comfort. Not that he would've allowed them after what they'd done. His father had been his sounding board, his adviser, his confidante.

And he was gone.

Of course, there was their housekeeper with whom he shared a close bond. But she was an employee.

And there was Duke, his childhood friend. They'd talked, but Duke was just a young man like him. He didn't have the answers to life's questions.

Like how would he handle a manipulative family and keep his sanity?

The car horn beeped, and Mason opened his eyes, sighing.

They'd arrived at the family residence. Security men rushed to open the gates after verifying the new arrivals.

The car drove into the enormous premises situating two detached buildings. The front building was his parent's residence, while the one at the back was the staff quarters and guest house.

Mason had been using one of the apartments in the BQ but had moved into the main house during his father's funeral so guests could use the BQ. So, his clothes and personal effects were still in the primary residence.

As soon as the car stopped, he pushed the door open and stepped out. Sophie followed him, shuffling across the seat to exit at his door.

"Welcome," one of the security men said.

"Is my mother awake?" he asked. Except for the outdoor security lights, the main house was in darkness.

"No. She went to bed a long time ago."

"Good," he muttered and turned to Sophie. "Come on."

Then he halted as he noticed she still had his shirt on. He doubted she had anything suitable for the days ahead in her bag.

"Benji, come here," he ordered, and the man sauntered over after he decanted from the car.

"I need you to go to Mama Binye first thing in the morning," he continued. "Tell her that we need some ready-made clothes. Stylish clothes, oh. Not Mary-Amaka or Mama Nkechi style. Tell her to bring at least five—"

"Five?" Sophie interrupted him in a loud whisper. "How long am I staying?"

"I don't know yet. We'll see." He turned back to Benji. "The clothes should be a size ten—"

"Twelve," she cut in again. "Does Mama what-was the name-again?"

"Binye," Benji replied.

"Oh, yes. Mama Binye. Does she have shoes as well? I just need something lower than these." She pointed at her high-heeled platform sandals.

"Yes, tell her to send some sandals as well, size ..." He glanced at Sophie, brow raised.

"Size seven, and she should throw in a handbag or two, too," she said.

Huh? He frowned and opened his mouth to tell her to piss off, that she wasn't getting handbags, but she started giggling, her face lighting up, her body rocking.

"Oh, you should see your face," she said between chuckles. "You should get a sense of humour."

He couldn't help the smile that broke on his face. The last time before tonight he'd burst into spontaneous mirth had been when his father was alive. A shiver went through him, and he felt like his old man was smiling too.

He wanted to reward her for putting a smile back on his face after so long.

"Benji, tell Mama Binye to add a handbag to the list too."

"Yes, sir," the man replied.

"Thank you. You're so sweet," Sophie said, giving him a glorious smile.

"No, I'm not," he said but chuckled, shaking his head. He was so far from sweet he could be described as bitter kola. "Come on."

He headed for the servants' side door rather than the front door. There was a risk of waking his mother if he used the front door.

He knocked on the window of the ground floor bedroom of the servant who slept in the main house. A few minutes later, the corridor light came on, and the side door was opened. A middle-aged woman stood there rubbing his eyes.

Ms Baguthur, or Ma Bagu as they fondly named her, was a long-term housekeeper and the only living person in this house he would do anything for.

Warmth suffused him when he saw her wearing the pink nightie and robe he'd bought for her. Her hair was wrapped in a scarf. When she looked up and saw him, a wide-toothed smile broke on her face.

"Mason, nwa m. Nno," she welcomed him like a son in Igbo language. There were days when she was more of a mother to him than the one who birthed him.

"Ma Bagu, ewe na iwe na m kpọ tere gị," he apologised for waking her as he stepped into the corridor.

"Ekwukwala ya. Mụ nwa chere na m agaghị ihu gị ruo mgbe tere aka. Nke a ị loghachiri, obi di mụ ụtọ." *Don't mention it. I thought I wouldn't see you for a long time. But, since you've returned, I'm happy.*

She moved to the side, allowing him to enter fully and looked at Sophie with enquiring eyes. "Onye ka gị na ya so?" *Who is with you?*

"Ma Bagu, onye a bu Sophie," he replied, introducing his companion.

"Ọ bụ enyi gị nwanyị?" *Is she your girlfriend?* Ma Bagu winked and grinned at him.

"Ehm…" His cheeks heated as he blushed. Why the hell was he blushing? The older woman could reduce him to a teenager again, in a good way. But why couldn't he tell her that Sophie was a prostitute he'd hired for a few days.

Perhaps because it was incorrect and not the entire truth. He didn't want to lie to the housekeeper.

"Ọ dịghị otú ahụ. Mụ na Sophie anaghị ayi oyi. A hụrụ m ya n'okporo ụzọ. O nwere ndị chọrọ imerụ ya ahụ." *It's not like that. Me and Sophie are not dating. I saw her on the street. Some people wanted to hurt her.*

"Eyaa. Ị na-enyere ya aka. Ị bụ ezigbo nwa." *Oh. You're helping her. You're a good kid.* She turned to Sophie and waved her in. "Ada, bata n'ime ụlọ." *Daughter, come inside the house.*

"Good evening, ma." Sophie curtsied, her gaze bouncing between him and Ma Bagu. She looked uncertain as if she couldn't understand what was happening.

"Nno, nwa m." Ma Bagu replied. "Ọ na-aghọta Ìgbò?"

He'd assumed she did but didn't know if Sophie understood Igbo.

"Come inside," he said in English, and she stepped across the threshold as he pushed the heavy metal-reinforced door shut and engaged the triple locks. "Do you understand Igbo?"

"Only a little bit," she said.

"O si na o naghị aghọta, so obere," he said for the housekeeper's benefit.

"Welcome," Ma Bagu said in heavily accented English, making Mason smile.

She was going out of her way to make Sophie comfortable. Igbo was her comfort zone, and she rarely spoke English. So, her use of a foreign language now meant she liked Sophie. She walked along the corridor and entered the first door to her left. "Come into the kitchen. Are you hungry?"

"Ma—" he started but was interrupted.

"I'm not talking to you. I know what you're going to say." Ma Bagu tilted her head and placed her hand on Sophie's shoulder. "Don't follow these young men. You hear? They will survive on cigarettes and alcohol. Meanwhile, we women have to build our energy to keep up with them. Abi, I lie?"

Sophie smiled and shook her head, giving Mason a cheeky grin. "It's true, ma. I could eat something."

"Ehen. Now you're talking." The housekeeper dragged Sophie with her, and Mason had no choice but to follow them into the massive modern kitchen as she turned on the lights. She pointed at the small round table in the corner for four people. "Ngwa ṇọrọ odu. Sit down. I won't be long."

Sophie looked at him first as if to check that it was okay. He nodded, and she pulled out a seat, settling in it. He took another one beside her. They faced Ma Bagu as she pottered around, humming a tune.

Sophie leaned towards him, her thigh brushing his, making his skin tingle.

"She's nice. She's not your mother, right?" she said in a whisper and swallowed.

He chuckled. "No, she's not."

His mother was a whole different kettle of fish. She would not offer to cook for Sophie. That was for sure.

Sophie nodded and whispered. "But this is your family home. Your mother is here, and your brother is coming too. Are you sure it's a good idea for me to be here?"

The uncertainty in her voice got to him, and he clenched his hands. "This is my home too. I have the right to invite whomever I choose."

His brother and mother had denied him so many things, but he wouldn't allow them to deny him the pleasure of Sophie's company for as long as he wanted.

However, Sophie was stubborn and bloody-minded. A wrong step could land her in deep waters.

He leaned close to her and issued a warning. "But you better remember this. If you want to leave this place intact and alive, keep away from my brother and do what I say."

SEVEN

"If you want to leave this place alive and intact … do as I say."

Mason's words spun in Sophie's mind as she stirred under the multi-patterned quilt the next morning. She blinked awake and tried to get her bearings in the unfamiliar surroundings.

Bright sunshine filtered through the edges of the pewter-grey blinds covering the black-framed three-panel casement window. The walls were painted two shades lighter than the blinds—a cloud-grey colour. The built-in wardrobe panels to her right were ash-grey with chrome handles and a full-length mirror in one column. The double bed was in the middle, the wardrobe to the right, and the window to the left. Two doors led off the room—one next to the cabinet led into the ensuite bathroom while the other led into the hallway. The only splash of colour in the room was from the quilted duvet cover, a multicoloured Ankara pattern.

The room was like the man, contradictory and confusing.

She recalled coming up here last night after Ma Bagu had made food for them—yam swallow with okra-periwinkle soup filled with shrimps and fresh fish. That had been the most delicious food Sophie had ever eaten. A smile broke on her face as she remembered licking her fingers to savour every morsel and drop of the soup. Even Mason, who'd been reluctant to eat that late had finished his meal after Ma Bagu placed the steaming plates in front of them.

While they ate, Ma Bagu had woken another servant who'd run a bath for her. Apparently, something was wrong with the hot water heater in Mason's bedroom, requiring an engineer from the city to fix it. In the meantime, Mason used the family bathroom across the hall. However, he hadn't wanted Sophie to use that one. So, he'd instructed for hot water to be taken to his bedroom in a bucket for Sophie to bathe.

At first, Sophie hadn't wanted the fuss of waking a servant to attend to her. She'd argued that she could bathe with regular tap water. Ma Bagu had laughed and told her to accept the hot water. She hadn't understood until they came to Mason's room, and gratitude filled her. The place was freezing cold, the AC blasting out of the wall unit. He really had a thing for icy spaces. She'd been grateful for the hot water on her skin when she'd washed.

Mason wasn't in the room when she came out, towel wrapped around her body. Trying to stay warm, she'd discarded the towel and climbed under the duvet naked. She sighed with pleasure at the warmth and luxury of the sheets and comforter on her skin. She could barely keep her eyes open as sleep called to her.

Minutes later, Mason strode into the bedroom, his naked body glistening from his shower, barring the towel around his waist.

"I see you made yourself comfortable. Who said you could sleep on my bed?" he asked in a stern tone, matching his expression.

Her heart thudded, and she glanced around. "What? I … I thought—"

"You thought what? That because Ma Bagu fed you that you could do whatever you wanted. Get off the bed." his voice was cold and menacing as he stood over her.

What was wrong with him? Before he went into the shower, he was smiling. Now he was back to being menacing like he'd been in the driveway of the house in the city when Rocha had arrived. Why did he flip so randomly?

"Are you listening? Get off the bed."

Annoyed at the change in his behaviour, she shuffled off the mattress and stood. The cold air wrapped around her, and she hugged her body. "What did I do wrong?"

He stepped close, crowding her. "Did you forget my warning already? You do nothing here unless I tell you."

"But it's your bed. What's wrong with lying in it? We're going to fuck anyway," she retorted.

"You wish!" He ignored her and pulled the cover back, preparing to get into bed.

Her annoyance spiked. "I wish? We were downstairs eating food thirty minutes ago. We were laughing and joking with Ma Bagu. What the hell is the matter with you? All I did was lie in your bed, for fuck's sake."

He swivelled so quickly she barely had time to respond. He grabbed her by the neck, and she fought him, clawing his skin. He shoved her face down on the bed. She tried to push off, and he knelt on her back, his weight pressing her into the mattress.

She struggled as he reached for the bedside cabinet and opened the drawer.

"Mason, Mason, what are you doing?" she trembled as fear flooded her.

"Stay still," he instructed quietly, and she froze as a jagged knife appeared in his hand.

Shit.

"Did you forget my warning? You do nothing here unless I tell you," he continued. "Did you really think you could relax because a sweet, little old lady fed you? Do you not realise that nothing in this house is safe for you. Not me. Not Ma Bagu. I can slit your throat right now, and that sweet little old lady will help me bury your body, and the two of us will be back at that table eating fufu like nothing happened. That's how unsafe it is in this house. But giving you verbal warnings is not enough, so I'm going to carve the warning into your skin. So that every time it hurts, every time you move, every time you see it, you'll remember to heed my warning."

"No, Mason. I understand now. I will heed your warning," she pleaded, turning her head to see what he would do. Her heart was nearly exploding in her chest.

"Stay still, Sophie. This knife is very sharp."

Oh god, she cried silently, squeezing her eyes shut and bracing her body as the blade sliced the skin on her left shoulder. Pain burst through her as blood trickled down her back.

"Stay there," he said as he got off her back.

She didn't dare move as tears trickled down her face, which she hid in the duvet. How did she get into this situation? All she'd wanted was to get away from Bomba. But it seemed she'd landed in a worse place. Was she going to leave here alive? Would she become one of those statistics of girls found dead after spending an evening with a man? Heaven help her.

She heard him rustling in the bathroom then he returned.

"This is going to sting," he said before cold liquid dabbed the injury.

"Ouch," she flinched. "It hurts."

"I need to clean it and stop it from getting infected. Don't be such a baby," he chided and continued dabbing the cut with iodine, peroxide, or whatever he was using. She couldn't place the aroma.

"You cut me in the first place," she bit out angrily, turning her head to glare at him.

"For your own good. Next time you will listen and do as I say." He met her gaze and seemed unfazed by her attitude. He reached for some gauze and plasters.

"No, wait. I want to see what you carved into my skin."

"Okay." He shifted.

She pushed off the bed, wincing as she walked over and stared at her naked body in the full-length mirror. Behind her, Mason sat on the bed, watching. She'd already packed her braids into a bun at the top of her head when she had a bath. So, she stared at the wound unimpeded. It was shallow and no longer bleeding. There would be no permanent damage. At first, it looked like he'd carved zigzags until she saw it properly.

"Bloody hell. You carved your initial into my skin." She glared at him through the mirror, shock running through her. What kind of human being was this?

"Yes. You're my temporary property for the next few days. It should heal by the time you go home, and the scar will disappear." His earlier annoyance had disappeared, and he looked relaxed. The motherfucker appeared satisfied with his handiwork.

"You're fucking crazy, you know that?" she said, suddenly realising what all his warnings meant. He'd given her the opportunity to leave several times. Now it was too late.

He nodded. "That is an accurate description. Now come over here and let me dress the wound."

"You cut me, and now you're a nurse?"

He shrugged and stayed where he was, waiting for her.

It was the same thing he'd done in the car when he'd forced those orgasms out of her. He'd provided comfort for her exhaustion.

His behaviour was confusing and scary. He caused pain, and yet he soothed her. Warmth pooled at her core as desire thrummed in her veins.

Much as she hated to admit it, she liked the hurt-comfort aspect of him. She wanted him, and thinking about the orgasm in the car didn't help.

She glared at him, reluctant to let him touch her again because she wanted him to fuck her. But he was right. If he didn't dress it, it would get infected. Finally, she dragged her feet over to the bed and sat on it.

"Lie face down, like you were."

She glared at him but did as he said. She didn't want him to pull out that knife again. Who knew what part of her body he would carve next?

He gently applied the gauze and square patch on her skin, his touch feathering and arousing her. After he finished, he tugged the edge of the duvet up. "Get in."

Her heart rate spiked. She glanced at him. "You want me in bed?"

"Yes." He cleared the first aid kit and returned it to the bathroom.

"But you told me to get out of it, and now you want me to get in it." She was getting whiplash, trying to keep up with him.

"Yes. Like I said. You can do things when I tell you to do them," he said from the ensuite.

She shook her head and grabbed the condom pack from her bag before crawling into bed. She was glad for the warmth and luxury it provided. Looked forward to having him between her legs too.

He returned and got into bed, pulling the cover over him. Then he flicked the switch above the headboard filling the room with darkness.

Oh, he liked to do it in the dark. Okay. Some light came through the edge of the blinds, anyway. He lay on his side, facing away from her.

"Mason—" She reached for him.

"If you touch me, I will chain you, and you will sleep on the floor," although he said it quietly, she knew he meant it.

"Okay. Good night," she muttered and shifted to the other side of the bed so she didn't have to touch him.

***

Now awake, Mason wasn't in bed or in the bathroom. When did he wake up? She hadn't heard him get up or leave the room. She must have been exhausted. Thankfully, the AC had been switched off, and the room was warm. She shuffled along the bed and went to use the WC. Everything in here was sparkling clean, another luxury. When she finished, she flushed and washed her hands.

Wondering about the time, she returned to the bedroom naked and reached for her phone to check the clock. The battery was dead. So, she pulled out the charger and plugged it into the wall socket beside the bed.

The squeaking door made her straighten. Expecting Mason, she swivelled only for her eyes to widen in horror.

A middle-aged woman dressed in a flowing white lace boubou walked in. Instantly Sophie knew this was Mason's mother. Dripping in jewellery, she carried herself regally, almost gliding across the room, shaved hair and face with a hint of makeup.

Sophie grabbed the duvet and covered herself, curtseying. "Good morning, ma."

The woman ignored her. "Doctor, you can come in and do your tests."

A young man walked in, wearing shirt, tie and trousers with a stethoscope around his neck and carrying a box. He looked too young to be their family doctor. But that was beside the point.

"What's going on. I don't need a doctor. I'm not sick," Sophie replied, her gaze bouncing from the woman to the so-called doctor.

"That's left to be seen, young lady. I can't allow you to infect my children with whatever disease you're carrying," the woman replied, turning her head to someone outside the door. "Rocha, come and hold her down."

The skin on Sophie's skin mottled with goosebumps, and a cold finger travelled down her spine as Mason's brother appeared in the doorway.

EIGHT

This could not be happening!

Sophie stumbled back involuntarily as Rocha entered Mason's bedroom, followed by another man. Both were muscular, intimidating men, certainly bigger and scarier than the doctor. Three men and a woman stared at her with intent and malice.

Mason's mother had brought a fucking army to take her down. Why? She'd never interacted with the woman before. Never given the woman reason to think she would need so many people to subdue her.

Unless, of course, Rocha had mentioned the incident in the driveway of the city house and how Sophie had slipped past him and gone with Mason at the last minute. Maybe Rocha was the one who'd insisted on being here and brought reinforcement.

Considering the sneer on his face and how he looked down his nose at her, it was the most likely option. This was payback for her snubbing him last night.

Shit.

Her shoulder hit the wall, jarring the wound, and she winced in pain.

"If you want to leave this place alive and intact … do as I say."

Just like that, she remembered Mason's warning. He'd been right. The knife cut acted as a reminder. But what would he want her to do in this situation?

"I'm here with Mason, and he didn't tell me anything about a doctor coming to do tests." She hoped mentioning Mason would stall them at least until he got here.

Mason, where are you?

"He sent you a text message about the doctor!" Rocha shouted.

"A message." Her heart thudded in her chest, and she glanced at her phone plugged into the charger. "My phone battery was dead. I didn't see a message."

"That doesn't mean the message doesn't exist. It's your own fault." Rocha leaned under the bed, and metal rattled as he yanked something out.

Cold sweat broke out on Sophie's skin, and dread filled her as she stared at the metal chain with cuffs in his hands. Mason really had a freaking metal chain under his bed. His threat to chain her last night hadn't been a joke.

"I'll do whatever the doctor says. You don't need to chain me. Doctor, please," she hoped the man had an ounce of decency in him and wouldn't stand by and watch them chain her. He was in a caring profession, after all.

"You will lie on the bed and open your legs?" The doctor asked in an unaffected voice. Placing his box on the table on the other side of the bed.

Sophie swallowed the lump in her throat. "Yes, but can I have some privacy, please. Let the others leave. You don't need them."

"Okay. But Mrs Maduka will stay for your own good." He glanced at Mason's mother, who frowned but nodded.

"Rocha, don't go too far," the older woman said.

Rocha's smirk stayed as he walked out with the other man.

"Can you close the door," Sophie said, still trying to delay the outcome. She didn't want to submit herself to whatever this doctor would do to her.

"Don't waste my time, young lady!" Mrs Maduka snapped.

"Okay," Sophie muttered and shuffled to the bed. She climbed on and held the duvet to cover her body. Her shoulder hurt with the movement reminding her of Mason. If Mason sent a message to her about a doctor's visit, she must do this because it was about survival.

The doctor brought out items from his box, metal objects, as well as huge fucking syringes.

Sophie's pulse rate sped up. She hated needles as much as she hated knives—any sharp objects against her skin. She clutched the duvet cover to her chest, trying not to panic as her body trembled. She squeezed her eyes shut as the doctor tied a small elastic belt around her arm. She didn't want to look at what he was doing.

"Make a fist," he said, tapping her elbow and the back of her hand to find her veins.

She obeyed, trying to regulate her breathing. She'd survived Mason's cut last night. Okay, only because he'd held her down.

Perhaps she would need those men to hold her down too.

No, not Rocha. She didn't want Mason's brother touching her. Mason wouldn't want his brother touching her. There was a tug of war between the brothers, and she'd inadvertently chosen a side—Mason's. The fresh, hurting brand on her left shoulder proved she belonged to Mason for a few days. Crazy, but a fact she would have to stick with if she wanted to survive.

"Drop the duvet," Mrs Maduka's voice cut through her thoughts.

Sophie's eyes fluttered open, and she frowned, confused. "Why? The doctor is only taking my blood. He doesn't need to look at my naked body."

The older woman glared at her, and Sophie realised her mistake.

"Don't speak unless you're asked a direct question."

Mason had said that to her when his brother had arrived in the city last night. She assumed that instruction applied to his mother too.

Her question was valid, though. She had no problem appearing naked in front of people. But when she visited the mobile sexual health clinics that provided a free service for prostitutes, she was still accorded dignity and privacy. She never had to strip her clothes completely.

Still, this situation wasn't about care or dignity.

Mrs Maduka was proving a point. She could make Sophie comply with whatever she wanted—willingly or forced.

It was about humiliating Sophie and causing her discomfort.

Anger flared inside Sophie. The woman had no right to treat her this way. She'd done nothing wrong. She might be a prostitute, but she was also human. Someone's daughter. Someone's sister. She didn't deserve the humiliation because she was in the woman's son's bedroom.

The doctor inserted a needle into her vein, and Sophie flinched.

Don't be a baby. She reminded herself using Mason's words.

She was strong and would survive whatever these people did to her.

She flung the duvet aside, glaring at Mason's mother and spread her legs, exposing her pussy to the woman's gaze. "You wanted to see what your sons are fighting over? Well, take a good look."

The doctor made a choking sound, drawing Sophie's attention briefly. He had finished drawing blood and seemed fixated on her body, too, the pervert.

"Well, doctor, you wanted me to spread my legs. Is it so you can stare at it too?" she mocked him.

He lowered his gaze in embarrassment and grabbed a metal object similar to what they used at the clinic to do her cervical smear—a speculum, a nurse called it. He attached a headset with a torch and flicked it on. "You need to face me so I can examine you."

She moved so he was facing her vagina, but her glare still stayed on Mrs Maduka. She wanted the woman to see that she wouldn't be cowed, not by a man fiddling with her vagina while she watched.

To be fair, the woman didn't flinch or bat an eyelid. Instead, she stood there, watching the doctor poke and prod Sophie, including her anal passage.

"You can cover up now," the doctor said after he withdrew the instruments from her body. "Mason wanted you to be vaccinated. Have you had the HPV or hepatitis B vaccines?"

Sophie slowly tugged the duvet over her body, shocked that Mason wanted her to be vaccinated. "No. What is HPV?"

"Human Papillomavirus is an STI which causes cervical cancer, but the vaccine will prevent it."

The thought of getting cancer scared her. But vaccines meant more needles.

More to the point, Mason wanted her to have the vaccines, and she had to obey him. Still, he was looking out for her by trying to stop her from getting cancer. He didn't have to do this. It was costing him money. Did he care about her? He must do. Maybe that was why he was so adamant about her heeding his warning. He wanted her to survive this visit with his family because he cared in a crazy way.

"Yes, I'll have the vaccines." She shifted and sat up, back to the headboard.

"And a tetanus shot…" The doctor brought out the vials and syringes.

"Tetanus?" her brow rumpled.

"For your … injury." He indicated the dressing on her shoulder. He seemed to know that the wound was not an accident. Did Mason mention what he'd done?

"Okay." Sophie pursed her lips and braced herself as the man injected the medicines into her body. She'd had so many sharp objects against her skin in the last 24 hours she hoped she didn't become traumatised by it.

The doctor packed up once he was done. He strode the door.

"I will fast-track the tests with the lab and send you the results as soon as I have them," he said to Mrs Maduka.

"Will I get a copy of the test results too, doctor?" Sophie asked. The tests were about her. She should see the result, even if she wasn't paying for it. Well, the whole freaking process of being examined was a kind of payment on her part.

He cleared his throat. "Of course, Ms Sophie. I will send a copy to you via this address."

Then he walked out.

Sophie stayed on the bed, expecting Mason's mother to leave too so she could get dressed.

"Rocha, bring the koboko and the boys to hold her down."

"No fucking way." Sophie jumped on top of the bed and scrambled across towards the bathroom. She wouldn't lie there and take whatever they were about to dish out.

Before she could reach the bathroom door, Rocha stood there as if he'd anticipated her move. Of course, he would expect it. She'd done the same thing to him last night when she'd run into Mason's car to escape him.

He flexed the long flexible cane in his hand, and it made a zipping sound through the air.

She backed away as other men entered the room. Men she didn't recognise. "I did the examination. I did what you told me. Why are you doing this?"

"Oh, young lady. The list of your offences is long." For the first time today, Mrs Maduka smiled, and Sophie knew she was in for a world of pain. She'd defied the woman, and she had to pay.

She panicked, her body trembling, and tears pooled in her eyes. "Please, I didn't mean to be rude. I won't do it again. Please, Rocha."

"Me? You want my help? Okay." Rocha smiled and turned to his mother, handing her the koboko. "Mum, let me talk to her. It's okay. I'll handle it."

His mother eyed him for a few seconds and nodded. Then she stepped out of the door with the other men.

Rocha closed the door and ambled towards Sophie. "You know you should have taken the three hundred grand I offered you last night. You wouldn't be in this position right now. You would have been in your own home, doing whatever you do during the day." He stopped and raised his hands as if a thought occurred to him. "Oh, I hear you are homeless. Still, with the money, you could have been in a hotel room right now, not here about to be punished. This is what choosing my brother does to you."

Sophie kept retreating until she was stuck in the corner of the wardrobe and the wall. "I only went with him because he'd picked me first. If you'd been the one to pick me first, then I would have gone with you instead."

He grimaced and shook his head. "Yet, if I'd picked you first, I would have been happy to share you with my brother, something we've done several times before. Yet, somehow, this time, my brother doesn't want to share you. Can you tell me why?"

"I don't know. I'm not in his head. I can barely predict what he would do, let alone why he's doing it. He cut me last night for no fucking reason. How—"

"Wait a minute. He cut you? With his knife?" His eyes narrowed.

"Yes."

"I want to see it."

"No. It's going to hurt."

"Let me fucking see it, or I'm not helping you."

"Fine." She sighed and turned her shoulder so he could peel the plaster off the edge of the wound. It hurt, and she gritted her teeth through the pain.

"Fuck!" he swore aloud when he saw the wound and backed away as if it was a snake and would bite him. He paced towards the door and scrubbed a hand over his head.

"What is it?" she asked, confused about his reaction.

"Look, I'm going to make you a one-time offer to get out of here. I'll take you somewhere safe. Somewhere away from my brother. He's not okay in the head, you know. You saw the chain he keeps under his bed. He's already cut you once, and he'll do it again."

"So, what's the deal? What do you get for helping me?" She wasn't naïve enough to think he would do anything for her for free.

"I want to know that you won't run away once I get you out of this house. So, I'm going to fuck you right here."

"In Mason's room. On his bed. Are you crazy?"

"It'll be our secret."

"Ours and everyone standing outside the door."

He smiled. "Yes, they'll know too, but they will keep the secret."

Huh? Then the image of Mason standing in the driveway alone while Rocha's men stood on the other side watching him replayed in her mind.

"So, you can all make fun of him when he's not there," she said as the reality of the situation dawned.

Smirking, he nodded and pursed his lips. "Yes."

"No," she said quietly.

Rocha was cruel for fun. Something Mason wasn't unless the person deserved it.

"What?" He jerked back.

"I won't let you use me as a weapon against Mason. He might be crazy, but he doesn't deserve what you're doing to him."

"Nothing in this house is safe for you ..." Mason's warning played again. If she went with Rocha, she would end up dead in a ditch. If he could do these things to his brother, he would have no problem killing her.

"You know that means my mother will flay your skin." He raised his brow.

"Bring it." She taunted, straightening her spine. She was shitting scared, but she would not give him the satisfaction of seeing it.

He growled and advanced towards her, hand raised.

"Touch me, and Mason will break your hand!" she shouted.

He stopped as if realising she had spoken the truth.

"He's not coming to save you." He gritted out. Then he grabbed her hair, bending her backwards painfully, making her eyes water like he was ripping the strands out.

She fought him, kicked him the way she'd seen Mason kick Bomba, and he released her. Then, before she could back away, he slapped her, and she collapsed on the floor.

She didn't know when the door opened. Then she was lifted as she fought, and they chained her across the bed, hands stretched at one side and feet at the other.

Soon Mrs Maduka stood over her while Rocha and the men watched as the woman set Sophie's back on fire with each cane stroke.

She buried her face in the duvet and wept. Even after the caning stopped and they left her alone, chained, and naked, she wept.

NINE

Mason woke feeling hot and realised a supple female body curled into him. He glanced down into Sophie's sleeping face, and a smile curled his lips.

He'd warned her not to touch him when he'd gotten into bed, and she'd shuffled to the far side. Yet, somehow, she'd ended up curled into him. To be fair, the room was freezing, just the way he liked it. However, she proved to be the opposite and didn't enjoy the arctic blast from the aircon. Hence she'd subconsciously sought out the nearest source of heat—his body.

He'd threatened to chain her and make her sleep on the floor if she touched him. Yet, the punishment was far from his mind this morning. Instead, he stroked his fingertips along her arm in a slow caress, moving upwards from elbow to shoulder. She stirred and exhaled into his chest but didn't wake up.

The smooth feel of the water-proof fabric on her shoulder had his dick hardening and his pulse rate skyrocketing. She bore his mark under the dressing. Last night he'd branded her with his knife, carved his initial—M—into her skin. It wasn't deep enough to scar permanently. Over time it would heal and flake, and fresh epidermis would replace it like it never existed. Like he never existed.

A weight settled on his chest. For a few seconds, he struggled to breathe.

Why was he filled with dread about the brand on Sophie's skin disappearing? He'd marked her knowing it would be temporary. Just like he'd brought her here, knowing she would only stay for a few days.

Nothing in life lasted forever.

A lesson he learned the hard way with his father's death. He'd assumed his old man would live long and be in Mason's life until he became a father. Now, that dream was gone.

A lump sat in his throat, and his eyes smarted, tears clouding them. He withdrew gently, not wanting to wake her, not wanting her to see him being vulnerable.

People assumed many things about him. Mostly that he was unfeeling and crazy. Perhaps he was both things. Sure, his brain was wired differently from other people's. But his late father had made him feel sane. The man had never used his idiosyncrasies against him. Had only shown him right from wrong. Shown him respect. Taught him about honour and loyalty. About protecting his responsibilities.

Grey light filtered through the blinds as he grabbed a towel and walked out of the bedroom across the corridor to the family bathroom. He flung the towel over the chrome rail, used the WC, flushed it, and entered the walk-in glass cubicle. He turned the faucet and stood aside as water cascaded from the showerhead. He waited until steam rose before he stepped under the hot spray.

Although he loved a cold room, he loved a hot shower, a tale of two extremes like his life.

And just like in his life, some of his actions might seem extreme. Branding Sophie, for one. He understood how people would view his actions. Sophie had called him "…fucking crazy …"

He smiled again as he grabbed the soap bar from the holder and started scrubbing his body.

He'd agreed with her description of him. His father had once warned him:

"Son, the Yadili life is like being in a constant state of war. There will be war rooms and battles, even truces. But make no mistake, you can never fully relax. The minute you do, you've lost the war. The enemy will take what you're trying to protect."

He'd been a teenager then and perhaps hadn't fully understood the implications.

Now, he did. Hence his brand on Sophie.

In this house, it was the only way to put his claim on her, short of putting a ring on her finger.

Sure, there'd been a pleasure for him in the process. Holding her down while she struggled and cutting into her skin had been exhilarating. That bit had been for him.

However, Sophie walking around the house with that mark would protect her from all the predators around here—and there were plenty of them.

Because no one would dare touch something that belonged to him when he'd so clearly labelled it as his.

Everyone feared crazy Mason because they could never predict his reaction.

He stepped out of the cubicle and dried his body. He took his toothbrush from the cupboard over the sink, applied paste and brushed his teeth. Done, he stepped out of the bathroom and halted, his back tingling.

Ma Bagu stood in the hallway, dressed in a matching Ankara skirt and blouse of Mama Binyerem's trademark style—modern and mumsy. Reminding him about the clothes coming for Sophie. He didn't want her dressed like Ma Bagu. He stifled a smile.

"Good morning, Ma Bagu," he said, wondering why she stood in the hallway. "Nke a i guzoro ebe a, ihe nile adịkwa mma?"

"Morning, nwa m. Gaa yiri uwe. Achọrọ m ka mụ na gị kpàrịta ụkà." *Morning, my child. Go and get dressed. I want me and you to have a discussion.*

"Okay. I'm coming. Ana m abịa," he replied and entered his bedroom. He moved lightly across the room, grabbing clothes and putting them on. He wasn't that fussed about his appearance. He was a jeans, t-shirt and trainers guy.

Sophie seemed fast asleep, and he didn't want to wake her. She'd had a long night, and they'd only gotten into bed around three. The time on his wristwatch said it was six-thirty.

Dressed, he left his room and went downstairs. He found Ma Bagu in the kitchen with two other domestic staff. They greeted him as Ma Bagu ushered him through the back door, down the narrow passage at the back of the staff quarters, and out the back gate into the rear garden. On one side, they were surrounded by trees—oil palm and plantain. The other end was rows of okra plants with blooming flowers. This was where the okra from the soup had been harvested. Ma Bagu was a keen farmer. The land was his family's for as far as the eyes could see.

She walked to a bench along a path separating the trees from the shrubs. He sat down beside her and waited for her to speak. The sun rose to their left and the house to their right.

She didn't keep him waiting long and spoke in Igbo. "I have a message from your father."

"My father." He sat straight, although he wasn't surprised. She was a spiritualist. The modern term was medium. She'd conveyed messages from his late dad before.

"Yes. I was communing with the spirits last night after I met the girl your brought home. You have a fondness for her—"

"I do?" This one shocked him. He liked Sophie, but he wouldn't call it fondness. Fondness implied importance and longevity—none of which he could apply to the prostitute he'd brought home.

"Yes, you do. You might not know it yet, but—" she prodded his chest "—your heart accepts her."

"O dị egwu." *It's ridiculous.* He scoffed, chuckling. "Ma Bagu, I don't even know anything about her except that she's a prostitute, and I saved her from her pimp."

"Your heart accepted me when you knew nothing about me," she interjected.

"But that was different."

"How is it different? You didn't know me. You saw what they were doing to me. When no one else stopped to help, you did. You saved my life."

He'd been a teenager who'd snuck out of boarding school on a lowdown jolly in a taxi when they encountered a mob in the street. They'd stripped a woman they'd claimed had eaten her unborn children and husband, whipped her and hung a sign around her saying she was a witch.

Mason barely remembered his reaction except for some of what the taxi driver and Ma Bagu said afterwards. First, he'd told the taxi driver to wait and had gotten out. Then, crazed by what they were doing to someone who wasn't fighting back, he'd jumped into the fray, grabbing a metal pole off someone and smashing people's heads. The crowd had dispersed quickly after that, afraid of the mad person in their midst who looked like he would kill everyone in the vicinity.

The taxi driver had grabbed a fabric off a woman with a double wrapper and covered Ma Bagu. Mason had put the woman in the taxi and had taken her to a hotel. From there, he'd called his father, who'd shown up and brought him and Ma Bagu home.

"You brought me to your house and convinced your parents to let me stay. Without knowing much about me," Ma Bagu continued."

Mason's mother had been furious with him for skipping school and getting into the melee. She'd wanted to kick Ma Bagu out, but Mason had made a deal with her. He would submit to his mother's punishment if she allowed Ma Bagu to stay.

Now, he shook his head, not wanting to remember what had come afterwards.

"You spoke the truth." He sighed. There were similarities between how he'd saved Sophie and Ma Bagu. "But what has it got to do with my father."

"As I said, I noticed your fondness for her which means you're vulnerable where she's concerned. So, I wanted to commune with the spirits to find out if any darkness is hanging around her that could affect you."

"And what did you find." He shifted to the edge of the bench.

"Your father showed up. You remember how he said he would return to you through reincarnation?"

"Yes, I remember." He sat still, waiting for the rest.

Months ago, soon after his father passed, Ma Bagu had mentioned that his father noticed how heartbroken Mason was and would reincarnate as Mason's child. At the time, Mason hadn't put much stock in it since he wasn't dating, although it had soothed him that his father was looking out for him.

"Your father said he's chosen the woman who will bear your son. He chose Sophie."

Mason couldn't help the burst of laughter out of him as he stood and paced away, shaking his head. He'd been indulging Ma Bagu's visions, but this one was beyond ridiculous.

He turned back to face the old woman. Her expression wasn't amused at all.

"Ma Bagu, what you're saying doesn't make sense. Sophie is a prostitute that I saved. She's not my girlfriend. Or my date. I haven't even … slept with her like that." At this rate, he wasn't even sure he would have sex with Sophie. Oh, he was attracted to her, but…

"But when you do, it will enter."

"How? I'm not about to have sex with a prostitute without a condom." He wasn't that crazy.

Ma Bagu shook her head, looking annoyed. "Some people believe in Immaculate Conception. Yet you don't believe that a manufactured product like a condom can malfunction? Hian. If I didn't know you, I would've said you're a fool."

He stiffened. "Ma Bagu, what are you saying? Are you prophesying?"

She rolled her eyes upwards. "Do I have water in my mouth? I'm telling you that if you have sex with Sophie, condom or no condom, she will get pregnant. And that child will be your father reincarnated. I've finished talking."

She stood in a huff and started walking back towards the house.

Mason sat in shock for a few seconds as the words sank in. He could have his father in his life again. The idea sent a burst of joy through him. His father was coming back. This time as Mason's son. He would do anything for that child. He would give the world.

Excitement made him jump up, and he ran after Ma Bagu.

"Mama, ewela iwe. Chere nu. Don't be angry. Wait, now." She stopped midway through the path, and he hugged her from behind. "Daalu." *Thank you.*

"Anula m," she said, nodding, her mouth curling into a smile as he came around to face her.

Then the reality of the situation hit him. "How am I going to make Sophie understand?"

"Slowly," Ma Bagu said. "First thing is to show her this world you inhabit. Your family. Your life. Once she understands, the rest will fall into place. And you must prepare for fatherhood. You must sort out your priorities and set your house in order."

"True." He nodded and knew precisely how to do it, his mind mapping out everything he needed to do as they walked back to the main house.

He left Ma Bagu in the kitchen and went to the dining room. His mother sat at the table with Rocha, who looked like he'd just arrived from the city.

"Good morning, Mother, Rocha," he greeted in a cheerful tone. "How are you?"

They both raised their heads, looking at him suspiciously.

"I'm .. fine, Mason … good morning," his mother's shock was evident at the head of the table.

"Morning," Rocha eyed him as Mason pulled out the chair opposite his brother.

He couldn't blame them. He hadn't shared breakfast with them since his father died.

"Are you okay?" his mother asked.

"Yes, I'm feeling wonderful this morning. Thank you for asking," he replied, reaching for the covered dishes. "And how about you Rocha? I see you just arrived. I hope the drive was safe."

"Yes, the drive was good." His brother exchanged looks with their mother.

Mason pretended not to see it as he stacked steamed plantain and egg stew on his plate. "That's great. It's a beautiful day. The sun is out. Have you seen Ma Bagu's okra field? It looks wonderful and flowering."

"This one you're in such a good mood. Your toy must be excellent," Rocha said as he grinned.

Mason didn't take the bait. He was in such good spirits. Knowing his father hadn't abandoned him, he could forgive his brother's jabs.

"Mother, I have a guest staying for a few days," he said instead. "Her name is Sophie. I will ask Doctor Amaechi to come and check on her."

The physician wasn't Mason's first choice, but he was at the family's beck and call and would drop everything else if needed. He specialised in OB-GYN and was the one they used to handle any indiscretions involving Rocha's women.

Mason had never had to use the man until now because he never dated, and he rarely had penetrative vaginal sex involving his dick. For him, sex was about control and restraint rather than release. It was about pain rather than pleasure. Of course, he always used a condom, and most of the women were sex workers.

But things were changing, apparently.

"Why does she need the doctor? Is she unwell?" his mother asked, frowning.

"No. I just want him to examine her and make sure she's fine. It's just a precaution. Is that okay?" He didn't need her permission. He would pay the doctor directly if required.

But he was trying to keep his mother sweet. So, she would be nice to Sophie in turn. He needed his family to be nice to her. He wanted to remove all the obstacles which would prevent Sophie from accepting his proposal when he eventually asked her to be his baby mama and wife.

"Sure," his mother replied. "That's fine."

"Good. Please do me a favour."

"What is it?"

"I have a meeting with Chief Odili, and then I'm going to see Duke afterwards, so I won't be here when the doctor visits. Please stay in my room with Sophie when Dr Amaechi gets here. I don't want him alone in the room with her."

"Of course. I'll be happy to do that."

"Great. Thank you so much, Mother." He pushed his chair back.

"Are you not going to finish your breakfast?" his brother asked.

"No. I want to get to Chief's house early. There's something important I want to talk to him about."

"What is so important that you won't finish your meal?" his mother asked.

He grinned and settled back into his chair, leaning forward. "I've decided to take the Yadili oath and swear allegiance to Chief."

His mother's eyes widened. "You're serious."

"Wow." His brother said.

"Absolutely," he said. "I've been putting it off for so long. I only regret that I didn't get to do it before Dad died."

The impending prospects of fathering a child made him realise he had to settle down and plot a path for his life. And every member of his lineage took the oath for the secret organisation at some point.

"That is wonderful news." His mother's eyes sparkled with pleasure, something she rarely directed towards him these days. "I'm pleased that you made this decision. Finally, you can become part of the brotherhood and not be treated like an outsider."

He doubted some people would stop treating him like an outsider because he took the oath, but who knew.

"I'm happy for you, bro," his brother said.

"Thank you," Mason said. "Will you come with me to Chief's house?"

"No. I have some other business to handle. But I'll see you when you return, and we will celebrate with Sophie too."

Mason heard the taunt in Rocha's tone as he lifted his head. They locked gazes, and Mason kept his face expressionless.

His father's voice played in his mind. *Don't give away your position.*

In order words, he shouldn't reveal how important Sophie was to him.

He forced a smile onto his face. "No, brother. The celebrations will not involve Sophie. She is out of bounds."

Rocha's eyes widened, and he pursed his lips. "Okay."

"Ehm, does your guest know that the doctor is coming?" his mother asked. She must have noticed the sudden tension.

"No, she doesn't." Mason pulled out his phone and sent a message to Sophie's phone. "I've sent her a message informing her of the visit."

He pushed off his chair. "I'll see you both later."

"Okay. Bye." His mother said.

"Bye," Rocha muttered.

When he reached the door, he stopped. "One last thing. No one else should enter my bedroom except Mother and the doctor."

His mother twisted in her seat. "Why? What if the girl refuses the doctor? The boys will need to hold her down."

"Sophie knows better than to disobey my instruction. She won't."

"But what if she doesn't? If you really want the doctor to examine her, then she might have to be restrained. Of course, if you don't want me to do it, you can wait until you are available and get the doctor."

"No, it can't wait." He didn't know how long he could restrain himself from having sex with Sophie. And he didn't want her getting pregnant without a health check first.

His mother was correct. Sophie was defiant and could refuse the doctor.

He sighed. He would have to allow his mother some leeway in restraining her.

"Okay," he said finally. "You can have two other people there. Just to restrain her. Nothing more."

"I hear you," his mother said, and he detected a note of triumph as he walked out of the door.

His spine prickled with dread, and he sent another message to Sophie, this one of caution.

Obey my mother.

TEN

Mason returned to the house later that evening feeling accomplished. He'd first had a productive day meeting with Chief Odili, who had welcomed his decision to become a full member of the Yadili network. He'd been a Yadi associate as a student but hadn't taken the formal oath once he'd graduated.

The sun was setting, the sky a mix of orange and violet.

Benji parked the car in his spot, but Mason didn't leave immediately.

"Did Mama Binye bring the clothes for Sophie as I requested?" he asked.

Benji had been with him all day, but he'd been instructed to get the message to the seamstress who owned a shop in the town. "Yes, she did. I told her to text me as soon as the items were delivered, and she did."

"Great," Mason replied.

He liked this about Benji. The man was straightforward and got things done. Hence, Mason preferred using him as his security. He was older and didn't mess around like the other men who worked for Rocha.

Benji came around and opened the car door.

As Mason stepped out, he stopped in front of the man. "Benji, I want you to work for me permanently. To become my second."

The man rarely smiled, but his lips curled upwards. "Yes, I would like that."

"Good." Mason grinned, too, stretching out his hand. "We'll work out the details later."

"Of course, thank you." The man shook his hand, and Mason patted his shoulder.

He headed towards the portico. However, Ma Bagu came around the side passage before he could enter through the front door.

"Good. You're back," she said in Igbo, a note of urgency in her voice.

"Yes. What is it?" he asked, the hairs on his neck standing erect.

"Come," she indicated for him to go along with her.

Mason followed her through the side door.

"It's Sophie," she said in a low voice once they stepped inside. "The girl hasn't come downstairs. She hasn't eaten anything all day."

"Why?" Mason asked, frowning.

"I don't know. Your mother banned everyone from going to your room after the doctor visited."

Mason's breath quickened, his suspicion rising. "Where is my mother?"

"In the dining room, about to eat dinner," Ma Bagu said.

"Okay." He turned to Benji, who stood just outside the door. "Make sure no one leaves this house. Do you understand me?"

Benji nodded. "Absolutely."

He hoped the man knew enough about how he operated to understand what he needed him to do.

Then Mason took the steps two at a time as Ma Bagu followed at a slower pace.

He reached the top and walked down the landing to his bedroom. He pushed the door, and the suffocating feeling in his chest returned.

Sophie lay stretched across his bed, naked and face down, hands and feet cuffed to the metal chain under his bed. She wasn't moving, and he couldn't tell if she was dead or alive.

He hurried across the room, placed his fingers against her neck to check her pulse and he noticed the marks on her back—cane welts. His stomach rolled.

Fuck! His mother had cancd Sophie.

His body tensed, and he ground his teeth.

He hadn't given his mother permission to do this. Restrain her, yes. But not this. She'd been locked like this for hours. Not at all what he'd wanted.

Ma Bagu walked in and calmly went to the other side of the bed. She fiddled with the locks around Sophie's ankles.

He knelt beside the bed and undid the cuffs around her wrists. Her limbs would be sore and stiff from being locked in this position for so long.

As he dropped the chain, the sound of the clonking metals woke Sophie, and she groaned and stirred. She tried to roll over but cried out and opened her eyes instead. Her face was covered in tear tracks, and her eyes were red. There was a swelling on her left cheek. Someone had hit her face.

His anger boiled, and his hands clenched into fists.

When she met his gaze, she flinched and moved away, dragging her body across the bed, away from him.

"Sophie," he reached for her as a bitter taste filled his mouth.

"Don't fucking touch me," she cried, obviously in pain as she tried to sit up, face in a grimace. "You let them do this to me!"

She was right to accuse him. He'd left her. But he'd thought they would respect the sanctity of his bedroom—his ownership claim of her. He'd miscalculated, perhaps too arrogantly. Nothing was sacred to his family, obviously.

"Nwa m, jiri nwayọọ, take it easy," Ma Bagu said in a calm tone from the other side of the bed. "Make I help you, please."

Sophie panted heavily for a few seconds. Then she nodded. "Ma Bagu, you can stay. But I don't want him here."

"No—"

"Mason, go. I will take care of her," Ma Bagu interrupted.

He gritted his teeth in frustration, reluctant to leave Sophie. However, Ma Bagu would care for her, and he had other matters requiring his attention.

He marched to the wardrobe, unlocked the hidden compartment, and withdrew the handgun. Then he opened the side drawer and took the leather sheath containing the Damascus steel hunting knife with a reverse saw serration. He tucked both behind him into his belt and covered them with his t-shirt before heading downstairs.

Benji stood in the corridor by the kitchen and patted his trouser pocket. "The gates are locked."

"Good. Cover me." Mason could handle his brother and mother himself. But he'd been stupid to relax, to underestimate them this morning. He would never make that mistake again.

He walked down the corridor, Benji closely behind.

In the dining room, Rocha and his mother sat at the table like this morning, laughing and chatting. His brother was in dress shirt and trousers. No obvious place to hide a weapon. He didn't need to get his hands dirty because others around him carried weapons.

Mason walked in casually, going straight towards them instead of to the other side of the table.

"Mason, welcome," his mother said when she looked up and saw him. "How did it go with Chief?"

"Good. Chief sends his regards," he replied and grabbed the bottle of water, fiddled with the cap and poured water into a tumbler. He lifted the glass and dumped the liquid on his mother's head.

"Mason!" she cried in shock.

"What the hell?" Rocha jumped from his seat to intercept him. He was so fucking predictable, and Mason knew he would be quick to defend their mother.

But Mason was quicker, his knife already in his hand and slashing diagonally, catching Rocha's arms as he lunged for him.

"Sit the fuck down," he ordered his brother, who clutched his arm, blood seeping through his shirt and fingers. "Benji, keep your gun pointed at my brother. If he moves, shoot him in the leg."

Mason grabbed his mother by the neck, yanking her from the chair.

"No way." Rocha twisted in his seat to glare at Benji, who had drawn his weapon. "Benji, I fucking pay you."

"No. Your late father paid me. But you've hardly paid me since he died. Now, Mason made me a better offer."

"How dare you." Rocha leapt from his seat towards Benji.

The bodyguard fired a shot into the fabric upholstered chair next to him, making him jump back. "That was a warning shot. Sit down, sir."

Mason almost smiled. It would teach his brother to treat his team better.

An

"Mason, stop this madness!" his mother shouted. "Your brother needs the hospital."

"No one is going anywhere until I get answers." Mason tightened his grip on her from behind, the blade close to her jugular. "What was my instruction to you this morning?"

"You are the one who came in here and asked me for a favour. I did you a favour!"

"I told you to watch over Sophie while the doctor was here," he gritted out. "So why was she chained?"

"The girl defied me and was rude. She refused the doctor."

Mason paused. Why would Sophie refuse after he'd instructed her to obey his mother? "She refused the doctor?"

"Yes, at first. We had to make her. You said we could restrain her."

"Only while the doctor was examining her. I never told you to whip her!" His grip on her tightened, and she gurgled, struggling to breathe. "If you ever touch her again or do anything to hurt her, I will kill you."

"You won't fucking dare it!" Rocha shouted.

Mason turned his glare on his brother. "Are you fucking stupid? Don't you realise that the only person that kept me on a leash was Dad? Now he's gone. Nothing will stop me. You've already done the worst you can do to me by not letting me be at his bedside while he was dying. But you see Sophie? I will kill every last person in this house if she gets hurt again. If you don't know what I'm capable of doing, dare me and find out."

He turned to his mother, who was gripping his forearms, trying to push him away. Her eyes bulged as she choked. "Are you listening to me, Mother?"

She nodded, her eyes watering and going red.

He loosened his grip. "I want to hear you say it."

"Yes … I won't touch her again," she choked out.

He released her. "Now, tell me everybody that was in my bedroom today."

"What?" His mother trembled, her wide gaze going to Rocha.

"I said, name the people who were in my bedroom today."

"Well …" she hesitated. "It was me and the doctor."

"Who put the chains on Sophie?" he gritted out.

She named two men but didn't mention Rocha. Typical.

Mason swapped the knife into his other hand, stepped up to Rocha and punched his face. His brother hit his head on the table, clattering everything and smashing a porcelain dish. "Mother may try to protect you as always. But I know you were in my bedroom. I saw your handiwork on Sophie. She belongs to me. Mine alone. You saw my brand on her, yet you dared to touch her. That punch was for the one you gave her. Next time you won't live to regret it."

He left the dining room, calmer than he'd entered it. Revenge violence soothed him.

His mother rushed over to the slumped Rocha who required a trip to the hospital for his injuries. Of course, the dining room furniture would need replacing due to damage from blood stains and a bullet hole.

Mason didn't care. As he stepped outside through the side door, he quickly phoned Duke requesting a security crew. Then he turned to Benji. "You need a team. Duke is sending men over to support you. I want you to find the two men that were in my room this morning and chain them up. Can you handle that?"

"Of course."

"Good. Send one man to stand outside my bedroom door in case anyone tries anything."

"Done."

"Thank you." He took a step into the house and paused. "When you get a moment, let me know how much my brother owes you. My father never underpaid staff, and it's wrong for my brother to sully his legacy. I will make up any arrears you're owed."

"Thank you. I appreciate your efforts," Benji replied.

Mason nodded and went upstairs. He would have to find out how many other staff had been underpaid since his father's death.

It was one thing if the Maduka family had fallen on hard times after the old man died. But they owned properties and investments that kept them living in luxury. So, there was no reason to pay the hardworking employees less than they deserved.

For now, he had more pressing matters, though. Sophie.

He opened his bedroom door and found her still on the bed, under the duvet, eyes closed. Ma Bagu sat in the armchair, watching her. A tray of food lay on the table untouched.

The old woman looked up and pressed a finger to her lips indicating for him to be quiet. Then she got up and came over, tugging him into the corridor before shutting the door. "She's sleeping. I cleaned the wounds and gave her something to relieve the pain and help her sleep. She didn't eat much, though."

"Thank you. I'll take over after I shower," he said, entering the room to grab toiletries.

When he returned from the family bathroom, Ma Bagu took the food tray and left.

Dressed in shorts and a T, he settled in the armchair, placed the gun next to the lamp on the bedside table, and watched Sophie sleep.

She was his, damn it, and he would make sure every damned person knew it.

ELEVEN

Sophie woke to a dark room, although light came through the corners of the blinds. It was daylight and probably around midday. She was used to sleeping through the mornings because most of her work occurred at night. It took her a minute to remember her location as she tried to move. Her back hurt.

From Mrs Maduka's koboko strikes. The horrible woman had left her locked in chains all day.

She remembered Mason coming home last night and unlocking the cuffs. She'd seen his angry face and clenched fists, directed at his mother. Not caring, she'd just wanted him out of the room. She'd been pressed and needed to use the toilet.

She'd refused his help, not wanting him to see her bent over and hobbling to the bathroom because of the pain piercing her body.

Yesterday had been torture. In all her years of working with Bomba, she'd never endured anything as painful or humiliating as what Mason's mother and brother made her suffer yesterday. Her former madam, where she'd worked as a house help, had been mean. Still, Mrs Maduka's cruelty and brutality remained unmatched in her experience.

Why had Mason allowed them to torment her?

Surely he'd known what his mother and brother were capable of doing.

Okay, he'd warned her that nothing was safe in this house. So why hadn't he been here when the doctor arrived if she'd required supervision.

Hissing and wincing, she shuffled to the edge of the bed closest to her and stood gingerly. Although her ankles hurt where the cuffs had been, she could stand without bending over in pain like last night when she'd gone to the toilet.

She turned on the overhead lamp and walked to the full-length mirror. Her breath hitched. She'd been in such pain yesterday she hadn't thought to examine her back. Now she stared in shock.

Welts lined her back diagonally, the skin swollen, broken and oozing liquid. There was discolouration from bruises. Her back would hurt for many days if not weeks.

She shuffled to the bathroom and sat on the WC. Afterwards, she washed her hands and brushed her teeth, things she couldn't do without Ma Bagu's help last night. First, the old woman had rubbed cream on her skin, numbing the pain. Then, she'd given her a bitter drink, allowing her to sleep through the night.

She turned on the shower cubicle. She always had a morning bath. Despite knowing the water would sting her damaged skin, there was no reason to change her routine.

There wasn't any running hot water in this bathroom. So, she would have to leave Mason's bedroom to use the hot shower in the main bathroom. But she wouldn't risk bumping into any of his family again. In fact, she needed to leave this house at the earliest opportunity. Mason's room wasn't even safe for her. This was where she'd been assaulted by his family.

She would not trust Mason again. Didn't even know why she'd trusted him after the things he'd done.

Sure, he'd saved her from Bomba. Still, he loved inflicting pain as much as the rest of his family did. He'd carved his initial on her skin with a knife!

She stepped under the cold water and winced. Grabbing the soap, she rubbed the lather on the front, avoiding her back. The last thing she needed was soap stings as well as water. She didn't stay long, stepping out as soon as she'd rinsed off the soap lather.

She took the large towel, wrapping it around her body gingerly.

Then she went back to the bedroom. There were shopping bags with clothes sitting beside the wardrobe. Ma Bagu had mentioned Mason ordered them from the local seamstress's shop. Sophie doubted anything in there would be backless and not chaff the raw skin.

She took the jar of petroleum jelly from her bag and rubbed some over the parts of her body she could reach without hurting. It was still painful to stretch her arms, to bend her body. Not to mention her aching wrists and ankles.

She pulled on a fresh pair of panties when a tapping alerted her to the opening door, and she tugged the towel over her body.

Mason walked in, carrying shopping totes, and greeted her. "Good morning."

She ignored his greeting and glared at him.

He moved from the door, and a young woman entered, carrying a silver food tray.

Sophie recognised her from last night. She'd brought her meal up when Ma Bagu was here.

"Good morning," she greeted and walked over to the bedside table, placing the tray on top.

"Thank you," Sophie said before the girl retreated.

"You can go too," Sophie said as Mason shut the door after the girl.

He ignored her and smiled instead. Striding over, he placed the bags on top of the duvet. "These are for you."

"I don't want them," she bit out, clutching the towel against her chest with clenched hands.

"Are you not going to look at them first? Chief Odili's daughter sent them over. It will be rude to reject them."

She stiffened, remembering what they did to rude people around here.

"What? Is she going to cane me if I don't accept them?" She made a clicking sound in her throat.

His chin lifted, his stare sharp. "Don't be silly. No one is going to cane you."

"Of course not. Unless you permit them like you did yesterday."

"Yesterday was a mistake. I didn't give my mother permission to cane you."

He sounded sincere, but she couldn't accept his words. They didn't soothe her one bit.

"And yet she did. Why was that?"

He puffed out a heavy sigh. "She said you were rude. I warned you to obey her. Why didn't you?"

"So, it's my fault that your mother is a cruel bitch."

"I didn't say that," he rushed his words, muscles rigid and neck corded.

Interestingly, he didn't argue about his mother being a cruel bitch. No violent response was directed at her to prove he was exactly like the rest of his family.

Still, what right did he have to be frustrated? She'd been the injured party.

"So, what are you saying then," she goaded.

"She had no right to cane you," he said quietly, in a matter-of-fact tone. "I told her to restrain you for the doctor's examination if you resisted. And I sent you a text message to behave so she wouldn't have to restrain you. Of course, I expected you to comply."

"I didn't get your goddamned text message." She would have complied if she'd seen it. "I didn't even know about it until she and the doctor and Rocha came in here."

"You didn't get my text message?" He rubbed his chin, and his eyes narrowed.

"No, I didn't because my phone battery was dead. I plugged it in just as your mother walked in yesterday."

"Oh. I didn't realise," he said as if it all made sense. As if it explained what happened afterwards. "But as I said already, I've dealt with my mother and brother. They won't lay their hands on you again."

What did that even mean?

"And I'm just supposed to take your word for it."

"You should." He stiffened, looking affronted. Like she'd tarnished his honour.

How could a violent man have any honour? How could anyone from this family have any decency?

"In order words, I don't have a choice," she said because it was a take-it or leave-it situation.

He said nothing and opened one of the bags. He was dismissing her, moving on as if the clothes would compensate for her raw back and emotions. What else should she expect?

For a moment, she was distracted by the beautifully multi-coloured clothes he took out—halter neck tops, dresses, skirts. The fabrics looked expensive—silk and satin and would feel soft and luxurious against her skin. Best of all, the tops and dresses were backless and wouldn't hurt to wear.

But if Chief Odili's daughter sent her backless clothes, she knew about the flogging.

Sophie's cheeks heated. It seemed everyone knew about her humiliation and torture. She felt claustrophobic and needed to get out of the room, out of this house.

"I need to get out of here," she said, reaching for her bag and pulling out a pair of hotpants and boob tubes.

"Those are not suitable for you to wear," Mason said.

"Why not? They are my clothes," she retorted.

"Yes, when you were advertising your wares. But I've already bought the goods. You're here, and you belong to me. So, there is no need for you to advertise."

Her anger flared. She'd almost forgotten he saw her only as a prostitute and his property for a few days. Someone to be discarded when he'd had his fill. If she wasn't permanently damaged by then.

"But I don't want to wear hand-me-downs from a mafia princess."

"They are not second-hand. I asked Sahara to order them from a boutique in the city and have them delivered here for you."

Oh. Her mouth dropped open, her righteous indignation fizzling out. He'd ordered the clothes specifically for her. Nice of him. But she didn't say it.

Instead, she grabbed one of the tops, a blue-yellow flowery silk halter neck with clasps. It felt luxurious on her skin, and warmth bloomed in her belly. He'd spent a lot of money on these items. This was his way of apologising for what happened, even if he hadn't said it.

She tugged it over her neck and reached back to secure it, but her breath hitched as her arm ached.

Mason stretched his arms to do it, and she moved away.

"Stop it," he growled. "You know I'm not going to hurt you."

"Do I?" her voice rose with emotion.

They glared at each other. When he reached for her again, she grabbed the items on the bed and threw them at him.

"Haven't you hurt me already?" She pounded his chest with her fists.

He caught her arms, restraining her, pinning them over her head as they toppled onto the bed, him on top.

Pain bloomed in her back, and she froze, his face hovering above her. They both panted, his breath fanning her cheeks. The rugged plains of his body bore into her, making her feel him from chest to thighs. The atmosphere changed, suddenly charged with sexual electricity. He stared at her mouth, and she held her breath, thinking he would kiss her. She wanted to taste him, feel the slide of his tongue.

Instead, he jerked away, sitting up on the bed.

Disappointment washed over her. Then she gasped as he scooped her onto his lap. His touch was gentle, surprisingly, his fingers caressing the skin on her nape as he secured the clasp of the halter-neck. She had no bra on, and the soft fabric rubbed her nipples, making them taut and sending tingles down her spine. Desire for him rushed in her veins.

Her heart raced as he lifted his hand and placed it around her neck. At first, she thought he would squeeze like he'd done in the car two nights ago. Instead, he tilted her chin up.

"Look at the mirror."

She obeyed him, looking up. Their reflection loomed large and erotic. He was fully clothed in jeans, a t-shirt clinging to his torso and trainers on his feet. She was partially dressed in a halter-neck top and black thongs.

He used his powerful thighs to spread her legs, exposing her crotch and the wet patch. From the top of her shoulders, he trailed his fingers down her arms, wrapping them around her wrists. Then he placed her palms on her knees.

"Keep your hands there," he said in a husky voice against her ear, his breath feathering her skin.

"Okay," her voice was weak, her pulse rate accelerating.

He feathered his fingers up her arm and down the sides into the opening of the top, cupping her breasts. Her skin tingled as he moulded and manipulated her nipples.

Whimpers escaped her lips and she tilted her head against his shoulder, pushing out her chest. One of his palms travelled down her belly and cupped her pussy.

She rolled her hips, grinding her bum against his hard erection encased in his jeans while his fingers worked her labia, gathering her juices and stroking her clit.

The ache on her back bloomed as she rocked against him, a reminder of her situation. She shouldn't let him do this.

"Seeing you like this makes me so hard," he whispered.

"Seeing a woman battered and bruised makes you hard?" she taunted, angry at herself for finding him attractive, for craving the way he touched her.

He bit her earlobe and pinched her clit.

"Oh," she cried out in part-pain part-pleasure, rocking into him.

"Not just any woman. My woman."

"I'm a prostitute, not your woman."

"You are my prostitute. Mine."

The way he said it was so profound. Like he genuinely believed she belonged to him beyond a few days. She shuddered.

Closing her eyes, she allowed him to work her body, pleasure fizzing in her veins, sending heat from her core to her extremities. This orgasm would be as intense as the one in the car, like nothing she'd felt before she met him. She could feel it as her body wound tight.

"Open your eyes," he commanded, and her lids fluttered open.

The fierce expression on his face reached into her soul. Suddenly she wanted to be connected with him in a way they'd never been.

"I want you inside me." She moved her hands under her bum to his belt buckle, and he froze.

"No," he said.

"Why not? You're as hard as a fucking rock. I want you inside me."

"If I fuck you, you're going to get pregnant."

She giggled.

"No, I'm not. You're going to use a condom, and I'm on contraceptives. So don't worry." Although she needed a top-up injection soon.

Needing the condoms, she bent to reach into her bag on the floor beside them.

He tugged her up, and his expression was serious. "What if none of that works? What if you get pregnant?"

"As I said, don't worry about it. I'll get rid of it," she said dismissively. She supposed he was worried about getting a prostitute pregnant and dealing with the consequences.

"Excuse me?" He froze, looking shocked. "Did you just say you will kill my baby?"

Huh? What was going on? Was he pulling her legs? She stared at him in confusion. "You really don't expect me to have a baby for a client, do you?"

"Sophie, I'm not talking about anybody else. I'm talking about me, my sperm. My baby in your womb."

His voice held sweetness and naivety, a vulnerability she'd never seen in him.

Still, how did their sexy times suddenly become a conversation about pregnancies? What was he really expecting her to say? She was a sex worker, and he was her client for a few days. Nothing changed.

In fact, an hour ago, she'd been thinking about how to get away from him. About how to run. She hadn't wanted to have anything to do with his crazy family.

Sure, she was attracted to him despite his family. And he made her feel like no one else made her feel.

But pregnancy? No way. Babies were not in her near future at all. So, there was only one answer for him.

"Mason, the answer is still the same. Sorry, I'm not going to have a baby for you or any other client."

Hopefully, this was just a crazy joke, and she'd passed the test.

ROUGH DIAMOND 2

DEAL & CLOSE

Frenemies and desire, a lethal cocktail.

Mason is a Yadili fixer. Like his name implies, there's never been a challenge he couldn't cut, dress, and lay to rest. Those close to him fondly call him Mace—a heavy club with a spiked metal head—for a reason. He will rip the heart out of anyone who crosses him. However, when the treacherously seductive Sophie comes to him for a favour, the grudge he's suppressed for a decade threatens to spiral out of control.

Sophie holds her own in the ruthless Yadili world. She set up the Haven Project to provide safety for her workers. Still, someone is intent on destroying her. So she has little option but to ask the dangerously desirable Mason for help. He offers her a deal she can't refuse. But making a bargain with Mason is akin to dealing with the devil. Still, better the devil she knows, especially one she's resented for ten years.

Together, Mason and Sophie must battle to survive all manner of betrayals. That's if their thinly veiled animosity for each other doesn't consume them first.

ONE

Present day

The black metal gate rattled as Sophie rapidly tapped her knuckles against it. Excitement fizzed through her veins, heightening her senses. A light breeze fluttered the hems of the multi-print Ankara pantsuit's wide-leg trousers. She ignored the urge to tug the loose blouse to prevent it from clinging to her dampening skin—the downside of abandoning her air-conditioned vehicle on the street. She'd been in Lori Osa for six months and was still unused to the heavy humidity of its rainy season. On days like this, she missed the arid weather of hilly Opal City she'd called her home for the past decade.

Stepping back, her high-heeled sandal pushed a pebble. It rolled down the inclined concrete slab concealing the drains running along the outside of the duplexes surrounded by high brick fences in this middle-class residential neighbourhood. The road must have been resurfaced recently with its intact upper charcoal asphalt. Then again, the incumbent governor grew up in the area. The least he could do was give them good roads, even if he wasn't doing much else for the state's citizens.

She lifted her dark sunshades and glanced up at the overcast sky. Rain was imminent. Still, the dull, grey weather, humid heat and ugly Nigerian politics wouldn't dampen her energy. She'd been looking forward to this visit for weeks. Since she got the news from her mother that her younger sister had given birth.

The pedestrian gate creaked open, and a young man in a red t-shirt, jeans trousers and white trainers appeared. He held one white earpiece attached to a white cable disappearing behind him, in his back pocket and smartphone.

"Good afternoon. Who do you want to see?" he said, staring at her curiously. He was probably her sister's neighbour's son.

"Good afternoon. I'm here to visit Mr and Mrs Idowu," Sophie replied, lifting the bags in her hands from the baby shop.

"Oh, okay. You can come in." He stepped away from the entrance, making way for Sophie.

"Thank you," She entered the paved courtyard surrounded by a brick fence leading to the modern two-storey pale-grey duplex but didn't go further. She wasn't sure which one of the two residences was her sister's. "Are you their neighbour?"

"Yes." He smiled, locking the pedestrian gate. Then he waved her towards the front entrance of the first house. "Auntie Bimpe is in 11B."

"Thank you," she replied and walked to the dark-grey door. She pressed the bell attached to the wall.

Two minutes later, she heard the metal locks disengaging before the door opened.

"Sister!" Bimpe gasped softly. She was dressed in a blue floral top and long flowing black skirt, her hair in braids packed into a bunch at the back. "We were not expecting you today."

She looked flustered and not pleased to see Sophie.

Sophie's belly knotted with regret. Perhaps she should have waited before coming to see her sister or called ahead. Still, each time she'd called or messaged, Bimpe had given Sophie an excuse to not visit, making her suspect something was wrong.

"My niece is a month old, and I still haven't seen her. I can't be in the same city as you and only get to see her photos on social media," Sophie replied. "Are you going to let me in, or are we going to do this visit at the door?"

"Sorry." Bimpe fidgeted with her skirt, biting her lips. Then she stepped aside, her body posture rigid. "Come in."

What was that about? Something was definitely off with her sister. Was it the stress of dealing with a newborn?

"Are you okay?" Sophie asked as she crossed the threshold into a small alcove.

The staircase to the next level up was right in front. The entrance to the right led to a kitchen. The open plan area to the left included a wall-mounted TV entertainment unit, low sofas and a six-seater wooden dining unit.

"Yes, I'm okay," Bimpe replied quickly, waving at the sofa. "Please, sit."

She sounded defensive, but Sophie didn't call her out on it. She didn't want to add to whatever was troubling her sibling. Instead, she settled on an armchair. "How is David?"

"He's fine. He's upstairs and will be down in a minute. Let me get you something to drink. Is juice okay?"

"Yes, thank you." She hadn't been expecting to find David home today. Part of the reason she'd chosen to visit midweek instead of the weekend. She'd hoped to talk to Bimpe privately to get to the root of any problem.

"Okay. I'm coming." Bimpe walked towards the kitchen.

Sophie watched her disappear through the kitchen door, unable to shake the feeling that something wasn't right with her sister.

She'd been nine years old when Bimpe arrived as a baby after their parents had tried for years to have more children. So, Sophie had always been the big sister looking after her baby sister. Then a few years later, after their father died from kidney disease, Sophie minded her sister while her mother ran her small shop. Still, they'd struggled without her father and his income as a bus driver.

When, as a young teen, she'd been sent to live with and work for a wealthy family, she'd conceded that her mother would have fewer mouths to feed at home. Therefore, her sister wouldn't struggle.

And later, when Bomba introduced her to the business of selling her body for cash, she sent money to her mother for Bimpe's school fees. All because she'd never wanted her sister to go through the difficult situations she'd been through. Hadn't wanted her sister to prostitute for a roof over her head or food in her belly. Sex work wasn't for everyone, and sheltered Bimpe wouldn't have survived the harsh realities.

Sophie had been the one who'd paid for Bimpe's university tuition and maintenance expenses. Now, her sister was a graduate and had gotten a job at a fintech firm through Sophie's connections—one of her clients was the CEO. A year ago, Bimpe had gotten wed to David, who Sophie also helped through another client link. Now, they had a daughter who was about a month old. They lived a good life—the mod-cons in an expensive home in a middle-class city suburb attested to how well they lived. A far cry from the low-income housing project where Sophie and Bimpe had been raised in.

Sophie's chest expanded fully with each deep, satisfied breath because she had contributed to her sister's success. She loved that she'd attained a position of influence where she could positively affect the lives of her family and friends. She had given Bimpe the opportunities she'd never had. The opportunity to attend school without worrying if the school fees would be paid. Access to modern conveniences other young people her age were using—mobile phones and laptops. Even the expensive data bundles so Bimpe would have internet access for study and research.

Yes, Sophie had sacrificed a lot to make it happen. First, while she'd worked for Bomba. Then later as she made the transition to becoming a Yadili associate. Agreeing to work for Chief Odili, the Odili family's godfather and a prominent Yadili network member, had created opportunities and opened doors to success for her. But in return, she'd had to work hard to deliver on the contracts she'd been assigned.

As Madam, she was now in charge of the Odili bordellos in the southeast. But, since the Odili's started expanding their empire into the southwest, she'd moved to Lori Osa to work on the project. Hence the reason for living in the same city as her sister for the first time in twenty years.

Bimpe returned with a carton of mango juice and a glass, placing them on the small table beside the armchair. She poured the yellow liquid into the tumbler before settling in the adjacent sofa.

Sophie shifted forward, pushing the shopping bags towards her sister. "These are for the baby. What's her name?"

She hadn't been invited to the naming ceremony. She hadn't made a fuss then because she'd assumed her sister had her hands full with a newborn. Moreover, it wasn't a big deal. Naming ceremonies were for the husband's family. Plus, Sophie's mother had been there.

"She is Amelia Jumoke." Bimpe picked up the bags and glanced inside without taking out the items. "These are lovely. Thank you."

"You're welcome. She has beautiful names. Where is she? Let me see my beautiful niece." Excitement laced her words. She'd told everyone who cared to listen about her new niece and the anticipation of holding her for the first time.

Her maternal instincts were triggered when she saw the cute photos of her sister's newborn on social media. Unfortunately, her job and lifestyle meant she would never birth a baby. Still, her mind had travelled to the one offer she'd had to bear a child. The one offer which could've changed the trajectory of her life. She'd thought getting to hold her new niece would clear her head and stop all the recent bittersweet emotions clouding her mind.

"She is sleeping." A man came down the stairs—Bimpe's husband, David. He was in his early thirties, and Sophie felt like a big sister to him, although he had siblings.

He must have been eavesdropping at the top of the stairs. His sudden appearance spiked Sophie's suspicion, but she forced nonchalance into her tone. "David, hi. How are you?"

"Not good," he said rudely. "Didn't your sister tell you? This is not a good time for a visit. Amelia is sleeping, and Bimpe should be taking a nap and resting. You should have called before coming."

He stopped at the bottom of the stairs, unable to look her in the eyes.

Sophie's incredulous gaze bounced from David to Bimpe, and her spine stiffened. Shocked at how the man had just spoken to her, it took her a few seconds to find the right words.

What the hell was his problem? Surely her sister could spare her a few minutes. It wasn't like she visited them frequently to warrant this attitude.

She didn't even have to pick up the sleeping baby. Just see her.

"What is really going on?" She stood, unable to bite her tongue. "When did I start needing to book appointments before seeing my sister or my niece, for that matter? Bimpe, I'm sorry that I disturbed your nap, oh. But seriously, what is going on here?" When her sister opened her mouth, she raised her hand. "And don't tell me it's nothing because this shit right here is so wrong."

Her sister wouldn't meet her gaze.

David flinched and bristled. "How dare you shout at me in my house?"

Sophie narrowed her eyes, tilting her head. "Bimpe, David, this is me, oh. Big sister Sophie. What is going on?"

"If you must know, you are not allowed in this house," David said, bracing his hips.

"Why? What's wrong with me?" Sophie asked as her spine iced over, filling her with dread.

"I've said my own." David hissed and stomped up the stairs.

Sophie turned to her sister and sat on the sofa next to her. "Bimpe, what did I do wrong? Why am I not allowed in your house? Talk to me."

She was a rational person. She just needed an explanation because this was new.

"I'm sorry, sister. But David doesn't want you coming to the house because of your job." Bimpe clenched her jaw and turned away.

"Wait, oh. My job?" Her body tensed, and heat flushed through her. "You mean the job that I worked my bones weary to put you through school, to make sure you lacked for nothing." She jumped off the sofa again. "The same job that gave me the connections to help your husband secure his job. That job was good when you needed my money. Now, you both are doing well, and all of a sudden, it's not good enough for you."

"Sis, it's not just your job. It's the fact that you're forty and not married. His family think you will be a bad influence on me. That I will start following men and cheat on David."

"His family, what? So, this is the reason you won't let me see the baby. The reason you didn't invite me to the naming ceremony. What about Mama? Is she a bad influence too? Wasn't she supposed to be here helping you with the baby?"

"David's mother will be here by the weekend. Mum couldn't leave her business for too long. So, she came for two weeks."

Sophie suspected it was just another excuse. David's family didn't want Bimpe's family hanging around for too long.

Sophie shook her head. "I can't lie to you, Bimpe. I'm disappointed in David. I thought … Anyway, it doesn't matter. As long as you're happy." She walked to the armchair and grabbed her purse. "I'm going, and you won't see me here again."

"Sis, I'm sorry," Bimpe called out.

Sophie ignored her, refusing to acknowledge her apology or show Bimpe how much she hurt. She'd handled many disappointments in life. This was just another one.

She'd sacrificed so much for Bimpe, and the woman couldn't let her see her niece. So, what if the husband's family was being troublesome. To hell with them. Her sister should stand up for her. Just like Sophie had always stood by Bimpe.

But it was her sister's life, and if she didn't want Sophie in it, so be it.

This was the reason she kept most people at a distance. People always disappointed her and rejected her. The only working relationships she indulged in were transactional.

She swallowed the lump in her throat, unbolted the side exit and sashayed out of the premises.

Her assistant, Ziga, was leaning against the SUV. With her natural locs pulled into a bunch with a hairband, she wore her trademark attire—black cargo trousers, a black T-shirt under the dark unzipped jersey hoodie and chunky military-style black boots. She straightened, opened and held the back door. "How did it go?"

So much had changed in Sophie's life. She was no longer the girl who'd struggled to scrape together enough money for transportation to escape her pimp. Now, she was her own boss and a big enough babe in the business to warrant a personal assistant-slash-bodyguard.

Sophie shook her head as she climbed in. "It's fucked up. That's how it went."

Ziga came around, climbed into the driver's seat and met Sophie's gaze in the rear-view mirror, eyebrows drawing together. "Is there something I can do?"

Sophie's relationship with her assistant was more than just employer-employee. They worked well together. Ziga understood her vision for Haven and supported her in establishing a safe campus for sex workers. They'd become good friends over the eight years since they met.

Sophie had been excited about meeting her niece but unsure what to buy. Ziga had driven her to the shopping mall and had suggested gift ideas because she had an adoptive daughter from her partner's previous relationship. The girl was now six years old, and Ziga had been in her life since she was about a year old.

"Short of knocking some sense into David. Can you imagine he doesn't want me to see my niece? In fact, he said I wasn't welcome in the house." Sophie couldn't hide her disbelief, her stomach clenching.

"Ah ah. The same David of yesterday? Is he on drugs?" Ziga's mouth gaped as she blinked rapidly. She'd known David for the same duration as Sophie, meeting him on the same day for the first time when Sophie visited her sister at university about four years ago.

"I don't know, oh."

"And what did he say was his problem with you?"

"Ah, my job, oh. Apparently, I'm a bad influence on Bimpe and will lead her astray."

Ziga barked out laughter and turned in her seat to face Sophie. "You're serious."

"I'm serious. David … David told me to my face that I'm not allowed in his house. Because at over forty and without a husband, I'm a bad influence. Okay, oh." She puffed out a heavy breath as tears smarted her eyes.

"Boss, you know all you have to do is say the word, and I will arrange him for you. Just say the word," Ziga spoke quietly and with confidence.

A smile broke on Sophie's face. She had no doubt Ziga could inflict terror on David on her command. Still…

"Abeg, leave him. If you touch him and he dies, my sister will never forgive me. Let's leave them. Hopefully, they will come to their senses soon."

"Okay, Boss. But the offer is still there whenever you need it."

"Thank you. Just take me to the apartment. I just want to forget it all."

Ziga nodded, settled in her seat and started the engine. She drove away from the kerb and down the street a few seconds later.

Sophie relaxed into the seat, pulled out her phone and checked for her next engagement. There wasn't must else to do until this evening.

She'd only been in Lori Osa a few months and resided in one of the properties belonging to the Odili family, another job perk.

She'd spent the time recruiting and training the escorts working in the Lori Osa bordellos. When Duke Odili had first approached her about setting up a high-class escort service about ten years ago, she'd jumped at the chance to be her own boss and not answer to the likes of Bomba. The deal meant the Odilis would fund it and provide protection, and Duke would provide oversight. However, running the operation would be Sophie's remit and responsibility. The catch? She would pay Duke a fixed amount every quarter as a return on his investment in her venture.

There had been a few hiccups along the way. However, considering how she'd become involved in the business, she hadn't regretted joining the Odili outfit.

Never mind her roller-coaster forty-eight-hour experience with the Madukas ten years ago. In the intervening years, Duke had been promoted from capo—the same level as the Maduka brothers—to underboss. Instead of the capos reporting directly to Chief Odili, they now accounted to Duke.

Sophie agreed with the promotion. Of the four Odili proteges—Duke, Maddox, Rocha and Mason—Duke most embodied the qualities of a great leader. He had empathy, was open in communication and was an excellent teacher. Duke could be stern and uncompromising, but he was fair and approachable, hence very popular amongst associates and employees.

As for the rest of the F4, or Fierce Four as they were known. Maddox was too hostile. Rocha was too malicious. And Mason? He was too damned merciless.

As an Odili associate, Sophie worked with them since she directly reported to Duke too. On the upside, she hadn't seen the Maduka brothers since her move to Lori Osa recently. Mason was in Opal City, responsible for the casinos. Rocha was in Iguocha in charge of the imports and exports. However, Maddox was the Odili enforcer and had relocated to Lori Osa with Duke.

About a year ago, Duke had gotten involved with Carla Owo, the daughter of the Lori Osa kingpin, John Bull Owo. A cartel war had broken out between the families, leading to the death of Carla's father and only sibling, Marlon. Hence, Duke's relocation to Lori Osa. However, setting up the Odili operations in the megacity was dangerous and challenging. Duke needed Maddox's unrelenting military expertise.

One thing she liked about working with the Odilis, they all progressed together. When one person succeeded, they encouraged everyone else to grow. However, two tenets should never be disregarded: loyalty and respect.

She'd abided by those tenets and had succeeded in her business venture. She had earned money and connections, loyal employees and respect among associates. Everything she wanted.

Is it all you want? A tiny voice nagged, and she shifted uncomfortably.

What else could she possibly want?

Mason!

She shivered and tugged the Pashmina shawl she kept in the car for this purpose around her shoulder. She needed the AC to stay cool. However, the frosty air reminded her of Mason. Of what happened a decade ago.

Feeling conflicted, Sophie remembered the conversation with Duke Odili on the night she agreed to work with him.

"We value loyalty above all else," Duke said as they sat in his apartment lounge in Iguocha. "I know about your affair with Mason, and I respect you for your resilience. You stayed true to Mason and rejected Rocha's advances even when it seemed the only way out of a tormenting predicament. To be honest, it's the reason you survived the tussle between two brothers."

Shocked, Sophie gasped, her body flashing hot and cold. "You know about that."

She'd accepted the news about her forty-eight-hour affair with Mason would spread amongst his friends and the Yadili men at his family residence then. However, she hadn't expected Duke to know the intimate details of what went down in Mason's bedroom involving Rocha or his mother.

"Of course. Chief had to arbitrate the issue between the brothers. There cannot be bad blood between members of the Yadili brotherhood, certainly not amongst the Odili family. We all swore to watch out for each other. If you'd gone with Rocha after Mason marked you, he would have been obligated to kill you because you would have been untrustworthy."

"What?" The bombshells came thick and fast. She struggled to process his words. She'd suspected Rocha would kill and dispose of her if she'd gone with him, purely because of his maliciousness towards Mason. However, this implied Mason could have killed her for sleeping with his brother. "Are you saying I can't have sex with anyone else because Mason branded me?"

He chuckled light-heartedly. "Of course not. When the scar heals and disappears, you're free to choose other lovers. But it cannot be someone in the Odili family unless it's Mason."

She shook her head, dismissing the idea, knowing Mason wouldn't touch her. She'd spent forty-eight hours with him and hadn't seen him naked. There had only been two sexual encounters, none involving his genitalia. The first time she'd climaxed. The second ended with no satisfaction for either of them.

A decade later, Sophie still wasn't getting any satisfaction sexually. Oh, she was having sex. But it was nowhere as fulfilling as the orgasms she'd experienced in Mason's car when he'd driven her insane with pain and pleasure until she'd climaxed to exhaustion.

No, nothing had come close since. Never would, it seemed.

The buzzing phone caught her attention, and she reached for the item beside her on the upholstered seat. The caller ID indicated it was Chiamaka, who she'd put in charge of the Opal City operations while she was away. Unfortunately, the woman rarely called her, although they had a weekly video catchup.

So, Sophie's spine stiffened as she answered the phone. "Hello, Chiamaka."

"Madam, we have a problem," the woman replied without preamble.

TWO

Drumming burst through the dusk air, a steady pounding beat accompanied by deep, resonant notes of the metal ogene double bells and the rhythmic dun-dun of the udu clay pot.

Chief Sylvester Odili grimaced and glanced at his gold wristwatch. "The music is loud tonight. Since when did they start using amplifiers at the festival?"

The sixty-seven-year-old man with salt and pepper hair and a gold-embroidered royal-blue linen tunic-trouser suit sat in a white gazebo outside his three-level mansion in Umudike, surrounded by mown lawn and trimmed hibiscus hedges.

"They installed loudspeakers because there will be a concert this evening," Mason Maduka replied before fireworks exploded, lighting the night sky in white, blue and orange sparkles.

Illuminating the faces of the people around the six-seater, oval, slate-grey metal table with the old man—Rocha, Duke, Maddox. Of course, Mason too.

The Fierce Four or F4

That's what they'd jokingly named themselves ten years ago when Chief officially inducted them into the Odili family as members of the Yadili secret organisation. They'd all taken oaths of allegiance to him, amongst others.

However, he'd selected them as the most promising apprentices and his potential heirs.

As Chief's proteges, he'd allowed them to develop different aspects of his business empire. Through the years, they'd expanded Odili Holdings and had been promoted to captains. Or capos as they were known.

Each captain headed his own enterprise, which could employ the public. However, they also commanded a Yadili team comprising a second-in-command and a security team.

A year ago, Duke defeated The Baron, John Bull Owo and took over his operations in Lori Osa, earning his promotion from Captain to Underboss or *Osote Onye-isi*. Tonight, they were gathered for the first time since Duke was named Chief Odili's heir. Now he reported directly to Chief while the rest of them accounted to Duke.

"A concert?" Chief asked.

The annual weeklong Umudike reunion celebrations ended tonight, and the musical ensembles were usually more traditional.

"Yes, Uncle," Duke replied. "I hired famous musicians to perform tonight. It's all part of the project to promote the annual reunion celebrations amongst young people. Celebrity culture is a big thing these days. Young people will be more invested in coming to their hometowns more regularly if they know there will be exciting activities and opportunities to see the celebrities they follow online performing on stage."

"That's good. Sahara mentioned something about it. So, who are the musicians?"

Chief Odili's daughter, Sahara, had already left for the festival with her friends. Mason and co would join them after this meeting with their godfather.

While Duke explained the people providing the entertainment for tonight's festivities, Mason allowed his mind to drift. He glanced at the other men at the table. Hand-picked to represent the best of the next generation of Yadili.

Despite many challenges, they'd achieved so much in the past decade, proving their positions as chief's favourites.

Maddox was the oldest and sat opposite Mason. His father was also Yadili and a high-ranking member of the country's military. Yadili members existed in every sector of the population, making them so influential. Maddox was also military-trained but had retired from active service. These days he applied his martial expertise elsewhere and had recruited, trained and led a private army for the family. He was the most experienced among the Fierce Four. If age was a determining fact, he should be the leader. However, age meant jack-all without cash and connections, otherwise known as C&C, to back it up.

The level of influence one wielded mattered most, according to Mason's brother, Rocha, who sat next to Maddox on Chief's immediate left side.

Rocha was the second oldest. If it were up to him, he would appoint himself Leader of the F4 since he supposedly had more C&C than his F4 cohorts.

Mason didn't believe his brother's bullshit.

Sure, Rocha had cash and connections. He controlled the Maduka family's substantial property investments while their mother focused on her political career. He also handled the import and export business of Odili Holdings and lived in the same city as their godfather. Proximity to the Chief gave him easy access to the old man and his connections.

However, a problem between one of Rocha's boys, Okenna and the daughter of a Customs officer resulted in Odili imports being held at the Iguocha port for a year, leading to a considerable revenue loss. The problem had since been rectified by Kane, a recent Odili family recruit Okenna had met in prison.

Until Chief's recent announcement, Rocha had been vying to become the Odili heir. Although he'd congratulated Duke on the promotion, privately, Rocha—and their mother—thought Chief had chosen the wrong candidate. Arrogantly, Rocha believed he was the best of the F4. According to him, Duke wasn't ruthless enough to become a Yadili underboss, let alone a future godfather. In addition, he was younger than Rocha by a few months.

A double standard, proving his brother's egotism and envy.

Maddox didn't deserve to lead because he was older than Rocha. Duke didn't deserve to rule because he was younger. Obviously, this ruled Mason out, too, as the youngest of the F4.

At the time, Mason expressed his disgust at his brother's secret rantings with their mother. Eventually, he just shook his head and left the house, unable to tolerate their malicious whining.

Of course, he disagreed with his brother's assessment of Duke. Their leader shouldn't be the most vicious person in the team for it to be effective.

Tonight, Duke sat beside Mason on Chief's immediate right-hand side, wearing a matching tunic-and-trousers set to the rest of the F4. The coral-bead necklace identified him as the group leader, while the rest wore coral-bead bracelets given to them by the godfather when they'd been appointed captains.

Duke was a natural-born leader, who displayed empathy and fairness, and the team respected him. Moreover, he was astute and innovative.

About a decade ago, Duke and Mason, as best friends, had partnered to create Maximo Ventures, which became the umbrella company for their business interests. They developed the Maximo Hotels and Casinos—their flagship in Niru Town, a suburb of Opal City. For the last five years, Maximo Ventures outperformed the other Odili Holdings companies.

So, Duke fucking deserved his promotion to underboss because he'd won it in blood, sweat and hard cash.

Mason had earned it, too but had no desire for the top position. He was too damned bloody-minded to make a great leader.

Chief had made the best decision for himself and the Odili family.

Under Duke's leadership, the clan thrived, which meant more C&C—money and influence—for everyone.

The other F4 members played vital roles too.

Maddox as the enforcer, who kept the crew in line, managed the Odili security and trained the apprentices in martial arts and combat skills.

Rocha was the ambassador, representing them at Yadili meetings and fostering relationships with other families.

Mason was the strategist and trouble-shooter, exploiting legal loopholes for the clan's benefit. As a result, associates sought him out and trusted him to resolve their business challenges.

"I know you all want to get to the fun part of the evening. So, I won't keep you too long." Chief Odili cleared his throat. "Ten years ago, when I chose the four of you as my potential heirs, some of my peers derided me for picking youth over more established candidates. I ignored them because I saw bright futures in you. Today I walk with pride because you have all proven me right. Odili Holdings has had its best financial years since its inception. I am very proud of you all."

"Thank you, Chief," the men around the table chorused.

The old man was correct. The F4 had flourished in the past decade.

Even Mason. Aside from the professional success, he'd come into his own, and so much had changed for him. More in charge of his emotions. And calmer.

To think that once upon a time, he'd been reluctant to take the Yadili oath. Not because he had anything against the secret organisation per se. But he'd classed himself as a lone wolf. He liked to think for himself and act for himself. He was a maverick and didn't like taking orders. The only authority he'd accepted and respected was his father's.

Then his old man died, and things changed.

He'd become lost in his grief, exacerbated because his mother and brother had connived to keep him away from his dying father. The misery had eaten away at him.

Until one chance encounter brought Sophie into his life.

And for a moment, he'd glimpsed the possibilities for his future and an existence with her. He'd wanted a life with her.

But she hadn't wanted one with him.

Even now, a sharp pain registered in his chest, and he balled his hands into fists under the table. As much as he'd tried to move on, he'd never forgotten the pain of her rejection, of her choosing a life without him. A life where she could have hundreds of men—

"Following your recent successes, I think we are ready for some expansion," Chief's deep voice drew Mason's attention again.

"Expansion? This sounds interesting." Rocha shifted in his seat, rubbing his palms together. A smile broke on his face for the first time tonight. "Onye Isi, what do you have in mind?"

"Following the recent deal Duke made with Don Himba regarding Xandra and Ebuka Njoku, I have it on good authority that the Don is looking to make a match for his daughter Zoe and an alliance with a strong outfit. The loss of the assassin and the death of his enforcer has weakened him, and he is looking to strengthen his position. I was approached informally to see if I would be interested in offering one of my capos, and I'm considering it."

"You are considering it?" Duke asked as the rest of the guys gasped in differing degrees.

Rocha slunk back into his chair, looking everywhere else but at the old man sitting at the head of the table. He'd lost interest along with his earlier excitement.

Mason's spine prickled at his brother's conflicting behaviour. But he suspected the reason.

"Yes," the Odili godfather said. "I think alliances with powerful families are important. Although Duke's father- and brother-in-law are no longer alive, the Owo family name still carries much weight. This will help to open doors with the western expansion of our business holdings. Likewise, an alliance with the Himba family will smooth the way for us to grow into the northern territories."

"But we have our hands full already with the expansion into the western region. Won't a northern expansion spread us too thin?" Mason spoke. His job was to spot the potential risks in their business ventures. This one had many potential pitfalls.

"I concur with Mason," Maddox leaned his elbows on the table. "Lori Osa is like a nest of mambas, and I'm focusing a lot of resources trying to contain it. I can't divert anything to a new project right now."

"Hmmm." Chief leaned into his seat, tugging his greying beard as he contemplated the words of caution for a minute or so. "I agree there are risks we need to analyse, but the rewards could outweigh them. We're not jumping into anything yet. But I don't want to dismiss this. So, since Duke is already wedded, he's out of the equation. Which leaves Rocha, Maddox and Mason. However, I've chosen Mason for this."

"Me?" Mason responded with a jerk as his heart slammed against his ribs. This hit him sideways, shocking him. Chief never assigned him any project which didn't involve the law. This one involved marriage, not legal intricacies. "Why me? Why not Rocha or Maddox."

Those guys were older and should be first in line for assignments like this.

"Bịa, nwoke m, are you going to argue with the godfather?" Rocha said smugly, capitalising on Mason's reckless reaction to publicly shame him. "Onye Isi gave you an assignment, Ị na-ajụ 'why me?' Hian."

Mason's muscles quivered, and instead of retorting, he ground his teeth. His brother sneered at him as if expecting him to explode.

A decade ago, Chief had settled their quarrel over what happened after their father's death and Sophie's arrival. Mason had promised he wouldn't draw his brother's blood again. Neither brother would do anything to harm the other. Otherwise, they would be summoned to the masquerade judge, who punished offences severely.

However, there were moments like this when Rocha seized any opportunity to belittle Mason, expecting him to lose his temper and do something rash. Rocha wanted his brother to fall on his own sword. To cause his own demise.

The other men said nothing, waiting for Mason's response. They could intervene but didn't. Sometimes a man had to stand alone and prove his mettle.

Mason had lived with his brother's manipulations all his life. Thirty-five bloody years. His brother had always been a trigger for his temper, but Mason had the perfect disabler. The perfect antidote.

"Don't let anyone control you through your emotions," his father's words rolled over his mind like a soothing balm.

He sucked in a deep breath and let it out slowly. Then he turned to his godfather, "Onye Isi, ewe na iwe. Ndị bc anyị sị onye na aju ajụjụ anaghị efu."

Chief, don't be angry. Our people say a person who asks questions doesn't get lost.

Chief burst out laughing, making the others— including Rocha—chuckle, too, defusing the high tension in the air.

"I kwuru eziokwu," the old man said when the laughter died. "You spoke the truth. This is the reason I chose you for this project. When the time comes, we will need someone who thinks outside the box to handle the Himbas. And that person is you, Mason."

THREE

Fate was a fucking bitch sometimes. When it hit Sophie, it drove a fucking wrecking ball right through the middle of her carefully orchestrated life, causing devastation.

"How did this happen?" Duke's voice rang in Sophie's ear from the other end of the phone.

Two days after the disaster that was Sophie's surprise visit to her sister's house in Lori Osa, she was back in Opal City.

Of course, misfortunes occurred in her life in pairs—Bomba and Mason, Rocha and Mrs Maduka. Prime fucking examples.

The same week she experienced her sister's snobbery, she had a professional fire to extinguish.

"I wish I knew," Sophie said with frustration, pacing the office on the top floor of the Haven building overlooking Lake Niru in the distance. The four-storey building with twelve apartments constituted the Haven campus where the thirty-six sex workers lived and sometimes worked. Usually, she would take great joy in looking out the window and enjoying the view. Yet she couldn't appreciate any of it today.

"I guess it wasn't such a great idea staying in Lori Osa for so long," she continued.

Two days ago, she'd received a phone call from Chiamaka, the coordinator overseeing her business in Opal City. State officials and law enforcement had invaded the premises and arrested everybody on site. The charges ranged from prostitution to money laundering.

Sophie immediately called her legal adviser, who started advocating for the release of the sex workers and dropping the charges against her.

Arrests had been made before. Typically, it took one phone call. Sometimes, money exchanged hands, and they would be freed.

Then she'd boarded a flight back to Opal City without Ziga, who had to stay back in Lori Osa to handle some matters in Sophie's absence.

Sure enough, everyone who'd been arrested was released two days later.

However, the charges against Sophie hadn't been dropped. According to her lawyer, there was a threat of her bank accounts and assets being frozen.

This was new and a considerable threat to her freedom and livelihood.

She had enough savings to cover her expenditures, even with no income over the past week. However, if her assets were frozen, she would lose the financial independence she craved so much.

Then there was the matter of her arrangement with Duke Odili.

She'd agreed to set up the high-end bordello in Opal City on the stipulation that she would retain complete control of the business after an accrued period. So, Haven Services Ltd was hers while Duke was an investor via his investment company, Maximo Ventures. She paid them a fixed amount every quarter, and they left her alone to run the business.

It guaranteed her maximum autonomy. However, this also meant she stood on her own when trouble hit.

"But I thought you had someone competent handling the operations over there," Duke sounded confused.

"Of course, I did," she replied. At least she'd thought Chiamaka was competent before giving her the coordinator job. But some feedback she'd received since her return wasn't favourable on the woman.

There'd been complaints about Chiamaka assigning jobs to escorts who'd opted out of those assignments.

Sophie had set up a system allowing the call girls to opt out of specific jobs. Each person had their talents but also had limits. Those limits should always be respected. For example, she'd never wanted anyone to feel bullied or coerced into performing sexual acts. This was one of the many aspects of working for Bomba which had appalled her. So, she'd ensured the escorts could pick their clients.

Nevertheless, Chiamaka had overruled that arrangement in Sophie's absence.

Now Sophie could be arrested on people trafficking as well as sex trafficking charges.

"I hope to resolve the matter as quickly as possible," she continued, scrubbing a palm over her face. Unfortunately, this situation raised her stress levels. "In the meantime, I called you because I will need a deferment for the next quarter's payment due in a few weeks."

"Deferment?" Duke said the word as if it was a ridiculous concept. "You know we run a tight ship, Sophie, and we don't do deferments. Payments are due when they are due, regardless. It's what you signed in the contract."

Her stomach quivered with unease, and she settled into the armchair, leaning forward. "I know. I just need a little time to get my house in order."

Duke said nothing for a few seconds, leaving her with a sudden dread he would reject the idea.

She squeezed her eyes shut, her breath becoming shallow.

What would she do if he didn't agree? Not paying was a deadly option she couldn't contemplate. She would have to dig into her savings to pay him and hope her problems were resolved soon enough to cover other expenditures.

"What does Mason have to say about it? How long before you're back in business?" his voice cut through her panic.

Instead of bringing relief, her heart skipped a beat. "Mason has nothing to say about it. I haven't spoken to him."

"You haven't? So, who do you have dealing with the authorities for you?"

"I have my own team working on this."

"Hmmm. I would rather you contact Mason and let him deal with your problem. He's in Opal City and is better than whoever you have working on this."

Sophie bristled, tapping her shoe against the hard flooring. She didn't want to touch Mason with a bargepole, let alone have him involved in her business. Duke implied he was the only one good enough for the job. As if Sophie couldn't select a competent fixer.

"Thank you for the suggestion. I understand what you're saying, but—"

"It's not a suggestion," he said in a deliberate, stern voice. She'd heard that tone before, usually directed at other people. This was the Yadili underboss. "You seem to forget that while I can't tell you how to run your business, I have a stake in it. Mason is the best fixer on that side of the River Niger. More to the point, he's the only one I trust to protect my interests. So, if you want your upcoming payment deferred, you will contact him immediately so he can get to work and fix your problem."

Shit. This wasn't good. Not what she'd wanted at all. Her unease returned, sending a chill down her spine.

"Duke, are you saying you don't trust me to protect your interests?"

They usually had a great business partnership. However, if he didn't trust her, their working relationship would be in jeopardy. She could become easily disposable.

His silence stretched for seconds, making her aware of the whooshing of blood between her ears. Her grip on the phone tightened. Then he exhaled.

"Sophie, I am not saying I don't trust you. In this business, there are degrees of trust. It's rarely measured in absolutes. Look, your company is among the best performing in the Odili portfolio. It doesn't yield the most, but it provides a steady income stream. Now, you're telling me the revenue could disappear altogether. Surely you can see why I want to protect the investment and sort the problem out sooner than later."

He had valid, solid points. He was trying to protect his asset, and Mason *was* the best, no doubt.

Out of options, she sucked in a deep breath before exhaling slowly. "Okay. I'll contact Mason."

"Good," Duke said, sounding pleased. "I'll defer your payment by one month, and this time only, I will waive the late-payment interest. Don't make me regret it."

The muscles on her shoulders relaxed as the tension left her body. "You won't. Thank you so much."

He was being extra nice to her. He didn't give other debtors the same grace.

"You're welcome. Keep me updated."

"I will. Bye."

He hung up, and she slouched against the chair, feeling lightened.

However, a glance at the phone in her hand made her sit up. She would rather not speak to Mason, but it was better than seeing him face to face. The man's presence messed with her equilibrium.

She lifted her phone again and scrolled through the contacts until she reached the one she needed. A tap of the call button resulted in three short beeps followed by an automated message, "The number you have dialled is not in use."

She tried again and got the same message. Did Mason change his phone number? It was possible. The number she had was from ten years ago. Users kept their numbers even when they changed phones. But it seemed Mason had disconnected his old line.

Still, all wasn't lost. She had alternative contact for him via his hotel-casino. Someone there would connect her to him.

As expected, the phone rang on the other end, and someone picked it up.

"Good evening, Casino Maximo. How can I help you?" a soft voice sing-songed.

"Good evening. This is Madam Sophie from The Haven. I need to speak to Mason Maduka. Can you put me through to him?"

"I'm sorry, Madam. Unfortunately, Mr Maduka is not available. Can I take a message?"

"No. Just tell him it's me. He will take my call." Well, she wasn't sure. But considering she hadn't called him directly in ten years, hopefully, he would be curious to speak to her.

"I can't do that. Mr Maduka is currently entertaining guests. I can leave a message to call you back when he's free."

"Never mind," Sophie said, hanging up in frustration with a sigh.

She would have to go over there and see Mason personally. There was no time to delay. Since she'd committed to using Mason as the trouble-shooter, she needed to get him onboard soon so he could start working immediately.

The sooner she spoke to him, the sooner he would fix the problem. Then, life would return to normal, and she could run back to Lori Osa, far away from him.

She walked down the corridor into the apartment where she'd lived since The Haven complex was built. Her top-floor residence had an unimpeded one-eight-degree view of the Niru Lake and Town, a prominent suburb of Opal City.

This apartment was a testament to how far she'd come from her humble beginnings.

She wouldn't lose it all and would do whatever was required to protect her lifestyle, including facing up to Mason after a decade.

She clenched her jaw, pressing her lips together as determination gave her mental focus. She entered the bedroom and selected a new outfit from the wardrobe—a black zip-front unitard jumpsuit and high-heeled sandals. Matched with a fitted blazer, this was her power suit and never failed to induce men to eat from her palm.

Once she changed her clothes and retouched the elegant makeup, she stood in front of the full-length mirror. She brushed back her hair, keeping her trademark off-centre parting. Then she pulled it into a ponytail and held it with a black velvet scrunchie.

Her appearance screamed, 'You better pay attention to me and listen to what I have to say'. The exact effect she wanted to have on Mason.

She needed him to see nothing of the young woman he'd met ten years ago. The person his family had tormented and he'd discarded so readily.

He needed to see the boss she'd become. Ruler of her own domain.

They would meet as equals.

She wasn't begging him to rescue her or give her money. No. She would hire him for a job, and he would be compensated with cash. Nothing more.

Mental pep talk done, she left the apartment and took the lift for the quick journey to the ground floor. Her heels clicked on the concrete floor as she walked across the foyer towards the front desk, where Chiamaka stood, talking to the receptionist.

They operated check-ins and check-outs to track which escorts—and guests—were in residence. Hence the welcoming desk. The sign-in book proved beneficial during a fire incident three years ago.

One of the guests had thrown a cigarette into a bin, igniting the other items. The smoke triggered the detector and the alarm. The building was evacuated per the fire procedures, and the check-in book ensured everyone was accounted for afterwards. Thankfully, the fire hadn't spread beyond the room in the second-floor apartment.

"Madam, you're going out?" Chiamaka asked. As she swivelled, the tresses of her fringed, front-lace wig flipped with her. She wore a backless, draped-collar, body-hugging, burgundy mini-dress and high-heeled shoes. She was a beautiful woman who'd learned to maximise her assets by copying Sophie's fashion style.

But Sophie didn't mind the woman's imitation. It was flattering, if a little creepy, sometimes. Sometimes, she'd change her outfit at the last minute because Chiamaka wore an exact copy.

"Yes," She replied. "Have you confirmed which boys are covering tomorrow's party at Maximo?"

They had an event, prebooked before the police raid, for tomorrow night which she couldn't afford to cancel. So, she'd personally called each escort to persuade them to work.

A few wanted to move on after the authorities showed up last week, and she couldn't blame them.

However, each escort's tenancy agreement for their residence at Haven penalised them if they broke the contract without giving one month's notice to the landlady—Sophie.

Sophie had waived the penalty and told them she would allow anyone who wanted to leave to do so without losing their deposit. She didn't want to lose some of the best people who worked for her. Still, she couldn't hold them ransom if they wanted to pursue alternative careers. Better to release them from their contracts and keep the goodwill.

Her generous approach seemed to work, and they recanted the wish to depart.

However, their biggest concern was Chiamaka as coordinator.

Sophie had guaranteed she would resolve the problem and had thrown in financial incentives to boost their incomes. Happy escorts made happy clients. Satisfied clients spent more dough, meaning she would recoup the extra expense.

So, the escorts had agreed to participate in tomorrow's party. Thankfully.

In the meantime, Sophie reassigned Chiamaka to handle logistics and ensure adequate security. The last thing she needed was one of the girls getting assaulted while an investigation was hovering above her. Not that she wanted the girls attacked ever.

"Yes, we're ready," Chiamaka replied.

"Good. If you need me, you can reach me on my phone," she said and sashayed out of the building into the night air.

She would find a more permanent solution for Chiamaka once she resolved the other matters. The woman obviously wasn't a good team leader.

She walked towards her SUV parked in the concreted front courtyard. Her chauffeur, who doubled as a bodyguard, scrambled from the chair beside the security guards. He pressed the fob to unlock the vehicle and held the back door for her to slide in.

Then he hurried around, got into his seat, started the engine and drove forwards as the security man opened the gates. Sophie had instructed him to always have the car facing the entrance, a neat trick she'd learned from Jide, Duke's driver and personal guard.

"When parked, always have the car facing the exit. You never know when you'll need a quick getaway, and trying to reverse could cost your life."

It made total sense in their business.

"Madam, where are we going?" her driver asked, pulling her attention as they left the driveway. He was deciding whether to turn left or right on the street.

"Take me to Maximo," she replied.

"Oh. Okay, Ma," he sounded a little miffed.

She couldn't blame him. She could walk it. A walkway linked the casino premises to their building from the back, which the escorts used when they needed to make a quick, discrete exit.

Sophie wasn't about to sneak around. Instead, she would walk in through the front door like the Madam she was and announce her presence.

The car turned left into the road. Across from Haven stood other commercial premises, beauty salons, hairdressers, restaurants, fashion houses, boutique hotels and more. None of these buildings existed—this entire area didn't exist—until Duke's and Mason's vision to build a gambling destination came to fruition with Maximo Hotels and Casinos. This created a whole new economic ecosystem of businesses feeding off the boom. The area had primarily developed in the last five years, from rural grasslands and hills to a thriving small town.

About two minutes after leaving Haven, the car stopped at the security barrier leading into Maximo. The team of five armed guards scanned the vehicle. This was necessary in this country because extremists and bandits always sought soft targets.

Once they were cleared, they went down the long driveway lined with palm trees until a circular fountain appeared with the statue of a woman in a wrapper carrying a clay pot in her arms. Invisible, water travelled through the woman's body, down her arms and flowed out of the vessel into the fountain. The water feature created a roundabout, and the hotel's front doors stood on the other side.

When the car stopped, Sophie leaned forward. "Park the car and wait down here. I will text you when I'm ready to leave."

"Don't you want me to come inside with you," he asked, twisting in his seat.

"It won't be necessary," she said, grabbing her purse.

"Okay, ma."

A guard stepped forward and held the car door open. "Good evening, Madam. "Welcome to Maximo Hotel and Casino."

"Thank you." Sophie sashayed towards the glass entrance.

The door attendant hurried ahead and opened it. Sophie nodded at him with a stiff smile. She walked through the security arch with the metal detector screens, and her skin prickled.

It felt like the devil was on her tail.

She hurried across the busy lobby of Casino Maximo, determined not to glance around. The buzz of music, conversations, and coins slotting into machines were temptations that had nearly consumed her when she'd first arrived here years ago. Never again.

Pressing the lift call button, she stood back, tilted her head and watched the blue digital numbers above the metal doors, trying to decipher which of the four elevators would arrive first. Finally, one to her right pinged, and she stepped in when the door slid open. She pressed her palm on the reader before punching the unique code that would give her access to the top floor of the building.

When the door closed, she lowered her eyelids and exhaled in relief. Why was she so jittery? It wasn't the first time she was in this casino. She'd frequented the place to see Duke when he'd been the Managing Director.

Now Duke lived in Lori Osa as the new boss of the territory, leaving one of his capos in charge of Maximo and the other casinos in the region.

Mason Maduka.

Her eyes flew open. Her heart beat fast, nearly exploding in her chest at the thought of Mason. The one man who made her knees weak both with desire and fear.

She hadn't seen Mason in months, as she'd been working on a project Duke had assigned her in Lori Osa. She enjoyed managing at an organisational level, which she did at Haven. However, she preferred the one-to-one experience of training others, which was the bulk of her work in Lori Osa in recent times.

As the lift stopped on the top floor, she took another deep breath and gave herself a pep-talk.

Pull yourself together. Don't show him any weakness.

FOUR

As soon as the lift door opened, background Afrobeat music mixed with conversation floated into the metal box. It sounded like there was quite a gathering on this level which consisted of the executive offices and the penthouse living space for the MD.

Head high, shoulders relaxed and chest out, Sophie sashayed out of the lift, her heels tapping against the hard floor tiles rhythmically.

"Good evening, Madam." Two security men stood in the lift lobby. One waved a wand over her body. Not like she could fit any weapons into the formfitting pantsuit with her ass and tits threatening to burst out.

Still, she opened her purse for the other guard, who stared into it and prodded her compact, lipstick and phone aside before waving her along. A bank card was tucked into the zippered section in the lining of her purse. She'd come a long way from the girl carrying worldly possessions in her tote.

"The party is on the roof garden terrace, and the stairs are at the end of the corridor," he directed.

Nodding, she headed towards the sounds. She knew this level well, although she hadn't been here for about a year. It couldn't have changed too much since Duke's departure.

As expected, not much had changed in the layout as she walked past offices. At the top of the short stairs, she spotted a familiar face beaming a smile at her.

"Madam Sophie, na your eye be this?" Benji stepped down towards her. He rarely smiled, so he must be pleased to see her.

Warmth filled her chest as she was enveloped in a bear hug. He was built like a bear, too—a lean, mean, fighting bear.

"It's good to see you too, Benji. And I've told you to stop calling me Madam. Me and you are on the same level."

They'd built a good rapport after she'd spent two days in Mason's house ten years ago. He'd been there the first day she'd met Mason. Had been there on her last day in Mason's home. After Mason abruptly kicked her out of his house, Benji drove her to Duke's house. Over the years, they'd become friends, even as her relationship with his boss had deteriorated and turned to resentment with time.

"You be correct Madam, nothing less." Winking, he stepped back and saluted her like she was a military general. Something he sometimes did.

Shaking her head, she laughed and then sobered. "How is Mason?"

If anyone knew Mason's frame of mind, it would be Benji. He was Mason's deputy and in charge of his security.

Was Mason in a good mood? Would he be receptive to her request?

She'd never been able to predict what he would do, so any help would be appreciated.

"He's doing well. He's sponsoring the staff party—" Benji waved at the terrace "—because they exceeded all their quarterly targets at the casino."

"That's good." Sophie exhaled in relief. "I'm going to grab a glass of champagne. Then I will wait in his office."

"Okay. I'll send him your way." He grinned and told her the code for the door.

She walked into the terrace busy with revellers sitting or standing in clusters, animated in conversation and merriment. Out of the corner of her eyes, she saw Mason talking to another man.

Her heart skipped a beat, and she licked her lips, refusing to turn or acknowledge him. She wanted him to come to her.

Instead, she accepted a flute of champagne from a server, swivelled and walked back down the stairs, heading to Mason's office. The gold plaque on the slab identified it as belonging to the Managing Director, with the Maximo Hotels and Casino logo underneath.

She punched the code into the door, and it clicked open. Her adrenaline spiked.

She shouldn't be here. She knew not to mess with the man who owned this office. Yet something about being in Mason's office without permission made her want to misbehave. Made her want to break the rules.

The room was freezing cold. Typical Mason space. She tugged the blazer around her, grateful she'd had the foresight to take it instead of coming out in just the unitard.

She didn't turn on the lights as she stepped further into the room. However, the neon glow of the hotel signs and display lights illuminated the office through the expansive glass windows. The maze garden interspaced with spotlights sparkled in the distance.

Even in the semi-darkness, it was easy to distinguish this as Mason's domain—the enormous metal, glass desk and bank of screens. The dark leather armchair behind the desk matched the low sofas in the corner. On the other side of this level was his apartment, accessed via a separate entrance. So, he didn't have far to go from work to home and vice versa.

The enormous painting on the wall caught her attention, and her breath hitched.

A new installation. It certainly hadn't been on the wall when Duke was MD.

She was tempted to turn on the light. But even in the dimness, she made out the feature—a couple in a cinch. The man cradled the woman by the waist and gripped her neck in the other hand. But she wasn't afraid. Instead, her throat was turned up and exposed in offering, her eyes closed, and her face obscured. A dark square patch covered part of the woman's left shoulder as if something had been scratched off her skin. The man faced the viewer with a fierce expression.

Those eyes, she would recognise anywhere. The man in the painting was Mason.

Her pulse rate accelerated, and her nipples tightened with need. Arousal flowed through her for the first time in a long while.

Although the couple weren't nude, it was the sexiest painting she'd ever seen.

A ball of jealousy dampened her arousal. Who was the woman in the painting? When did Mason start dating?

She couldn't read the artist-scrawled signature and wondered who'd painted it. Did Mason commission it? She hadn't even known he was into the arts. A pleasant surprise.

Perhaps the cold and brutal Mason she'd known had mellowed.

She giggled. It was impossible to imagine that Mason, who'd built a reputation for being calculating and savage over the past ten years, would suddenly mellow because of a painting. Or a woman.

He was a savvy businessman and had built a successful gambling business from nothing and provided opportunities for others. She doubted Haven would have been as successful without the clientele Casino Maximo attracted, who sought other services, ensuring the cash filtered down and building the ecosystem supporting all of them.

So yes, he was brilliant… and gorgeous.

Over the years, he'd lost the fresh face as his features became more chiselled and fiercer. His body had filled out and hardened like he was carved out of marble.

She sipped the champagne, the bubbles tickling her palate. Even after so many years, she wasn't a big drinker. But she liked the taste of quality champagne.

"What are you doing here?" a deep voice growled behind her.

Although Sophie was expecting him, her heart skipped a beat. Her spine stiffened, and her fingers tightened on the stem of the glass flute to stop it from slipping. Instinct dictated that she swivel and face him. *Don't turn your back on a wild animal.*

And in this business, no one was more savage than Mason Maduka.

Still, she took her time, taking a shallow breath and schooling her expression before swivelling to face him.

His massive silhouette blocked the door, broad shoulders, bulging arms stretching the fabric of his white dress shirt, and sturdy, long legs in dark trousers. Good to see that some things hadn't changed. Even with a business worth billions of cash, he still wore denim.

The hair on his head was clipped short, close to the scalp, and his jawline was darkened with a beard, trimmed tidily. His piercing gaze bore into her—eyes as dark as the night sky.

He stood there waiting for her answer, another surprise. He usually wasn't patient.

She swallowed the lump in her throat before speaking. "I have a problem."

"And?"

"And I need you to solve it."

"Not my problem." There was darkness in his voice, a baritone edged in steel, laced with whiskey, and lined by leather.

It tugged her insides, pulling at something deep inside her.

"I need you to make it your problem. I will pay you." Perhaps he thought she was here to ask a favour, which would explain his abrupt attitude.

"Still not interested." He didn't turn on the lights and approached the desk, walking around to sit in the armchair.

"Are you even going to hear me out? I need you to do a job for me. I said I will pay you." She bristled, palms clenching into fists.

"You can't afford me," he scoffed, looking away, dismissing her.

Her anger went stratospheric. He really was the most infuriating man she'd ever met.

"You know what? You can go to hell." She approached his desk and slammed the flute on the top, champagne sloshing over the edge. Then she leaned over it, glaring into his shadowed face. "I didn't want to come here in the first place. It is only because Duke requested it that I'm here. I don't need you."

"Go ahead and leave," his voice was calm and cold, his dark eyes glinting with contempt. "And you will lose everything, including the clothes on your back. Leave and see how quickly you become that girl walking the streets with nothing to her name but the items in her bag. The girl who was hopping into random men's cars."

A shiver travelled down her spine. "What did you just say?"

It was like he'd glimpsed her worst nightmare and was playing it back to her. Because she never wanted to go back to that life. To be at the bottom of the pile. To be the girl sucking dicks just to have a roof over her head.

"You heard me. What do you think will happen to you when you can't make your payments? Do you think Duke will let you walk away? Have you learnt nothing about this life over the past decade?"

He was right. Owing Duke money wouldn't end well for her.

But her eyes narrowed for a different reason.

"So, you know about the issues at Haven, and yet you don't want to help me?"

"Why should I help you?"

"Because ..." she started and trailed off. "Because we're friends."

"Are we?" He leaned back as if surprised, and the leather chair sighed softly. "That's news to me. Well, tell me one *friendly* thing you've done for me as a *friend* since the day we met."

She opened her mouth ... and closed it. She couldn't think of anything.

"Okay. We're not friends. But you know me. I'm a business associate. You should help me when I reach out."

He shook his head. "I don't have to help you. I don't help every associate that reaches out. It's not my responsibility to do so."

"For fuck's sake, Mason. Why are you doing this? Why are you being so difficult?" She flopped into the chair on the other side of the desk, feeling exhausted mere minutes into talking to him. And fearing the worst—losing everything she'd worked to build.

"You don't like it, do you? You don't like someone being unreasonable and not hearing you out when you've mapped out a deal that would be favourable to both parties?"

She lifted her head and glared at him. "No, I don't like it."

He nodded. "Now, you know how I felt ten years ago. I made you an offer that would have changed the trajectory of our lives. It would have been a good life. But you refused to hear me out. Refused to give me a chance. You preferred a different life. So, this is your bed. You made it. Now you must lie in it."

"What?" Her jaw fell, and her breath hitched as the penny dropped. "You're talking about your proposal for me to have your baby. Why is it still an issue? We've both moved on."

"Easy for you to say. I never forgot. I couldn't forget. You deprived me of something important. Something I wanted."

"Oh. My. God. You've been holding a grudge all this time when you could have had babies with other women," she shouted angrily.

Was he indirectly trying to ruin her life because she refused to have his baby? Okay, no law said he had to help her, but didn't he have an ounce of compassion? Where was the man who had rescued her from Bomba? The man who had threatened his mother and sliced his brother with a knife for hurting her. She'd found out what Mason had done for her the day she'd left his house. Benji had told her. Yes, she'd regretted not reaching a compromise with him. But she'd been unable to see past the fact she didn't want a baby at the time.

But to hold it against her all this while? To allow her to lose everything. That was pure malice.

Well, if he was going to play hardball, she could play it too.

After all, she needed him to fix her problem in less than one month. And babies didn't arrive in less than nine. Anything could happen before a child ever made an appearance.

Was having a baby such a bad idea? A little voice nagged.

No. No. This was about her business. Nothing else.

"Look, Mason. If you want a baby so damned much," she bit out. "Fix my business problem, and I'll have a baby for you."

FIVE

Finally, she was here. In his lair.

The moment Mason received reports indicating Sophie's business would get raided by the authorities, he'd known she would eventually show up here.

Oh, he'd known what was going down at Haven. Knew it was in trouble long before she'd found out.

Niru Town was his fucking domain. Every enterprise in this locality fed off the crumbs scattered by Maximo Hotel and Casino. Nothing existed in this rural location on the outskirts of Opal City except a village and farms. Then he and Duke built the hotel and turned it into a gambling resort.

The people who arrived here for work needed homes, so new houses were constructed, which developed the need for local shops and services and, in turn, schools and churches.

Since Duke relocated to Lori Osa, Mason became the king of Niru Town. Nothing happened around here without his knowledge. So, he'd known about Haven running into difficulties.

And he'd waited for a day like this. A day when Sophie Ojo, the procuress and managing director of Haven Services Ltd, would walk into his offices, requiring his professional assistance.

Mason noticed the moment Benji moved from his position at the terrace exit with a grin on his face, disappearing into the stairwell. His second rarely smiled in public and only with a handful of people.

A devilish smile pulled at Mason's lips because a quick analysis reduced the number to one. Two minutes later, that one person sashayed into the roof terrace.

Everything in Mason stood to attention, including his dick.

Madame Sophie, as she'd become known, commanded attention the minute she walked into a room. She wasn't a freaking wallflower. Hell, no. She became the focus of every male gaze in the vicinity. And every other eye, to be fair.

Because even if they didn't want to fuck her, they would either be jealous of her or crave the sensuality she oozed from every pore.

She knew the power she wielded, her hips swaying seductively as she walked up to the bar, and the server passed her a glass of champagne. She smiled, grabbed the flute, waited for a beat, swivelled, and headed out the exit.

A second later, Benji returned to his post, glanced in Mason's direction and nodded.

He got the message. Sophie was here to see him.

She'd walked into the terrace to bait him. A queen move. No doubt. She'd learned a few tricks since he'd found her fighting with her old pimp in the street many years ago.

Pride swelled his chest because he liked to think he'd contributed to her growth. To her survival. If he hadn't found her or taught her the dangers in plain view early enough, she might not have survived.

He waited a couple of beats and excused himself from the finance nerd giving him a status update on yesterday's revenue.

Mason would admit numbers were not his strongest suit. He was a lawyer by education and a strategist by profession. Duke was the one with an Economics degree and an MBA.

So, he'd recruited the most intelligent numbers person he could find who became responsible for providing daily reports. He knew their breakeven, therefore, which days were profitable or not. And if the prosperous days exceeded the not-so-profitable.

However, none of it crossed his mind as he followed the alluring scent of the woman who made his dick throb with need. He could barely control the anticipation fizzing in his veins.

"In your office," Benji said as Mason walked past, down the steps and along the corridor, the leather soles of trainers muted on the hard flooring.

He reached the open threshold to his office and froze. The dark space was only lit by the glow of the hotel sign coming in the window, illuminating the female figure in black.

She stood facing the almost-life-sized painting on the wall, scrutinizing it like she was in a museum. Like it was there for her pleasure.

How dare she?

A prickle of annoyance spiked through him.

The painting wasn't there for her pleasure. The last thing he wanted her to feel right now was amusement. No, far from it.

She'd stepped into hell, and the only thing left to do was burn.

"What are you doing here?" he demanded as if her presence proved surprising.

She took her time to face him and respond. "I have a problem."

Okay. She'd arrived with queen moves. Therefore, he should match her energy. He wouldn't make life easy for her. No, Madam.

He remained the grudge king. So, he levelled up the indifference and disdain as they bantered back and forth. Oh, he could do this all night.

Payback was a bitch.

First, she was in his face, her hot breath fanning his forehead as she taunted him fearlessly. His fingers itched, and he resisted the urge to wrap them around her neck and squeeze, to feel her restricted lifeblood pulsing against her skin, to see the fear flicker in her brown eyes as she choked.

Still, he kept his arms to himself and sat calmly. He'd learned how to control himself in a decade, to keep his temper in check.

Then he almost grinned when she flopped into the chair opposite him as if drained because he wouldn't budge or give an inch. He was being spiteful, tormenting her.

He was a sadistic bastard, after all. He'd warned her as such a decade ago when they'd first me, and she'd still stayed with him.

Suddenly, her eyes widened as she realised the reason for his malice.

"Oh. My. God. You've been holding a grudge all this time when you could have had babies with other women!" she screeched at him.

An angry tick started on his temple as his rage returned. What the hell did she take him for? Other people might be happy filling random wombs with their offspring. He wasn't one of them. He'd always been meticulous about where he released his seeds and ensured no one else would get to mother his child.

I wanted you, damn it! Not other women.

He resisted the urge to shout those words at her and watched the emotions chase across her features—confusion, regret and finally, rage.

Her fury matched his. Good. They were getting somewhere. She needed to experience precisely how he felt. They would both burn in this malevolent hell together.

"Look, Mason." Anger vibrated through her with every word. "If you want a baby so damned much, fix my business problem, and I'll have a baby for you."

His breath quickened, and his stomach knotted. Suspicion and dread swirled through him. Did she just threaten to use his child against him? Because there was no way she could have changed her mind on a whim about having his baby after she'd been so adamant.

He leaned back, pulled his knife out of the sheath and placed it on the table, the blade catching the light.

Sophie jerked upright as her breath hitched. Her widened eyes stayed riveted on the blade as if it would strike her any minute. For the first time tonight, her fearlessness vanished. She appeared ready to bolt.

Could she run faster than a knife thrown by someone with immaculate aim?

"Repeat what you just said," he said in a deceptively calm voice, although everything inside him jumbled up, and he rode tumultuous emotional waves.

She could threaten him with anything else, extort his business or life, and he would let it ride.

But one thing he would not tolerate was a threat against his child. Or any child under his protection, for that matter.

"Mason, it's fine. I'll go." She pressed her hands on the arms of the chair as if ready to rise.

"Don't make me repeat myself," he growled, his temper fraying.

She froze in place, eyes flicking from the blade to his face. Her throat bobbed as she swallowed, and her tongue flicked out and licked her bottom lip.

"I said I'll have your baby if you fix the problems at Haven," her tone was hesitant.

"Do you mean it?" he asked quietly, needing clarifications. His pulse raced in expectation, at the possibilities. Could he be finally getting his heart's desire?

"Of course," she said quickly. Too quickly. Triggering his internal alarm.

"When you get pregnant with my baby, will you carry it to full term and deliver him?"

"Yes, why not, if there are no complications."

"Complications?" He shot off the chair, unable to keep still any longer.

She jumped up, too, stumbling away from him as he approached.

"Mason, what are you doing?" she glanced around as if expecting someone to rescue her.

"Tell me what you mean by complications. Is that a euphemism for you terminating the pregnancy?" He walked steadily towards her, blade in hand by his side.

"No. No. I meant that sometimes a pregnancy does not go full term because something could go wrong. It happens quite often. I found out about it when my sister was pregnant," she said rapidly, trying to convince him.

Her back hit the wall, trapped beside the painting.

He knew about complications. His mother had two miscarriages before he'd arrived. But he'd wanted her to spell out her intentions or lies for the ancestors to judge her if she ever hurt his baby.

He swivelled, strode to the door, pushed it shut and engaged the lock. Then he walked back to his armchair behind the desk and lowered his body.

"Strip," he commanded in a low voice.

"What?" she sounded shocked.

He raised his brow. "You want to have my baby. There's no time like the present to get started with making him. Take your clothes off."

She hesitated, glancing around. Then she straightened and sashayed slowly towards him.

"Shouldn't you call your pervert doctor to poke and prod me first? You don't want to catch something nasty from me," she taunted, palms braced on her hips.

"If you don't strip, I'll cut the clothes off." He lifted the knife for emphasis. He was still suspicious of her and needed to keep her on her toes.

She unbuttoned the jacket and slipped it off her shoulders, draping it over the chair she'd vacated. He flicked a switch beside his desk, and the corner lamps glowed softly, revealing more of her.

The black one-piece body suit clung to every dip and curve of her body from a deep V-neck and the cleavage threatening to spill to the stretch of her wide ass and then narrowing down the legs.

His dick throbbed, and his spine tingled.

Damn. How did she get the outfit on in the first place?

She tugged the front zipper at the bottom of the V down to her crotch and peeled the outfit off like a second skin.

He couldn't take his hungry eyes away from her as her naked body came into view.

SIX

Sophie made an artform out of undressing, and Mason was fascinated for a few seconds. She peeled the outfit down her arms and chest in a sensual motion, keeping Mason transfixed as more of her cinnamon-brown skin came into view.

Damn. She was perfect.

He'd seen her naked before. But somehow, she seemed more perfect than ten years ago. Although he'd always desired more than physicality, his attraction to her had never been in doubt. He'd always wanted the whole package she presented—the feminine and the feisty.

Except when she talked about murdering his offspring. In those instances, the urge to protect superseded the craving for pleasure.

A bite of loneliness caused a thickness in his throat. A longing so intense he ached and struggled to shove down the feeling which simmered inside him for years. The isolation started when his father died.

He'd had respite briefly with Sophie's arrival ten years ago. She'd been his beacon of hope when he'd been surrounded by hostility at home.

Then she'd threatened to abort his baby if she got pregnant.

And he'd spiralled into anger and resentment—his twin companions for a decade.

At the time, he had no option but to ship Sophie off. Not too far away, though. The safest place he'd known to send her was to Duke, who understood Mason had claimed rights over her and was therefore obligated to protect her until Mason withdrew those rights.

Which would never happen.

He'd marked her once. He would do it again.

So, he'd waited ten years patiently. Oh, he'd had to learn patience.

Because what the fuck else could he have done? Fucked her? Gotten her pregnant? Watched her abort his kid? Never. Or coerce her into keeping the baby, making her resentful about it? Even worse. How was that a good way to bring a child into the world? With all the negative energy the mother carried during the pregnancy. Not a great start to anyone's life, let alone his son.

So, yes, he'd learned patience, and eventually, Sophie sought him out. She came here on her own. Offered to bear his child without his prompting. Although he didn't entirely trust she would deliver on her promise. But he would give her time to get used to the idea. He could be fair, too. There was a purpose to his madness.

She wiggled her waist, pushing the bodysuit down her hips. The black lace and satin bra barely contained her D-cup breasts. Her chest tapered into her waist before flaring at the hip.

She was performing a striptease without the music.

Still, he didn't need any external distractions. Instead, the fast tempo of his drumming heart provided the cadence to the moment. His nerve endings tingled, increasing his yearning.

She was everything he wanted. Her curves were more apparent, her body somehow more mature than a decade ago. Perhaps it was his imagination or just the confident way she carried herself.

She bent in a standing forward fold and tugged the zippers at her ankles to pull the outfit off her sandaled feet. He'd witnessed similar poses at the yoga classes held at the hotel gym.

Yet, he'd never experienced such a visceral reaction as his dick throbbed painfully.

He stared at her plump ass, and the thin scrap of black lace thong stuck between the brown cheeks, covering nothing and drawing attention to her puckered hole and glistening pussy.

"Fuck," he swore under his breath, losing his fight with restraint. He pushed off the leather armchair and strode around the table.

She tried to straighten as he approached.

"Don't move," he growled, and she froze, hands braced around her calves.

Gripping her hips, he pressed his body against hers from behind. Her high-heeled sandals aligned her butt to his groin. Ideal. Her clothes tangled at her ankles, restricting her movement. Even better. He could unbuckle his jeans, tug his dick out and fuck her in this position. Make her take his punishing thrusts whilst bent in half. Torment her the way he'd hurt for years.

His grip on her skin tightened, and she whimpered, shoving her bum against him.

Oh, she wanted him. His body. But that wasn't enough for him.

"I said, don't move." He gave her ass a hard swat.

"Ouch," she moaned and stopped wriggling.

A smirk curled his lips. He wanted more. So much more. To punish her and pleasure her. Wanted her to feel him everywhere. To remember the feel of his caress on her skin. Wanted to remind her what she'd missed in a decade. What could have been...

So, with one hand gripping her hip, he trailed the other over her spine. She sighed with pleasure as he pressed each vertebra. Her skin was smooth, flawless. No trace of the welts from his mother's cane on her back. No evidence of his brand on her shoulder. No proof that he'd once owned her, and she'd been a gratifying part of his life for forty-eight hours.

His chest hollowed out, and he took shallow breaths, fighting the despair.

She was here now. Nothing else should matter.

He shoved the unpleasant feeling aside and reached for her bra, unhooking it, allowing it to fall down her shoulders and arms. She didn't move or let it land on the floor.

Hmmm. Her compliance niggled at him, annoying him.

This was Sophie. She'd never been obedient. But, even if she wasn't fighting him, she was participating. There was always some resistance, some tension. Not this pliant state she currently inhabited.

It suddenly clicked. This was how some hookers behaved with him, believing he wanted their complete compliance.

Sophie was withdrawing, treating him like a random client. Like he was paying for her time.

Fuck that! He was Mason Maduka. He'd owned her body once. He would possess her again—body and soul. Forever.

He tapped her nape hard with his index finger. She startled, making him grin. She remembered how he would grip her neck. Good. He needed to keep her on edge, keep her focused on him.

She wore one of those lace-front wigs glued to her hairline. She'd been wearing them for years. He hated the damn things and had mentioned he preferred braids to wigs. Still, he would concede this style suited her, and because it was in a ponytail that currently fell forward, he didn't have to touch it or move it out of the way.

He focused on her skin, curling his body over hers and providing a cocoon. Then, he massaged the trapezius muscles linking the back of her neck and shoulders.

"Damn," she mewled, practically purring like a cat. "I forgot how good you were with your fingers."

Her words triggered his annoyance, and his neck corded.

He wrapped his fingers around her throat, clamped down and lifted. She had no option but to move with him, straightening with him. He kept the other hand clamped around her hips, holding her against him.

"So, you remember how good it was between us? Yet you preferred to give yourself to others for money," he gritted out, goading her.

Her mouth dropped open as she stiffened in shock. Then her eyes blazed with fury, and she shoved his chest. "Fuck you, Mason. I can fuck a million men, and it would be none of your business. You sent me away. Or have you forgotten?"

He said nothing. Didn't budge. Just tightened his grip and held her furious gaze while keeping his expression blank.

To speak would be to admit the dark, monstrous truth. He would've destroyed her if she'd stayed and aborted his baby. This, in turn, would have wrecked his soul.

"Your heart accepts her," Ma Bagu had once told him.

He hadn't understood at the time until he'd had to make the difficult choice of keeping Sophie or protecting her. Sending her away had saved her. Saved him. Saved them.

Now, it no longer mattered. She'd returned to him. And he would claim her like he should have ten years ago.

"I forget nothing," he said against her ear, swiping the skin behind the lobe with his tongue. "I remember how quickly you fell apart under my touch in the car on the way to my hometown."

"Fuck you!" She lashed out, catching his chest and upper arm with her nails. Her ponytail whipped his face.

The fight, the pain, only fuelled his desire.

"Yes, let's do that." He swivelled, taking her with him and deposited her face-down on the desk.

"Yes, let's!" She swiped everything off his desk, sending his laptop and lamp crashing onto the hard flooring. She twisted, glaring at him.

Yes, he liked her fierce and furious. She only inflamed his need for her.

Chuckling, he leaned against her, unbuckling his denim trousers and pulling his engorged dick out of his boxer-briefs. He ripped the skimpy lace thongs from her body, tossing them onto the table as she moaned.

Damn! She was driving him insane. Hot blood raced through his veins as his heart pounded in his chest.

He spread her open with his thighs, lined up his dick with her hot entrance, rubbing the head over her pussy lips. She was so fucking wet it would drip to the floor.

Despite her anger, she wanted him as much as he wanted her.

On the heady thought, he slammed into her all the way to the hilt. She tilted her head back and screamed in pleasure. Her grip on the table edge tightened, her butt pressed against his groin.

For a few seconds, he savoured the sensation of his dick inside her for the first time ever. The first time he fucked anyone without a condom. She was hot and slick, gripping him like a glove.

"Move, damn it," she demanded, clamping around him in ripples.

He lost control, taken over by primitive need, a need to rut ruthlessly. Gripping her hips, he pounded into her recklessly. She shattered with another scream, her orgasm rippling around his dick.

Good thing his office was soundproof, and the humming air-conditioner muted noises. Otherwise, someone might want to investigate. Still, Benji was out there, never far from him.

Mason didn't stop, didn't slow down, kept pounding even as her screams reduced to moans. He bent forward, pressing lips to her sweaty nape in open-mouthed kisses, tasting the salt of her skin, nipping and licking, then reaching down to stroke her clit. She whimpered, moving frantically against his body. She would climax again soon.

The urge to claim all of her made him lean forward and tilt her neck. He kissed her mouth with everything, hard and passionately, just as his hips pistoned fast and furiously.

Surprising him, she leaned into him, returning the kiss enthusiastically, her tongue tangling with his. She snatched a part of him with the kiss. A piece of his soul departed his body, entering her through their physical connection.

She broke the kiss and yelled, "Yes! Yes!"

And with it, his orgasm tingled over nerve endings even as hers rippled around his dick. Heat flooded him, and he ejaculated in waves, pouring hot cum into her, slowing his movement. Groaning, pleasure washed over him like never before, draining him.

He collapsed on top of her, bracing his weight with his arms against the tabletop. His head dropped onto her back, his breathing heavy like hers.

Overwhelmed with emotions he didn't quite understand, he pressed kisses to her shoulder, neck, and cheek. Then his heart dropped, and he froze.

What was the moisture on her long black lashes? Was she crying?

"Nkem, o gini?" he asked before he could stop himself. Igbo was his language of comfort and affection because of Ma Bagu. "What's wrong?"

Her muscles tensed, and she pushed against him. "Get off me!"

Her reaction confused him. In a decade, he hadn't had sex with someone he hadn't paid for, someone who wasn't prepared to take whatever he dished out.

"Did I hurt you?" he asked as he straightened, pulling out of her and tucking his semi back into his jeans.

He'd been so lost in the encounter. They'd seemed in tune with each other all the way. But perhaps he'd overstepped her boundary and had done something she didn't like.

She tilted her head back briefly before swivelling to face him. "Don't you fucking dare do that?"

She tugged her bodysuit over her hips without her panties.

"Do what?" Leaning against the desk, he lifted his hands in exasperation, watching as she dressed in jerky movements.

Once her blazer was buttoned, she grabbed her purse and stood still, hands on hips.

"Don't you dare be gentle with me? I know how you are with the girls. You are never gentle with them. This is no different. This is just another transaction. You fix my business problems, and I pay you by having your baby. Sex is just a part of the deal. Nothing more. Nothing else changes between us."

His blood ran cold.

They'd just had the most profound, most unguarded sex of his life. And she was dismissing him?

"No. Are you saying you felt nothing just now between us?" He couldn't even believe he was asking the question. For the first time after sex, he felt untethered, uncertain. He'd never been in this situation before. Had never been dismissed after sex. He'd always been the one to walk away.

Her throat rippled as she swallowed. "I'm saying it's only sex." She sucked in a deep breath and pulled her phone out. "What's your phone number? I tried calling you earlier, but the number I have was disconnected."

She was serious. All business. Okay. He could be all business too.

He allowed the coldness in his heart to spread through his veins like icicles. Tugging a drawer open, he withdrew a business card and tossed it on the desk. As she reached for it, he slammed his hand on top of hers. She froze, glaring at him.

"I'll fix your business problem," he said in a cold voice, his face devoid of expression. "In return, you will pay me by becoming my toy until my baby is born. Afterwards, you will hand over the child, and I'll free you from any obligations."

"No way!" she screeched.

"Take it or leave it," he said as he walked to the exit.

"Take it or leave it? We just fucked." She stomped towards him.

"Yes, that was just a deposit," he drawled, opening the door. "Deposits are non-refundable. You should've read the small print."

"What fucking small print?" Her eyes darted away, and she paced the room, her hand covering her belly briefly. "You know we just had unprotected sex. In a month's time, I could test positive for pregnancy."

"And in nine months, you can be free of me," he said flippantly, although the thought that she could be pregnant in a matter of weeks excited him.

Still, he waited for the veiled threat against the foetus. Something about complications.

None came.

Instead, she glared at him, shook her head and stomped out the door.

"You are fucking crazy," she yelled as she departed.

Finally able to vent, he slammed the door and growled his rage. The ball of black lace on his desk caught his attention, and he pursed his lips.

She wanted only sex?

They'd see about that.

SEVEN

"You are fucking crazy!" Sophie vibrated with anger as she walked out of Mason's office. The second time she'd yelled those words at him since the fateful night they met.

Unlike the first time, Mason didn't respond to her accusatory tone.

Instead, the door slammed in her wake, jarring her already shattered nerves, and she jolted. She turned and stared at the closed door, her mind a jumble of emotions.

Sure, she'd walked out, but did he have to let her go so readily? This proved how easy it was for Mason to shut her out of his life. Just like he'd done ten years ago. What did she expect?

The tears she'd been fighting whilst they'd been making love—having sex, damn it! —came rushing to her eyes again.

"Madam Sophie?"

Shit! Her muscles stiffened. She'd forgotten about Benji's presence. He was never far from Mason and probably overheard their argument while the door was open.

She blinked rapidly, pushing back the tears and dabbing her cheeks. With the sex and tears, she'd ruined her makeup. She'd been in such a rush to right her clothes and get away from Mason and the conflicting emotions evoked from having sex with him that she hadn't bothered to use his office bathroom.

Benji had seen her in worse states—naked in the back of the car with Mason while he drove them to Mason's hometown and covered in cane welts when he'd taken her to Duke's office a decade ago.

Right now, she felt as tumultuous and wrecked as that girl who'd had the rug pulled out from under her feet when Mason kicked her out of his home and life back then. She was fragile, jumping at the slightest sound and on the verge of bawling like an infant.

Don't be such a baby.

Those words had become her mantra through the years whenever situations got too dicey. She needed the bathroom to tidy up and compose herself before she walked through a hotel foyer full of people. But the nearest ladies she could think of was past Benji, by the lift lobby.

"Is there a bathroom I can use near here?" She asked, refusing to turn in his direction.

She didn't want him to see her this way. Despite her earlier assertion otherwise, she enjoyed how he called her Madam Sophie and didn't want to diminish his respect for her.

In this environment, respect was everything. She needed to hang on to some dignity—whatever was left of it.

"There's a bathroom at the end of the corridor. Just turn right. It's opposite the fire exit stairwell," Benji said in a subdued tone as if he recognised her current sensitivity to loud noises.

"Thank you," she muttered and hurried towards his indicated direction.

In the toilet cubicle, she shut the door, sat on the covered toilet seat, and gulped in deep breaths, trying to blank her mind of any thoughts, a technique she used to quell turbulent emotions.

Although the ball of despondent ache remained in her chest, she managed to grasp her composure. She left the stall and walked to the mirror above the sink. Running the tap, she wet her hands and pressed down on the stray strands of hair, retying her ponytail. Then she used tissues to clean her face and reapplied the mattifying powder from her compact. A dab of lip matte, and she looked as good as new.

Straightening her drooping shoulders, she left the ladies, some of her composure restored enough to keep a smile on her face when she sashayed past Benji, and he said, "Good night."

She stayed unflustered, although her body felt cold as she walked across the busy hotel lobby and into the warm night. The driver, who saw her as she exited, opened the car door and held it until she climbed in. Then he shut it, went around the front, and got in.

"Take me back to Haven," she said calmly, playing the Madame everyone expected.

"Yes, ma," he replied and started the engine before making the short trip around the block to the Haven building.

When she entered the front entrance, the receptionist sat at her station. No Chiamaka. Instead, a security man stood chatting with her.

"Madam, welcome back," the receptionist and bodyguard chorused, straightening to face her.

"Thank you. Where is Chiamaka?" Sophie asked, being all business.

She'd learned to keep up appearances a long time ago. These people depended on her for their livelihoods. She would never let them see her as erratic or insecure, especially when the company could be in trouble. She'd reassured them it was business as usual, so she needed to keep the façade.

Even if her entanglement with Mason or the lack thereof could lead to her destruction.

"She has a client," the receptionist replied.

"Okay," Sophie said. She'd thought as much. These were working hours. "I don't want to be disturbed tonight unless it's an emergency. Can you handle it?"

She needed time and space to think, and the constant routine interruptions would only add to her stress.

"Of course, Ma. Everything is under control," the woman replied.

"Good. I'll be at home." She headed up the stairs to her floor. Her legs felt heavy, and her body drained of energy.

When she opened the front door of her apartment, darkness greeted her with an eerie feeling. Shivering, she stepped inside and flicked on the lights. The modern living room came into view. Cream sofas with soft cushions and throws, rugs over the tiled flooring, and a separate dining area with upholstered cream leather chairs around a glass-topped light-wood table.

This was all hers, her space, her home. Beautifully furnished. Something she would never have afforded a decade ago.

She'd built a good life and acquired wealth. Could afford some luxury items. Okay, she wasn't at Otedola's level. But she was doing very well.

She tossed the purse on a glass side table, and the clacking sound echoed through the space, jarring her nerves again.

A thickness bloomed in her throat, and tears threatened to spill. The melancholic thoughts rushed back. She walked to the window, looking at the dark lake, a glint of silver in the distance.

She'd never been able to shake the feeling of isolation. She wasn't a solitary creature by nature, although she'd gradually had to become one to protect herself.

She had a family. But as her sister recently demonstrated, she'd been ostracized by them. They didn't think she was good enough for them anymore because they now had money. Her mother had never directly condemned her job. But since the incident at Bimpe's house, her mother had become distanced too. As if separating themselves from Sophie would make them more acceptable to her sister's in-laws.

Of course, Sophie had friends. Well, Ziga was an employee who was also a friend. They'd formed a strong bond, and Sophie trusted her. Still, Ziga had her own safety net—a partner and a daughter. More importantly, she was in Lori Osa and didn't know Sophie's history with Mason.

Then, there was Gabrielle, another sex worker Sophie had met recently. Last year, Gabrielle had helped Duke's team take down The Baron, who'd been the Lori Osa kingpin and Duke's father-in-law. Now, Duke was establishing himself as the new kingpin. Sophie and Gabrielle became friends and were currently working together to build a Haven franchise in the megacity. Still, Gabrielle was too fresh in her circle. Sophie wasn't sure she could bare her soul to the woman who was more of a mentee than a BFF.

This meant Sophie had no safety net, no one to share personal matters.

Sighing, she slumped into the nearest sofa and tipped her head against the backrest, staring at the white ceiling.

For a moment in her life—forty-eight hours, ten years ago—she'd opened to Mason. Had considered him to be her friend.

The moment he'd intervened in her fight with Bomba when no one else had even attempted to stop her old pimp, she'd trusted Mason to protect her. He'd even defended her against his brother that same night.

And despite what had happened with his mother, she'd still trusted him. Although he'd never apologised for his mother caning her, his actions had shown his remorse.

He'd been her friend, even if they hadn't defined what they'd shared back then. The easy camaraderie. Their jokes and laughter while eating the fufu and okra soup Ma Bagu prepared that first night. Even after Mason marked her skin, she'd still trusted him, somehow.

Because each time he'd directly inflicted pain, he'd soothed her. The comfort he gave was always full of affection, alleviated any ache, and made her want to bask in his embrace and caresses. Because no one else had ever paid her the same level of attention.

Not then and not now. Not even Bomba, who'd been a wham-bam-thank-you-mam man.

She'd thought Mason cared about her, even with his bizarre behaviour.

So, all those years ago, when Mason had shown up in his bedroom while she'd been recovering from the torture of his mother's caning with bags of clothes, she'd fought him, knowing the gifts were his way of apologizing for the pain she'd suffered.

Their fight had soon turned to caresses, and she'd expected they would make love.

Instead, he'd stopped touching her, and the conversation had strangely turned to pregnancy.

"I'm being serious, Sophie. I want you to have my baby," he'd said even more weirdly.

Her mouth had dropped open. She'd thought he'd been joking when calling her 'my woman'. But to even consider her as the mother of his child was just on the Yaba Left extreme. Totally insane.

Moreover, she'd just escaped the brutal clutches of one man, her pimp. Being chained to another man through pregnancy, one who seemed out of his mind no matter how much she liked him, seemed like the last thing she should do. Of course, *babies* hadn't been on her mind.

"I'm sorry, Mason. No, I don't want to have your child," she'd said, expecting him to lash out or choke her in anger.

Instead, his response had been unpredictable and distressing. First, he'd walked out of the bedroom. Minutes later, Ma Bagu arrived, helping her pack up to leave. Then she'd been in the car with Benji driving back to the city.

The devastation she'd felt that day. The despair. The fear. She'd never felt anything like it before. Not when she'd run from her former madam. Not when she'd fought with Bomba. For weeks she couldn't sleep properly. She cried. Lord, how she cried.

The callous way Mason discarded her broke her heart. She still could not understand why. She'd only spent two days with him. Yet she'd been heartbroken when he sent her away without a second look or a chance for an explanation.

Lord, she'd hated Mason for years because of it. Still did.

"So why the hell did you say you would have his baby?" she yelled into the room, jumping off the sofa as her agitation rose. "Hai. Sophie, you messed up!"

She crumpled on the floor, head on the cushion, her body trembling.

What had she done?

She'd been so desperate when he talked about her losing the business and everything she'd worked for. She'd had no doubts that if she didn't use his services, Mason would sit back and watch Haven crumble. The cold contempt in his gaze had said it all.

But losing the company wasn't the worst thing that could happen.

Owing the Odilis money was a painful death sentence. That was her biggest fear.

She was an asset now, which made her a tolerable associate. But the minute she became a liability, they would send her to oblivion with nothing. That's if they didn't kill her first.

And finding out Mason still bore a grudge because she hadn't accepted his proposal to have his child had confused her. Sent her spiralling into desperation. She'd blurted out the only solution in her mind.

"If you want a baby so damned much, fix my business problem, and I'll have a baby for you."

Once the words left her mouth, she'd realised her mistake and had tried to brave her way through it.

Of course, she'd thought he wouldn't accept her word. Or insist on her doing health checks like he'd done ten years ago, which would buy her time to back out and devise a different plan.

However, he'd latched on to the idea.

"Do you mean it?" he'd asked with the same naivety and sincerity he'd had a decade ago when he'd asked her to bear his child.

She'd had no choice but to say, "Of course."

The fear of Mason's knife was the beginning of wisdom. She didn't want the blade anywhere near her skin.

Leading to the biggest problem.

Now that she'd agreed to bear his child, she had to keep her promise.

Because the man who'd had no compunctions about kicking her out of his house when he'd known she was homeless would have no qualms about cutting her to pieces if she didn't keep to her side of the bargain.

But how could she keep to the bargain when their first time of having sex had been so profound and intense she'd sensed it in her soul? Felt as if they'd made love rather than mere sex. She hadn't even known when she'd started crying, floating in the cloud of euphoria.

Only became aware of where and whom when he'd spoken Igbo to her so tenderly that more tears had sprouted. Then she'd known she had to get away from him. Known she couldn't have him being gentle with her. Have him being nice to her. She didn't want to fall under his spell again. Didn't want to trust him.

Because he would only wreck her emotionally again.

It was only a matter of time. Nine months perhaps.

EIGHT

Sophie was back on Maximo Hotel's roof terrace. This time it wasn't the exclusive one above the executive offices. This garden gallery was an extension of the bar lounge, and tonight, it was reserved for a private party.

Middle-aged men occupied the low leather sofas flanked by female escorts. Champagne bottles, half-empty flutes and hand-crafted wooden platters with small chops covered the coffee tables. Afrobeat played in the background, and servers showed up, refreshing the drinks and nibbles.

"So, Sophie. Where have you been all these months?" Reginald Ifemelu asked. He was the sixty-year-old celebrant whose friends had organised this party. "Did you go to Dubai?"

His gaze seemed fixated on her boobs, and she tried not to roll her eyes heavenwards. Her role was to meet and greet and keep the clients sweet, ensuring everything ran smoothly. She usually spent a limited time at these events.

However, she didn't want to be here. The men's leering gazes made her skin prickle with unease, and she wished she hadn't worn the low-cut blouse, showing off her cleavage.

Still, Mr Ifemelu was a good client, generous with his wealth, although pushy sometimes. Handsome and stylish, he was a silver fox zaddy the girls liked to entertain. He and his friends kept her in business. Hence the reason she showed up for his birthday treat.

"No. I didn't go to Dubai. When you didn't take me there, what business do I have in Dubai?" Sophie replied with a nonchalant giggle, responding to the personal question while being purposefully evasive. Discussing her private life with clients was never a good idea.

"Dubai is a beautiful place for beautiful people like you," the man said.

"Yes, oh. I've heard it's beautiful, but I've never been." Not the entire truth.

She'd flown to Bahrain recently with five other escorts, briefly stopping in Dubai. The F1 Grand Prix event had been organised by Osagie Peters, known in Lori Osa as the King of Clubs.

"Then you must let me take you to Dubai. I have business there soon," Reginald said.

"Ah, won't your wife be upset if I go with you on a business trip," she replied jokingly, reminding the man why it was a bad idea.

He was married with kids at universities. He was a well-known local businessman, an importer/exporter as he preferred. Although, around here, it could mean he traded anything, including contraband. There were rumours he served a jail term in the USA for drug smuggling many years ago and got deported afterwards.

None of that mattered to Sophie as long as he paid well for their services.

He laughed aloud and placed an arm around her shoulder, shifting closer. "Don't worry about it. It doesn't concern her…"

Something prickled on Sophie's spine, and she glanced to the right, missing the rest of Reginald's sentence.

Mason reclined on a corner armchair near the bar. She recognised him although he sat in the shadows, face angular and cruel, sharp cheekbones and square jaw. His eyes glinted, staring straight at her, narrowed in disapproval. He wore navy denim, a white shirt and a brown blazer which matched his leather shoes. A gold watch gleamed on his wrist.

Her heart jolted as if she'd been hit by a lightning bolt. Heat tingled all over her skin, and she couldn't look away. Her attention homed in on him.

When did he get in here? None of her girls at the party had alerted her to his presence. But, then again, they shouldn't have to warn her because this was Mason's business. He could go wherever he pleased, although she didn't usually see him at these events.

More to the point, what was he doing here? She hadn't expected to see him so soon after last night.

Reginald's hand snaked down her shoulder towards her breast. His breath smelled of booze, and she suspected he was high on something else too.

She stiffened, shrugging off the offending limb with a giggle. "Sorry, Reginald. What were you saying about Dubai?"

"I said I will take you to Dubai on my next trip." He placed his hand on her thigh, which crept up her dress.

Still, she couldn't shake the burning sensation of Mason's gaze on her skin. His presence was a distraction, not helping her pay attention to the celebrant she was supposed to be entertaining.

She snuck a surreptitious glance at Mason, and a fissure of electricity rushed up her spine. His gaze stayed on her, unrelenting and impenitent.

It was weirdly thrilling, disturbing and infuriating all at once. Why was he even here? He wasn't a guest, and it didn't look like he knew this group of revellers personally.

She shivered, turning back to Reginald, trying to focus on him yammer on about all the different places he'd travelled.

But in truth, she couldn't concentrate. Instead, all her senses tuned into Mason.

She remembered last night, bent over the desk in his office while he fucked her vigorously. So damn good. His thickness filling her up. His demanding thrusts. His fierce kiss.

Her heart raced, her palms clammy. She wiped them on her dress, shifting in her seat as her pussy clenched.

Get your act together, Sophie. You're acting like he claimed your virginity!

"Sophie?"

"Hmmm…" she said distractedly as heat settled low in her belly.

"Is something distracting you?"

"No. Of course not." Her cheeks heated.

"Is there something going on between you and that small boy?"

"What small boy?" She pretended she didn't know what he was talking about, glancing around.

"The one over there in the corner who has been watching you for a while." He pointed in Mason's direction.

Shit.

"Oh. Don't worry about him. He does that all the time. He's just working."

"Okay. He's one of your boys. I was wondering how he got in here because I couldn't recognise him."

She stiffened, biting her bottom lip instead of correcting his wrong assumption.

"The 'small boy' is Mason Maduka, the managing director of this establishment, you dis yeye old man," she wanted to yell at the man who was suddenly pissing her off.

Some older people liked to disparage youngsters. Sure, Mason was in his thirties, and she was older than him by five years. But he'd worked damned hard and built Maximo from scratch with Duke. As a result, he'd earned recognition amongst his peers and deserved respect from everyone.

"In fact, you should warn him to stop looking at you like he does, as if he owns you. As if he has tasted you. Even if he has, you are still his madam. Isn't it?"

"Yes, yes. I will talk to him," she said instead of *"Mind your damned business!"*

"Good. Anyway, tonight, you will come back to my hotel room. I want to feel you."

His hand on her lap wormed between her thighs, making her skin crawl.

Time to get away from him. But she had to handle him diplomatically.

"Ah-ah, Reggie," she cooed, catching his hand and stroking the back of it. "You know I'm not on the menu tonight. The girls will take very good care of you. In fact, let me call them now so you can pick anyone you want, even more than one if you can handle it."

She shifted, about to stand.

"Of course, I can handle anything." Reginald grabbed her wrist, yanking her back onto the sofa. "But I'm the one who decides what's on the menu, and I want you. You know I can take very good care of you. In fact, I can buy a house and car for you. I told you I will take you to Dubai, and that's just the start. But if you want me to pay extra tonight, just name your price."

"No, I'm sorry, Reginald. But that's not how it works." She tugged at his fingers. Interesting how quickly some of these clients became assholes when they didn't get what they wanted. "You've used our services before, so you know you can't pick someone without their agreement. And as I already said, I have a prior engagement tonight."

His face puffed up in anger, and his snare on her wrist became painful.

"Well, it's my fucking birthday, and you are my birth—" Reginald's voice died suddenly.

Looming large above them was a very tall, familiar figure.

"She said no. Let her go," Mason's voice was deep and chilling.

"How do you know what she said from over there? Sophie, you see what I mean. Control your boy before I lose my temper," Reginald said arrogantly.

Mason said nothing as his hand went to the leather sheath attached to his belt.

Terror sent chills down Sophie's back. If he pulled the knife out, things would get bloody.

"Mason, no!" she ordered, praying he would listen as she got up again, tugging her hand free. "Reggie, I'll be back in a minute. Let me sort this out."

She placed her hand over Mason's on the knife's hilt and tugged him. "Come with me."

Mason and Reginald glared at each other for seconds before Mason followed Sophie. She stopped briefly where Chiamaka sat with another guest and whispered, "Go and sit with Reginald. Keep him occupied. I'll be back soon."

"Okay," Chiamaka replied.

Sophie walked down the stairs where Mason was already waiting. He pointed at the door, "In here." and pushed it open.

She entered, and he followed, shutting it.

Then she swivelled. "What the hell did you think you were doing?"

"You're asking me? What were you doing up there?"

"I was doing my job. Have you forgotten what I do for a living?"

"No, I haven't forgotten because you're bent on reminding me every fucking minute." He paced the small office. It must have been for one of the unit managers. Perhaps the bar manager. "Why are you even at the birthday party? You are the madame. The boss. You don't have to be there like the girls."

"Look, I don't have to explain my actions to you. But if you must know, Reginald requested my presence. It's his birthday party. He's a client, and what the client wants, he gets—"

"Over his dead fucking body. It's apparent he wants you, and there's no way he's going to fuck you."

"Like I already said to you. It's my job, and what I do is none of your business."

"None of my business? You could be carrying my baby."

"Your baby?" She threw her hands up. "There is no baby. We fucked last night. I'm not pregnant."

"You don't know that."

"Neither do you. Anyway, it's too early to tell, and it doesn't matter. Even if I'm pregnant, I still have to work."

He stiffened, going still. Then he shook his head. "You're not serious."

"Why not? You're not going to stop working if I get pregnant. Why should I?"

"You're telling me you're going to keep fucking other people while you're carrying my baby?"

Her skin prickled uncomfortably. After the way Mason fucked her last night, the concept of having anyone else inside her made her shudder. Still, he had no right to dictate to her. If she didn't want to sleep with others, it would be *her* decision. Not his. "My point is that whatever I do is none of your business."

He nodded. "Okay. And this man tonight. The Reginald guy. You're going to fuck him too?"

She shrugged, projecting nonchalance while her stomach curdled. After tonight Reggie had gone on her no-fucking block list. But Mason didn't have to know it. "I don't know. He's a good client, and you messed up matters. I'm going to have to smooth things over with him. If it means sleeping with him, so be it."

"So be it, indeed," he said in a calm voice. Too calmly.

She expected him to explode with rage. Instead, he stood quietly in contemplation for a few seconds while her heart raced in confusion.

"Okay," he said finally after puffing out a heavy sigh. "Do what you must do. I will do what I must. My mother once said I'd become a serial killer. It looks like it will happen. So go ahead, fuck anyone you like. But know this. I will kill every person you fuck from now on."

A dizzy spell overcame her, and she staggered as a chill travelled down her spine. "What?"

His set jaw, pressed lips, and intense gaze indicated his determination and sincerity.

"Let me spell it out. If you fuck Reginald Whatever-His-Name, I will kill him. If you fuck anyone else, man, woman, other, I will kill them."

"No way. You're just bluffing to scare me. How will you even know if I sleep with anyone else?" she muttered.

Surely, he'd lost his mind. No one in their right senses would say this. Should she call Duke to intervene?

"Am I bluffing?" He stepped forward, crowding her into the door. "I once threatened to kill my mother and brother because of you. Do you really think I will hesitate to kill some arrogant fucker who thinks he can have what belongs to me?"

"I don't—" she started, and he pressed his palm over her mouth.

"Argue with yourself all you like. Fuck whomever you wish. I won't stop you. But all you will do is create a hit list for me and turn me into a serial killer. I found out about your business being in trouble before you did. Of course, I'll know if anyone even sniffs at you in this town. And no, you can't leave town. I've already told Duke that you're not returning to Lori Osa for the foreseeable future."

"What the hell. You can't do that!" she yelled, her panic at his threat forgotten. Instead, her muscles quivered with anger.

"I did it. Get used to it." He reached for the door handle, his face a dark, impassive mask, his eyes like black ice.

He was leaving while matters remained unresolved. Things were snowballing out of control.

She panicked. "Wait."

He ignored her and turned the handle.

"Please!" She never thought she would beg him for anything. But him threatening to kill her clients was a red flag she couldn't ignore.

He paused and puffed out a heavy sigh. "What is it?"

She swallowed, her gaze darting around the office. "Why are you threatening to kill my clients?"

He rolled his eyes heavenward. "If you can't figure it out, I can't help you."

She clenched and unclenched her sweaty palms. "But you know this is my livelihood. My business. I have employees. I can't just stop working."

He whirled on her, his eyes blazing.

"For fuck's sake, Sophie. I'm not asking you to stop working. There are other things you can do instead of giving your body to others, come on! Do you know how I felt sitting there, watching that fucker put his hands all over your body? Do you know what that did to me? I don't think it's too much to ask for you to sit behind a desk for the next nine months and actually behave like a business owner instead of a hooker," he spat out angrily.

He'd just insulted her, and she wanted to tell him to go to hell. That she was a business owner and a hooker and proud of both.

But she bit her tongue and sucked in a deep breath instead. She needed to calm Mason's rage, not set him on a murderous path.

"Okay. Alright. I will find a way to work client relations from a distance and not be hands-on," she said, hoping to pacify him.

"Good. Now that's out of the way, we need to discuss when you're moving your things into my apartment."

"Hell, fucking no! I'm not moving in with you." She yanked the door open and got the hell out of there. She wasn't even going to argue with him about it.

The bomb blasts were coming thick and fast, but she had to draw the line of defence somewhere.

NINE

Two weeks later, Sophie sat in a judge's chamber in the State High Court surrounded by men in black robes and white wigs. Even Mason, the only other person not in a jabot, was still smartly dressed in a black suit and tie with a white shirt. He looked as distinguished as the other barristers presenting and arguing the case before the male judge.

Sophie was dressed in what she called her funeral dress. A long-sleeved black dress with a modest notched neckline and pleated skirt. She wore a black blazer over it. Her hair was styled into a neat chignon, and her face had minimal makeup.

They were in the courthouse because Mason petitioned the judge against the state authorities for the apparent wrongful search and seizure they carried out at the Haven building.

Sophie didn't understand all the legal jargons like fishing expeditions, unlawful arrests or illegal warrants that the barristers threw at each other.

Even more shocking was when Mason was introduced as Barrister Enyinnaya Maduka of Maduka & Ezeudo Chambers, one of the prominent law firms in the region.

She'd known Mason had studied law, but because of the Maximo business venture with Duke, she'd forgotten he also practised law until today. Seeing him speak so eloquently and confidently while he represented her left her in awe of him.

How could she reconcile the man she'd been arguing with days ago, who had threatened to kill her clients, to the one judiciously fighting for her legal rights? Evidence of the dichotomy and dilemma that was Mason. A man so contradictory that she was constantly in turmoil about how to handle him.

Three hours after arriving at the courthouse, Sophie stood outside in the afternoon sunshine while Mason shook hands with the other lawyers in his team as they congratulated each other.

They'd won.

Still, she remained tense because she didn't know the full implications.

A smiling Mason joined her, and they strode to the car. "You don't look very happy for a woman who won her case."

She climbed in as the driver held the door and waited until Mason joined her in the back seat before speaking.

"I'm sorry. I feel foolish for not understanding all the legal words."

She lowered her gaze as her cheeks heated in embarrassment. She wasn't as educated as him.

When she started working for Duke as a recruit, he'd made her return to school and complete her Senior School Certificate Exam years ago.

"Education opens the mind to all possibilities," he'd said.

Once she'd acquired the School Cert, she'd returned to him, asking him to mentor her because she'd had ideas about running an Odili franchise and becoming a captain. He'd agreed and told her to enrol for a part-time long-distance open university degree which was currently ongoing. She was good with the maths and accounting modules. However, she still struggled with any subject that involved writing essays and forming long, complex sentences. Words failed her sometimes.

"Hey, don't say that. You're not foolish." Mason's knuckles tipped her chin up, and she met his smiling gaze. "If everyone knows all the legal jargon, they won't need lawyers, and I'll be out of a job. Have mercy on me, please."

"You're not serious." She giggled, shaking her head.

"I am. But I'm glad you're smiling." The lopsided grin on his face was boyish and disarming. "You did very well in court today."

"But I did nothing. You and the other barristers did all the talking."

"You weren't supposed to talk. You did what you were supposed to do. You sat quietly and looked like a serious businessperson. We took advantage of the sloppy methods of the police. The Haven building is residential, not commercial, and they used the wrong warrant. As for the allegations of you trafficking people, they have no proof and, therefore, no case. The judge believed you were not guilty and ruled in our favour. So, you did brilliantly."

Warmth spread through her as his thumb smeared her bottom lip, making it tingle. Suddenly she was in a cocoon of just her and Mason, untethered from reality, strange buzzing in her ears.

These moments with him were rare with just the two of them, and the rest of the world faded. Right now, they weren't the mafia fixer and bordello madame nor the lawyer and businesswoman. Just Mason and Sophie.

She'd almost forgotten their lives could be simplified to those two profiles. A man and a woman. The last time she'd experienced it was in the back seat of another car a decade ago when they'd been driving to his hometown. They'd made a connection she'd been unable to shake off.

She got lost in the clarity of his obsidian-black eyes. The neatly trimmed beard gave sharp definition to his cheekbones. The curve of his full lips invited her to nibble.

Her body hummed with the need for him, coherent thoughts eluding her.

"Are you hungry?" he asked in a husky voice, his gaze fixated on her mouth.

He must be feeling the same way she felt. She wanted him so much her breath quickened.

"Yes," she said in a croaky voice and swallowed to clear her throat.

"Alright. Let me take you to lunch. There's a restaurant not far from here." He leaned forward and said to the driver. "Take us to Mona Lisa."

"Yes, sir," the driver replied.

"Oh, I didn't realise." she gasped as her cheeks heated, and she turned away in embarrassment.

"What is it?" Mason appeared confused, tilting her chin so he could meet her gaze.

"It's nothing." She shook her head.

"Tell me anyway," he said in a gentle voice.

She sighed, gesticulating. "I thought you meant something else."

She held his gaze, hoping he would read between the lines because she didn't want to say 'have sex' while the driver was in the car. Perhaps being in court and dressing modestly had affected her mind, and she didn't want to play the hooker. She liked the elegant proprietor persona, even if it would only be for a moment.

"Oh." His brows raised when he realised what she meant. Lips curved in a sexy grin, he leaned into her and whispered in her ear. "We'll get to that soon enough. But I want to feed my babies first."

Then he kissed her cheek, and her heart flipped over.

When he wasn't threatening to kill people, he was captivating. Irresistible.

"Babies?" she laughed, shaking her head. He really was obsessed. "How many babies are you expecting from me?"

"Well, now that you ask, I think five is a good number." His expression was deadpan.

"What!" She broke out in cold sweat. She was still trying to get used to having one, let alone five.

"Take it easy," he laughed. "I was only joking. One is enough."

"It's not funny." She swatted his chest, frowning. "You nearly gave me a heart attack."

"I'm sorry," he said, still chuckling heartily as he lifted her hand and brushed his lips against her knuckles. "I meant our little baby—" he pointed at her belly. "And you. You are both my babies."

"I'm your baby?" She felt breathless with surprise as her heart raced.

"Yes," he carried on caressing her knuckles with his lips, keeping his gaze pinned on her.

Warmth radiated through her body, and a grin broke on her face. Baby—that was a term of endearment for people in relationships.

Was he implying this thing between them was a relationship? That they were lovers rather than people engaged in a business transaction.

His words from days ago flashed in her mind, and doubt crept in.

She jutted her chin. "But you said I was your toy. And we know you share your toys."

"No, I don't!" he snapped, and she jerked.

Then he scrubbed a hand over his face and heaved a sigh. "Can I ask a favour? Please hear me out. For once, can we put down the weapons and jibes and act like a normal couple. I know we're not normal people. But can we at least pretend? Just for today. Let's pretend that I'm your man and you're my woman, and I'm taking you out to a late lunch to celebrate a successful case. We will eat good food, drink great wine and discuss anything that makes us happy. Afterwards, we'll go home, make love, and sleep in the same bed. I don't know about you. But I've never done anything like that. I'd like to try it with you. What about you? Would you like to try it too?"

One thing she would give Mason, he always spoke to her with sincerity and vulnerability. From the heart. There were no reasons to doubt his words except for her own insecurities.

She shouldn't do anything with him because even one day with him was a slippery slope into a deep hole she might never climb out of.

However, he'd never done the things he was asking of her with anyone else—a big attraction like a tempting, flashing sign. Pride expanded her lungs in deep breaths because he had chosen her to try these things. She couldn't resist being the first one, if only to claim the notch.

"Yes, let's pretend," she said with a shrug.

Vanity might yet prove to be her downfall. Then again, she made a deal with Mason, akin to dealing with the devil. So having a deadly sin as a character trait was par for the course.

"Great." He closed his eyes and relaxed into the seat, still holding her hand on his lap.

Watching him silently, she didn't need to pretend to admit he was handsome. Her handsome lover. Could she claim him as hers?

A compulsive need to claim Mason made her heart beat frantically. She brushed her thumb against his grasp, enjoying the feel of his skin as she moved their joined hands to his crotch.

His lips curled in a smile, although he didn't open his eyes. "If you keep doing that, we might have to skip lunch."

She giggled, effused with warmth. "Maybe we should."

His lashes fluttered open, and he grinned. "No way. I promised to feed my babies, and I keep my promises."

She opened her mouth to tell him there probably wouldn't be a baby and closed it. They were faking it for a few hours. What was the harm in letting him have the fantasy?

The car pulled into a parking spot outside a brown and white building, and the doors opened. Mason stepped out and came around to her side. He placed his hand on her lower back, directing her to the front entrance of the establishment.

Soft jazz music piped out of the speakers in the expensive eatery with seating for around one hundred people on the ground level. There seemed to be another section up a level. The place was almost empty. A couple sat at a window table. It was too late for the lunch set and too early for the dinner people.

A waiter approached them. "Good afternoon, sir, madam. Table for two?"

"Yes," Mason said. "But can we have it in the VIP section?"

"Of course, sir," the server replied, leading them up the stairs into the dining room with chandeliers hanging from the high ceiling and expensive paintings on the walls. Clear floor-to-ceiling glass covered the front. He pointed at a table in the middle, right under the chandelier. "Is this okay?"

"Can we have one by the window?" Sophie asked.

Mason nodded, and the server said, "Of course."

She approached a table with a perfect view of the front courtyard and the road. The waiter pulled out a seat, and she settled in it.

Mason undid his jacket, shrugged out of it and hung it on the back of the chair. Then he sat opposite her.

The server returned with the menus and left them to make their choices.

"Why did you want to sit by the window?" Mason asked. "You know the first table he showed us is considered the best in the house."

"I don't care about the best table. I just wanted a view of the road," she replied, glancing at the menu.

"Why? What's so special about this road?"

"Nothing. It's just that whenever I go to restaurants with … you know." She waved her hand, not wanting to say 'clients' since they were pretending to be something else. "I always end up tucked away in the back or corner because they don't want their wives or partners catching them. But today, since we're pretending. I can be the wife who gets to sit front and centre and gets shown off for the world to see."

He nodded with a thoughtful expression. "It makes sense. Enjoy the view."

"I will."

The waiter returned and took their orders. When he left, she spoke again. "I never knew your name was Enyinnaya. I like the sound of it."

"Thank you." He ducked his head as if he was blushing, the fleeting boyish innocence she'd glimpsed a decade ago returning.

"What does it mean?" she asked as her curiosity spiked.

"It means Father's friend."

"Oh. That's really lovely. I suppose your dad gave you the name."

"Yes, he did." His smile was bittersweet, his expression distant. "And our relationship lived up to the name until he passed on."

He loved his father. His sadness reached across the table and rattled the cage she'd placed around her heart. She remembered his loneliness on the night she'd met him. On the driveway, he'd stood apart from Rocha and his men, looking forlorn and forsaken.

An ache bloomed in her throat, and she extended her hand and covered his on the table. "You miss him a lot."

"I do. Some days more than others. He was everything to me. I became a lawyer because I wanted to be like him. I've tried to uphold his legacy. But some days, I feel like I'm failing him."

Huh? This was the first time she'd ever heard Mason sound doubtful. He was always so confident, and everything he did was successful.

"How can you say that? You're a prosperous businessman, a respected lawyer, and an honoured member of the Yadili network. How can you feel like a failure?"

He shrugged. "All those things are good. But he wanted me to have something more important. He wanted me to have a family, but I haven't succeeded."

"Oh." She supposed he meant because he wasn't close to his family. From what she recalled, his mother and brother were tight, and they excluded Mason. He was the pariah, just like Sophie was the outcast in hers. But that wasn't his fault or hers. "Well, keep working at it. I'm sure it will work out for you."

"Indeed." His lips curled in the most glorious smile, and her heart skipped a beat. "My father would have loved you."

"Really?" Warmth bloomed in her chest. She imagined his father as an older man with Mason's skin tone and smile, his intelligence and protectiveness.

"Yes. What about you? What type of relationship did you have with your father?"

She relaxed into the chair and stared out the window, not seeing the view. Her mind went back to her childhood, and a thickness clogged her throat. "I was young when he died, an adolescent. He was away working on an oil rig for long periods, and my mother stayed home with us. Each time he returned, he spent a fortnight with us. I knew he was my dad because I recognised him. But he was like a stranger. A fun stranger who brought gifts and played with me. Then one day, he left again and never came home. I remember things being good and then bad. I remember having a family one day. The next, I was sent away to another home. Sometimes I feel angry that he died and left us." She sighed heavily. "I'm sure that makes me sound like a horrible person."

"No, it doesn't." He reached across the table, his cool palm soothing her skin. "I felt angry too when my father died. In fact, the night we met, I was there because I was filled with rage and looking for an outlet."

Suddenly the camaraderie she'd felt on the night they'd met made sense. There had been a reflection of her in him. They had much in common—the loss of beloved parents, their status as outcasts, their rebellious natures and their determination not the be held down by life's challenges. They could have been kindred spirits.

The waiter arrived with a tray of their hot meals, placing them on the table.

They ate in silence, the crockery tinkling. A smile played on her lips as she watched him.

He looked up and caught her gaze. "What are you thinking?"

"I was remembering the last time we shared a meal. Ma Bagu's okra soup. I haven't tasted okra soup that sweet since then."

He grinned. "Her food is one-in-town. We can go and visit her soon if you'd like."

"Really?" She grimaced. "You think she'd like to see me after the way I left the last time."

"Of course, she'd like to see you. She keeps asking about you each time I see her."

"I don't believe that." She shook her head.

He grinned. "You'll find out soon enough."

Her heart warmed, and her spirits soared. The rest of the meal went smoothly, and their conversation flowed. For the first time in months, years, she relaxed in a man's company because there weren't any expectations to perform or entertain him.

As they left the restaurant and walked back towards the car, he leaned into her and said in a low voice. "Lunch was wonderful."

"Yes, it was. Thank you," she replied.

"I was thinking about fucking you in the restaurant."

Her stomach did backflips when his gaze swept over her.

She choked and coughed. "Why didn't you?"

He chuckled as they reached the car, and the driver opened the door. "Because normal people don't fuck in restaurants, and we're pretending to be normal."

"Good point." She giggled. He had a great sense of humour.

She climbed into the car and shifted as he slid in beside her.

"I can take you back to Haven if you prefer. But I'd like us to return to mine and fuck until daybreak."

He was showing her the compassionate, protective Mason of a decade ago. The one who gave her several chances to escape his brutal life. This time he offered the option to end the charade of a happy relationship.

She could go back to Haven … and do what? She couldn't attend to clients personally and had assigned herself to administrative duty for the foreseeable future. Or until this thing with Mason ended.

She had nothing to do tonight except answer phone calls and deal with emergencies. None of which appealed to her right now.

She would rather spend the time with Mason if their last time together indicated what was to come tonight.

"Back to yours, then." Anticipation made her skin spark like firecrackers. She couldn't wait for whatever the evening had in store.

TEN

After Mason instructed the driver to head back to Maximo, Sophie relaxed into the seat, holding Mason's hand, his touch soothing. The sun had descended, leaving the sky with purple and orange streaks. The streetlights were on. The car pulled out of the restaurant exit, the headlights shining on a car parked on the opposite side. She caught a glimpse of someone out of the front windshield.

A smartly dressed older man was getting into the front passenger seat of a car. The shape of his bald head and body appeared familiar. He glanced in her direction, and her breath hitched with recognition.

Bomba? No. It couldn't be. Bomba would never wear a European two-piece suit and tie. Then again, she hadn't seen the man in ten years. They lived in different cities and had no contact. Plus, she'd had Duke's protection, so she had never worried about the pimp taking her back. The Odilis wielded power in this region. No one would dare challenge them.

So, what was Bomba doing here? Her heart slammed into her chest. The side windows were blacked out, and she twisted in her seat to glance out of the back window as they drove past the man.

"What is it?" Mason asked, turning to look too.

"Did you see that guy?" She grimaced, facing forward again.

"Who is he?" Mason replied, releasing her hand. "One of your *clients*?"

She missed the warmth of his hand. This disdain in his tone made her look into his steel-edged, haunting eyes. All the earlier humour had disappeared from his face. Was he jealous? He didn't like her clients. Best not to mention, she'd thought she'd seen her ex-pimp.

"No. He just looked familiar," she muttered, uncertain about how she felt about him mentioning her clients.

Sure, she hadn't wanted to spend the afternoon with him initially. But the experience of hanging out with him and eating a meal had been fantastic. Not at all like her experiences with clients.

Mason had been respectful and attentive. He'd shown empathy when she talked about her father's passing and her family's struggles. He'd even shared his personal grief about losing his father.

Like her, he had dreams and doubts. He was human and approachable. They could be friends.

Moreover, he'd solved her business problem, and the judge had dismissed the case against her. So, he'd completed his part of their bargain in less than one month, saving her a lot of stress, sweat and tears, not to mention money.

This meant she had to keep her promise—bear his child.

Her chest tightened, and she blew out her cheeks.

Having a baby wasn't such a bad thing, was it?

No. She wasn't as opposed to the ideas as ten years ago. She'd thought holding her niece would dampen the maternal urge she'd developed recently. Since it would never happen, perhaps having her own baby would bring her the joy she'd sought elsewhere.

Still, nothing guaranteed she would conceive a child. That was for nature to decide. And it could take her weeks or months to happen. Or years!

Years? She placed her hand on her tummy distractedly.

Oh, God. Please don't make me wait that long, she prayed silently.

"You know you do that a lot," Mason's deep voice cut into her frantic thoughts.

"Do what?" Her face crumpled in a frown as her body overheated.

"You're very secretive," he said boldly, unrepentantly. "You like hiding your thoughts in your head when you can share them with me. What are you so afraid of."

Her back muscles tensed as she bristled. "It's so easy for you to say. I have to stay secretive to protect myself."

Mason always had a way of ripping her open whether she liked it or not, even without a knife. She should hate him because the last thing she wanted was to lay herself open to anyone.

"What are you protecting yourself from?" he drawled.

She suddenly wished she'd chosen to return to Haven and not his apartment. He'd offered a chance for her to escape him and his questions, but she'd decided to go with him.

She took a deep breath, held it and let it out in a whoosh. "If you must know, I'm protecting myself from the world, from people."

"Am I included in the people?" he asked coolly.

"Yes, you are," she answered honestly.

He shifted in his seat and faced her. "Did you know my job as your man is to protect you?"

"As you know, we're only pretending. So, you're not really my man."

"But I could be. Not just for pretence. Not just for a few months."

"You could," she whispered in a husky voice before she could stop herself.

"I could." He undid his seatbelt, shifting closer. He tilted his head, his smile disarming.

Damn. Just that smile alone had her mesmerised and hypnotised. She wanted him to be her man right here and now.

He closed the distance between them, his hand on her thigh moving upwards.

She glanced around the car. The driver was paying attention to the road, and it was dark outside.

Her clit throbbed, and she licked her lips.

"What are you doing?" her voice was croaky. "I thought we were being normal people."

"I'm being your man." He smirked, slipping his hand under the hem of her dress. His fingers teased her thigh, slowly leaving a blazing spiral of heat.

"The driver?" she whispered, trying to find an excuse to pull down the dress, yet excitement raced through her.

"Will keep driving." She could hear the laughter in his voice. He wasn't letting her off.

He was telling her that this was Mason. Not the pretend one who acted appropriately in the restaurant. This was the man happy to make love to her in the back seat of a car.

And she wanted it, even if she wouldn't admit it readily.

His eyes sparkled as he pressed his bulk to her, his fragrant cologne smelling of bergamot and citrus. She was pinned to the back seat, his hand on her collar, heavy but not suffocating. The other hand between her thighs inched up to her centre.

His body blocked the rear-view mirror, ensuring the driver couldn't see her. The blacked-out windows blocked streetlight except through the windshield. The spacious SUV meant it barely reached here.

Her legs fell apart, opening for him, willing him to where she needed him.

He was barely touching her and consuming her all at once. He was teasing her and killing her at the same time.

Touch me, damn it. She wanted to yell, but the words caught in her throat. She wouldn't beg him or fall apart so readily like she'd done ten years ago.

As if he could read her mind, his fingertips grazed her clit through the lace of her thongs.

Her resolve shattered, and she shuddered and gasped, her hands flying to his shoulders for support. Why did he always make her feel like no one else ever did?

He leaned close, his voice rumbling in her ear. "You're soaking wet."

She shivered, all inhibitions gone. "It's your fault. Stop teasing me."

He chuckled in her ear, making her smile. "You're my woman. I can tease you all I want."

And he did, his fingers tap-dancing on her labia over the panties for minutes that stretched like hours.

She could fight him. But what would be the point? She wanted him to tease and torture her. To provide his brand of pleasure and pain. Right now, if he asked her for the moon, she would gladly reach for the sky, pull it down for him and get burned while doing it.

Finally, he pushed the crotch of her thongs aside, parted her labia and trailed wetness from her slit to her clit.

Her mouth opened in an O as she gasped, hands clenching into his shoulders.

He pushed his fingers deep inside her, curled it and grazed her g-spot, thumb pressing her clit. Once. Twice. Then he repeated the pumping action in and out.

Press … Pump … Graze … Press … Pump … Graze. And so it went.

"Oh, God." She tilted her head back and whimpered, grinding her hips against his palm.

"It's not God. It's Eleniyan," he said with amusement, his breath whispering on her skin.

It took her a moment to understand. Of course, he remembered. She'd called him Eleniyan—boss of all bosses—when he'd saved her from Bomba and his gang.

Using the title again today seemed only fair since he'd saved her from prosecution and possible jail time.

"Eleniyan!" she cried out, falling into an orgasm.

He leaned back, his eyes darkening as he pulled his fingers from her body and licked her juices off. "Say it again."

"Eleniyan," she said huskily, catching her breath.

The car was slowing, and Maximo's glowing lights came into view.

The driver went round the back into the staff parking area. He drove into the spot marked 'managing director'. Then he opened the door for Mason, who climbed out and extended his hand to her.

Sophie hesitated as doubt returned. What was she really doing here? This charade of playing fake relationship could not last. Why not end it here and now and go back to being adversaries? The driver could take her back to Haven, or she could use the back alley and walk back to her residence.

Still, she missed Mason's closeness, his warmth and scent. Would one more night with him make a massive difference to her predicament? She was tied to him for another nine months at least. Maybe she could be his woman for the duration.

She slipped her hand into his palm, and he lifted her from the SUV. Pulling keys from his jacket, he opened a door, tugging her through the side entrance into a corridor lit by fluorescent bulbs. This was a staff hallway and seemed to house storage closets.

They entered the heavy goods lift and rode it to the top floor. But they exited in a different wing from the one she'd visited a fortnight ago. He guided her down a corridor.

Unease prickled through her. They didn't encounter anyone except two employees on the ground level before they entered the lifts. Why didn't they walk through the front entrance and the hotel lobby? It was as if Mason didn't want anyone to see that he was with her. Was he ashamed to be seen with her?

He unlocked a door to his penthouse and flicked a wall switch. Lighting from wall lamps glowed softly into the open-plan living area. Marble flooring gleamed with polish. Leather, wood and copper furniture blended the modern and artistic style, and the scent of flowers danced through the air from the large bouquet on the dining table.

Mason strode into the middle of the room, taking her with him. He stroked her face with the back of his hand. "Welcome to my place. Now yours too."

A flush of adrenaline went through her. He was offering his home to her, something no one had done before. He'd mentioned her moving in with him two weeks ago, and she'd dismissed it. But he was serious about sharing his home with her.

"Thank you," Her voice croaked, and her heart raced.

Then he leaned in and pressed his lips to hers. His lips were full but gentle, still faint. He lingered for a moment before pulling her to his body and deepening the kiss. His tongue flicked past hers. He tasted like coffee and cream, which he'd drunk at the restaurant.

"Nkem," he growled, reeling her into him and kissing her more passionately, more aggressively.

The kiss turned her on, making her want more of him. She grabbed his shoulders, legs wrapping about his hips.

His lips plundered her, and he grabbed her waist, walking her backwards until she reached a sofa. Then he pushed her into it, making her bounce breathlessly as he towered over her.

He yanked his jacket and tie off, unbuttoning his shirt but not removing it. His face was cast in shadow, eyes shining, making it hard to look away from him.

She watched with bated breath as his hands trailed over her figure, peeling her clothes off—the blazer first, falling aside. Then his fingers were at her back, pulling down the zipper holding the dress. Finally, he tugged the outfit over her head, leaving her in her bra and panties. With a flick of his fingers and wrists, the bra was gone, and her cleavage was free.

"You're so damn beautiful." Mason cupped one breast in his palm, tweaking the nipple.

She bit her lip, fighting not to cry out, her panties completely soaked through.

He pinched the nipple hard, twisting it. "I told you before never hide your pleasure from me."

Her spine arched, the back of her head hit the sofa, and nothing could hold back her scream of pleasure laced with pain.

One hand wrapped around her throat and squeezed gently. Enough to threaten danger. The other hand slid leisurely down her front. Dipped past the hem of her thongs. Into the part of her aching for him. He fingered her gently, eliciting hard-won moans. She gripped the cushions for stability, unable to keep quiet even if she'd wanted as her body turned to jelly.

With a feral growl, he yanked her panties down her thighs. Then, with one heavy palm on her neck holding her down, he unzipped his trousers with the other. Finally, he shoved her thighs apart, his hardness brushed against her opening, and she cried out.

He pushed inside her, filling her with one deep, powerful thrust, and she forgot everything, only feeling him.

"Sophie," her name was a prayer, a supplication on his lips.

It robbed her of control as he started fucking her slowly, surprisingly, grinding against her with each forward slam.

She raised her hips, trying to match his pace, to propel the action and stoke the fire inside her.

But his grip around her neck tightened.

"Nkem, am I doing it wrong?" he asked in a husky voice.

Warmth bloomed in her chest each time he used the endearment.

"No," she said through a parched throat.

"Then, don't try to control it, or I will punish you. Take what I'm giving you," he growled ferociously. "Do you understand?"

He pinned her down on the sofa, his face a mask of cruel and savage lust.

"Yes," she croaked, hating herself for giving up control even during sex. Yet loving him for denying her power.

This was the reason she ran from him. He always wrested control away from her, leaving her vulnerable and open to him. The way he loomed over her, larger than life, intensely powerful, dominating her. It was the scariest thing and the sexiest thing.

Satisfied with her acquiescence, he started pounding into her, each thrust forcing a moan out of her, louder and louder. She was wide open, soaking wet for him as he drilled into her, going deeper with each slam, making her eyes roll back and electricity skitter over her skin.

He leaned down, murmuring against her ear. "I bu nkem. You're mine."

Then he nipped her ear lobe, and his hips' actions became harder and fiercer, crashing against hers. The tempo increased, her orgasm coming closer, making her scratch and claw at Mason's back, tearing his shirt, and popping the buttons.

He didn't stop fucking her even as her throat became raw with all the screaming and moaning. He fucked her like no one else, took her brutally and gave himself totally.

Then he leaned over her and took her lips in a harsh kiss, and the orgasm broke over her, drowning her in wave after wave of intensity. She clenched and spasmed, and he pressed his body against hers, pinning her, anchoring her in solidity and comfort.

Just as the ripples ebbed, his climax hit, and he slammed into her one last time, emptying himself inside her, his head tilted back, his face screwed up in ecstasy.

"Nkem, stay with me. Tonight, tomorrow, for the rest of the week," he said in a breathy voice, panting. He lowered his body against hers, his arms braced around the cushion.

"Yes," she whispered, breathless too. Sure, she would go home eventually, but the solitude of her apartment could wait. And she would need clothes and personal items, but Chiamaka would bring those over. She always had an overnight bag packed anyway. A leftover from the days of carrying her life in a bag. *Old habits die hard.*

"Good." Mason pressed soft kisses on her sweaty skin, collar, chin, and lips as they caught their breaths.

This killed her. This tenderness after the most forceful, most exhilarating sex. This time she managed to keep the tears at bay because she realised this was how it would always be between them.

No one else would ever make her feel this way.

Her body now belonged to him.

But how could she keep her heart hidden from him for nine months?

ELEVEN

Mason woke to grey light coming through the window. He felt hot and stirred gently, trying not to wake Sophie, whose sleeping body was plastered against his. Weightlessness suffused his body as he stared at her.

She did this all the time. No matter what side of the bed she started off in, she always ended up clinging to him, her limbs all over him like an octopus. He stifled a chuckle picturing her as a marine mollusc.

She'd been sleeping in his bed thrice a week for the past fortnight. They'd agreed that she would live out of his apartment from Mondays through Wednesdays. He'd wanted her with him seven days a week, but this was a compromise he could live with.

Weekends provided the busiest times for Maximo and Haven, so it made sense for them to have time to themselves. Thursdays were transition days, and she spent the morning with him before heading to Haven after lunch.

The arrangement had worked well so far.

So, although it was Tuesday morning, his life over the past decade made him an early riser anyway. He juggled two jobs—one as a lawyer and the other as a business owner.

It had been a side hustle when he'd started working on the Maximo project with his friend Duke. His main job had been working as a lawyer in the Chambers his father had established.

It hadn't mattered so much, and there'd been less strain on his time. Duke had been the Managing Director of Maximo Hotel and Casino, with Mason as Head of Strategy and Development.

However, since Mason took over as MD in the past six months, his time on the project had grown exponentially. Now it was difficult to classify it as a side hustle. His lips curled in a smile at the thought of Maximo as a side gig, considering the billions in annual revenue.

He stared at Sophie's face. She always looked much younger when sleeping because she was most relaxed. Also, she'd removed the wig, and her natural hair was in cornrows making her appear girlish and cute.

He enjoyed these moments when she was asleep and could watch her uninterrupted. Mainly because they were hard-won.

Everything with her had been a challenge. Getting her to agree to have his baby, to have sex with him, to even be with him, and date him. Everything had been a struggle.

But she didn't fight him when she lay in his bed, especially when asleep.

Subconsciously she sought him out when she slept. Sometimes he thought it was the only time she sought his attention.

Then again, she came over here three nights a week of her own volition. So that counted too.

Still, he had doubts. Scepticism about whether she would go through with a pregnancy and give birth to his baby. Although they'd made a deal and she'd offered, he thought she only said it to get him to fix her business problems.

His phone on the bedside table beeped, and he grabbed it and switched off the calendar notification.

He pressed a quick kiss to her lips before gently rolling out of bed, not wanting to wake her. Still, she seemed a heavy sleeper and never woke when he moved.

He changed into his sports kit and wandered into his private gym. One of the advantages of being MD was this apartment and all the mod cons that came with it.

Even when Duke had been MD, he'd lived in a house he'd built at Hill Top, a suburb of Opal City. So, Mason had access to this apartment from Day One.

After his workout, Mason went into the bathroom for a shower. Then, body moisturised and deodorised, he tugged on a white cotton vest over his boxer-briefs as he entered the bedroom.

Sophie was awake and sitting in bed, the duvet pulled up to her chin. She still didn't like the cold.

"Good morning," he said, lifting the remote controller for the air-conditioner and pressing the button to reset the temperature to ambient level. He'd been making the concession for her since she partially moved in.

"Where are you going?" she asked, a frown corrugating her forehead.

He strode across the room to her side of the bed and leaned over her. "Nkem, aren't you going to return my greeting?"

"Good morning," she said, her face still rumpled.

"That's better." He pressed his lips to her forehead and stepped back. "Go back to sleep. You don't need to be up so early."

"But neither do you. Are you in court today?" she asked.

"No. I told you I had a meeting in Bakili today." He walked into his closet to get dressed.

"Oh, yes. You mentioned it." She sounded disappointed.

He felt an ache in his throat, which surprised him. Unexpectedly, he'd developed an emotional attachment to Sophie from the first night they'd had sex. A bond similar to the relationship with Ma Bagu but different.

Of course, ten years ago, when he'd met Sophie, they'd had a connection. But it had been simpler then. He'd liked her and had wanted to protect her. Then again, he'd taken her into the lions' den. Safeguarding her had been the only way to ensure her survival while surrounded by predators.

However, he didn't quite understand why he had this tenderness—or fondness as Ma Bagu had once described it—for Sophie, although he didn't fully trust her.

There were reasons not to trust her.

First, she didn't want to have his baby, though she'd offered to have it. Then she'd wished to have sex with other men, forcing him to take drastic actions to prevent her from doing so. Of course, she proved reluctant to live with him as a family, which only buttressed the first and second points.

Sure, she enjoyed their sexual encounters, but she didn't want to be a permanent feature in his life.

So, her disappointment left him conflicted.

On the one hand, he should shield himself from the impending desolation heading his way when she betrayed him like other family members.

Still, he couldn't shake the need to protect her, couldn't seem to harden the part of him that had grown tender towards her. He didn't like to see her upset. Never had done right from the first day he'd met her.

Once dressed in a two-piece charcoal suit and white shirt with no tie, he strode back into the room. She was still sitting up, her face furrowed.

"I told you to go back to sleep," he said, sitting on the mattress to put his socks and shoes on.

"What's the point of doing that if you're not here. I might as well go back to my place," she said.

He turned to face her, holding back from reaching for her because he wouldn't leave here on time.

"The point is that it's Tuesday. And Tuesday is my day. I decide what we do and how we spend the day. Unfortunately, I won't be here for part of it but will endeavour to return before the day ends."

His phone beeped with another notification. He unplugged it from the charger, pocketing it as he stood. "In the meantime, relax. Have a lie-in. When you're hungry, order room service. Do whatever you want to do in the apartment. I'll be back as soon as I can."

She puffed out a sigh. "Okay."

"You sound like you're going to miss me," he said with a smirk, leaning over her and pressing his lips to hers, kissing her lightly.

Her lips curled in a reluctant smile. "Maybe."

"Well, hold onto that thought and get as much rest as possible because when I get back, I will wear you out. You know how I love to fuck 'til the break of dawn."

"Yes." She giggled, lowering her head. "Don't keep me waiting too long."

He broke away from her reluctantly. He would miss their time together. But he had business he couldn't ignore much longer. "I won't. Enjoy your day."

"You too," she replied.

He headed out of the apartment. Benji waited for him outside. Although he was dressed in a suit, this was Yadili business, not a court affair.

"Is everything ready?" he asked his second as they took the lift together.

"Yes. Our team is already on site, providing cover," Benji replied.

"Good." Although the meeting was pre-arranged, he didn't want to be caught unawares.

***

Sophie took advantage of Mason's absence. She went back to sleep as soon as he left. When she woke again, the sun was high in the sky.

Hungry, she ordered room service before going into the shower. When she came out, she went to the overnight bag she'd packed and took her clothes out.

Although Mason wanted her to move in with him, she rejected living permanently with him. She was even reluctant to keep her clothes here when she wasn't here. So, she always packed a bag each time she stayed and took the bag with her when she left.

She didn't want to fall into the trap of believing this affair with him would last longer than a few weeks or months. Didn't want to even consider her body carrying his baby full term. Something would go wrong, so best to save herself the heartache.

Yet, Mason was gradually creeping into her mind. Into her psyche.

After the first time they'd spent three days in a row together, and she'd gone home, she'd looked forward to the next occasion. She was excited each time she got the call that his car was waiting outside her apartment. He always sent his driver and car for her.

A smile played on her lips at the memory.

And he always met her when the vehicle stopped in his parking spot. He would kiss her, carry her bag, and they would walk to his apartment hand-in-hand.

While she was here, making love seemed to be the highlight. But pottering around each other, watching TV, reading, and chatting with him made her feel good. Yesterday he'd helped her with an essay she'd been struggling to write. Gave her pointers on how to structure her words effectively. She'd completed the work and had submitted it online last night.

Now that he was away, she missed him, surprisingly. Mason had a way of making her like him even when she shouldn't.

Room service arrived with her brunch, and she was eating it while watching an African movie channel when her phone beeped with a message. Her heart skipped a beat, and she grabbed it from the table, hoping the notification was from Mason.

The ID and phone number didn't show. However, the message had an attachment. She knew not to click on random links sent by unknown numbers. She opened the note containing several photographs, and they started downloading.

The first one opened, and her spine stiffened.

The photo showed Mason with a woman Sophie didn't recognise immediately. He was smiling at her as they approached each other in what looked like a restaurant.

The other photos opened—ten in total—and it became apparent the camera had been clicking continuously. There were shots of Mason and the woman hugging, kissing, sitting opposite each other at a table, and chatting. From the time stamps, the photos were only taken about thirty minutes ago.

What the hell! Sophie jumped from the chair.

This was what Mason went to do? He went to see another woman? While he left her here?

She glanced at the photos again, and recognition dawned. That was Zoe Himba. The daughter of Don Himba, the godfather of the Himba clan.

Another message pinged:

In case you didn't already know. Mason is going to marry her. If you don't believe me, ask him. Or better still, call your boss and ask him.

What? Did Duke know about this?

Of course, he would. He was Mason's bestie, and there were no secrets between them.

Rage flowed through Sophie. She swiped the crockery off the table, smashing it all on the marble floor.

TWELVE

Sophie swore aloud as she paced Mason's living room. A glance at the clock showed it was just after one o'clock in the afternoon. Outside, the sky was grey, and rain plastered the window in sheets.

Her vision was blurry as she swiped her phone to look at those images again.

Mason had been gone for at least six hours. But considering he'd only met with Zoe recently, she assumed they would be together for a few more hours. The restaurant was a public space, and she supposed Mason would pull his 'behave like normal people' act. But they could go somewhere private afterwards. Would they have sex? Would Mason touch Zoe like he touched Sophie? Kiss her like he kissed Sophie?

Of course, they could do all those things if he was going to marry Zoe.

All while Sophie sat in Mason's apartment like a *mumu*.

Sophie clenched her hands into fists and screamed in frustration. Emotions stormed through her, all jumbled up. She swiped angry tears off her cheeks even as her chest ached.

Why had she allowed herself to be used by Mason again? Why hadn't she learned from what he did to her ten years ago?

He'd discarded her in the blink of an eye and kicked her out of his home.

She'd told herself never again. That she wouldn't fall under his spell again.

Yet, here she was again, about to be discarded.

And she could be pregnant for him.

"Oh, God." She clutched her belly and collapsed into a sofa, body trembling.

What had she done? How could she be so foolish? What would she do if she was pregnant?

She couldn't carry a child for nine months and give it up?

Hang on a moment. Was that what Mason wanted? For Sophie to carry his child, birth him and then hand the baby over to him and Zoe?

Over her dead body. They would have to pry that baby out of her dead arms. Because she would never hand her child to another woman.

Still, it might mean she would lose everything by backing out of the deal with Mason. But she couldn't do what her mother had done. Handing her child over to someone else, even if she was poor and couldn't afford to feed the child.

And considering she knew precisely how brutal Mason's mother and brother were, she couldn't trust them to care for her baby.

It would be better not to bring a child into the world in the first place.

Tears streaked down her face, her heart breaking at the idea. Regardless of her misgivings, she wanted a baby. Not just any baby. She … wanted Mason's baby.

Knowing Mason and his family, they would go to extreme lengths to take away her child.

No, she wouldn't let it happen. She had to do something. Something to protect her baby. She had to do something as devious as the Madukas would do to safeguard her unborn child.

She needed something she could hold over Mason the same way he used her business as leverage.

She got off the sofa, pacing again. But everything in here reminded her of Mason. He'd fucked her on the floor, against the wall. They'd eaten meals at the table, curled up on the sofa to watch TV and had more sex there too.

"Aaarrgh!" she yelled. She needed space away from his apartment to think.

She grabbed her phone from the sofa and made a call.

Her assistant answered after one ring. "Yes, boss."

"Come and pick me up from Maximo. The front entrance," she ordered.

"Oh. Wetin happen? I thought you were supposed to be at Mason's apartment until Thursday," Ziga said.

"Just come and get me," she snapped, not in the mood to discuss her predicament on the phone.

"Of course. I'll be there in ten minutes," her assistant replied and cut the line.

Sophie sighed and went to the closet to grab her overnight bag.

She'd asked Ziga to return to Opal City after she'd agreed to step back from dealing with clients hands-on.

After what had happened to Haven while she'd been in Lori Osa, she couldn't trust Chiamaka to run the place. She needed someone she could trust, and Ziga was it.

She'd arrived a week ago and oversaw the site while Sophie was at Mason's.

Sophie could ask her designated driver to pick her up. But in her current mood, she couldn't afford someone she didn't trust one hundred percent to see her in this state.

She cleaned her face in the bathroom mirror and applied makeup, reinstalling her wig. Mason didn't like her wigs, so she didn't wear them in his apartment. But fuck him.

She stuffed the toiletries and items she'd unpacked into the travel case. Then she grabbed her clothes and shoes that Mason had unpacked and hung in the closet, stuffing them in angrily and zipping the bag up.

He'd arranged their clothes as if they were a normal couple like he'd once said. Unfortunately, there was nothing *normal* about them.

If they were an average couple, he would take her out on dates regularly instead of practically locking her up in his apartment each time she was here.

She returned to the closet and grabbed the dress hanging in a clear clothing bag from the laundry. Unzipping the bag, she took the dress out and stripped off her yoga pants and top. Then she wore the short floral print dress with a plunge neckline and ties under her boobs. It clung to her belly and hips before flaring out, stopping midthigh. If she bent over, anyone around would see her ass and panties.

She'd bought it last week specifically for Mason. She'd barely stepped foot into his apartment before he'd shoved her against the wall, her bag abandoned by the closed door.

"Is this outfit for me?" He squeezed her throat, shoved his knee between her thighs, and spread her legs.

"Yes, I bought it two days ago. Just for you," she whispered in a husky voice, tilting her chin up to look at him as she humped his thigh.

"Yet, your security team saw you leave Haven. My driver watched you in the car. That's a lot of hard-ons." He pinched her nipple through the dress, twisting it sharply. The pain shot straight to her clit, and she screamed. "You're not even wearing a bra."

"You're the Torture King," she spoke through shallow breathing as the ache subsided, followed by a rush of warm pleasure in her veins as if she'd had a stimulant. "I learned to torment people because of you. As for the bra, you won't be able to do what you just did if I wore it."

She humped his thigh harder, recklessly, fireworks sparking over her skin.

"Sophie, don't you dare cum yet." He twisted her nipple again harder, the hand around her neck tightening.

Her eyes watered as she cried out. The early orgasm ebbed as pain washed over her.

They played these games. He edged her, overloaded her with pleasure and pain, took her close to orgasm and then withdrew it. But she loved it because the power dynamic was never static or one-directional. It flowed and ebbed, just like the pleasure and pain. She played along until she didn't...

"Eleniyan," she whispered, looking up at him with softened eyes. "I need you to fuck me."

"I know." He chuckled, his eyes sparkling with intense lust. He slid his hand between her legs, under her soaked panties. "You are being punished for wearing this dress outside. But you're enjoying it too much."

"Oh," she moaned aloud as his fingers caused havoc on her pussy. "Then punish me harder. Fuck me with your thick, long, hard veiny dick. Fuck me until I'm so exhausted I can't stand straight."

"I should fuck your mouth for being so damned dirty."

She'd thought he would do it as he'd never done it before. Never fucked her mouth or ass like other men.

Instead, he tore her panties off, the fabric ripping against her sensitive skin, making her whimper.

Then he unzipped his trousers and plunged into her hard against the wall. Her body slammed against the concrete as he took her savagely. She came fiercely and severally, and her body ached with exhaustion when he finally carried her to bed and let her sleep.

The next day, while curled together on the sofa, she asked him why he didn't do oral or anal sex with her. She knew he did those acts with hookers. Her girls had told her whenever he'd hired them. They kept track of which clients liked what to ensure they matched the right workers with the right clients.

"Do you want me to fuck your mouth or your ass?" he asked, not even looking at her as if he knew what her answer would be.

She shrugged. "Not particularly."

"Then, there is no point wasting my semen."

"Waste?"

"Yes, waste." He turned and grinned, placing a hand over her tummy. "I intend to breed you and breed you good."

Her pussy creamed, just remembering it all. Angrily, she shoved the discarded clothes into the travel case. Damn it, a dick was as good as another.

Girl, you've fucked enough men to know that's not true. A voice whispered in her mind.

Okay. Mason was great in bed. The best she'd had.

But he intended to breed Sophie and marry Zoe. That's the reason he didn't show Sophie off publicly.

Happy to hide her away, he didn't want other people to know that he was fucking her. Hence, they used the side entrance whenever she came here instead of the front lobby, where guests and staff could see them together.

He didn't want people to know he was fucking her because he'd intended to marry Zoe Himba all along.

Well, he can go to Hell. She knocked over a flower vase purposefully. The expensive white porcelain vase crashed onto the marble, sending shards, water, and tulips everywhere. It could ruin the plush copper-hued shaggy rug in front of the sofa.

Shame, she liked the rug, loved the feel on her knees and hands while Mason fucked her from behind.

Well, Mason was probably fucking Zoe right now. So, fuck him and his beautiful furniture. Fuck his apartment. If not that fire endangered innocent people, she would have set the place ablaze.

She dragged her travel case and handbag to his front door. Walking out, she slammed the door and sashayed to the central lift bay before pressing the button to call one. They did not use these lifts when she visited Mason's apartment. But to hell with him, she would not sneak out through the side door. Instead, she would go to the front lobby, where everyone would see her.

When the lift arrived, she stepped in and stood there, head high as it went down. Finally, it opened into the busy lobby. People were waiting to use the lift as she breezed past. Men smiled at her appreciatively. Women narrowed their eyes at her suspiciously. She didn't care, snapping her round hips provocatively.

"Hi, Sophie," a man in a tunic suit said, stopping her in the middle of the lobby. "How are you? I haven't seen you around for a while."

"Hello. I'm fine. Thank you." She said and carried on walking. She recognised him as a former client but didn't remember his name because it had been a while.

"Hold up." He held her arm.

She tugged her arm free and spoke sharply. "You know you're not allowed to touch me without my permission."

"I'm sorry. I didn't mean any harm." He raised his hands. "I just wanted to ask if I could spend time with you."

He seemed genuinely appalled that he'd upset her.

"No problem," she said as an idea occurred to her. "Remind me your name, please."

"Ah-ah, you forgot me already," he said, but it didn't seem like his ego was too bruised because she didn't remember his name. Then, smiling, he pulled a business card from his back pocket and handed it over. "My name is Osei."

"Osei, I remember." She smiled. "Would you like to meet me later this evening? Say 6pm at Maximo Bar."

"Sure. I would love to."

"Okay. See you later, Osei."

"Later, Sophie."

She swivelled and carried on, exiting the hotel as the concierge greeted and held the door for her.

Thankfully, Ziga was already waiting under the portico with her car. The door attendant put the luggage in the boot, then held the door while she slid into the back.

Once the door was shut, Ziga turned in her seat and asked, "Where to?"

"Take me back to Haven."

Her assistant nodded and drove the car around the fountain before heading down the long drive to the security gates.

They sat in silence for the few minutes it took to get to the Haven building and park the car. Ziga understood to leave her alone.

However, after they decanted from the vehicle and one of the guards came to carry her luggage, Sophie turned to Ziga. "Please come upstairs."

She needed someone to talk to, someone to back up her plans.

Ziga nodded and took the travel case off the guard before following Sophie upstairs. When they entered her apartment, she dropped the suitcase by the hallway leading to the bedrooms.

"What's going on?" Ziga asked. She must know that something was troubling Sophie.

Sophie shut the door and sighed. She walked into the living room and sat on the sofa. "Come and sit down."

The other woman walked around and settled on the adjacent armchair but said nothing.

Sophie sighed again before speaking. "This evening, I'm going to do something … something dangerous, and I'm going to need you to back me up."

Ziga shifted forward, her body posture attentive. "Yes, what is it."

"Full disclosure," Sophie started. "You know I told you that Mason and I were kind of dating after he helped me with the court case."

"Yes … and?"

"And that wasn't the whole story. Mason and I have a history that dates back ten years. I don't want to go into it right now. But he wanted me to have a baby for him back then, and I said no."

She waited for some judgement or disapproval from her assistant, who simply said, "Okay … and?"

"And …" she rolled her eyes heavenwards in frustration. She'd forgotten how Ziga liked hearing the full details before deciding. "When the problem with Haven happened, I asked him for help, but he refused. Flat-out refused. He's been bearing a grudge because I refused to have his baby ten years ago. Can you imagine?"

Ziga said nothing, one eyebrow raised.

Sophie continued. "Anyway, I had no other choice but to offer to have his baby. When I did that, he suddenly agreed to help me. And you know he did."

"Yes, he did. I still don't see the problem," her second said.

"The problem came today when I saw this." She pulled the phone from her handbag and went to her gallery, displaying the photos from earlier before handing the phone to Ziga.

The woman scrolled through the photos for a few seconds. "Someone sent these to you today."

"Yes, that is Zoe Himba in the photos. Mason met with her today. He's going to marry her."

"That's what the message says, but are you sure? Who sent you these photos? Did you have someone follow Mason?"

"No, of course not. Why would I have someone follow him? It's not as if I was expecting him to do this? To go to another woman. I didn't recognise the phone number."

Ziga frowned. "Well, it is suspicious that someone would send this to you out of the blue."

Sophie huffed. "It could be a member of his team who wanted me to know he was going to marry someone else."

"If a member of his team is betraying him, can you trust their motives?"

"I don't care about their motives right now. I care about what those pictures represent. Anyway, whose side are you on?" she said in an accusing tone.

"I'm just playing devil's advocate. I know seeing Mason with another woman would be annoying. But from what you just said, you only told him you would have his baby so he could fix your problem. So, you don't really want to have his baby, right?"

Sophie stayed silent for a few seconds. "Well, that's how I felt at the start. But now, I don't know. I wouldn't mind having a baby."

"A baby or his baby."

"Damn it. Fine. His baby. I would like to have his baby. But he will take the baby away from me, and I don't want that to happen. So, I came up with a plan."

"Okay. What do you have in mind?"

"This evening, I've arranged to meet an old client at Maximo Bar. At some point, I know Mason will show up. He showed up while I was entertaining Reginald Ifemelu at the party his friends had organised. So, I know Mason will show up this time. He doesn't want me to interact with clients. In fact, the last time he threatened to kill any client I sleep with—"

"What? He said that?" Ziga sat up straight, looking worried.

"He did. He said it right to my face that he would turn into a serial killer if I kept sleeping with clients. Why do you think I stopped taking bookings?"

"Na wa. This is serious."

"It is, and I want to take advantage of his threatening behaviour. I want you to come with me and sit at a different table. You will record everything Mason does so it can be used as evidence."

"Evidence, kwa? Wait, oh. Are you saying you're going to report Mason to the police?" Ziga looked appalled at the concept.

"No. But I need something to threaten him like he threatened me with losing Haven."

"Mba nu. I don't think this is a good idea. Do you understand the consequence of what you want to do?"

"Is there any consequence worse than having your child taken by force?" Sophie shouted.

"Look, I understand your frustration. But this could go seriously bad. What if he calls your bluff? This is Mason Maduka we're talking about."

"He won't, and it won't go bad. This is why it's happening in public. There's a limit to what he would do in public. I know something Mason fears more than he fears the police. He fears bringing his father's legal legacy into disrepute."

"Are you sure?" Ziga asked, still not looking convinced.

"I'm very sure," Sophie said as guilt curdled her stomach. Mason had told her of his fears in private, in his rare moments of vulnerability. Now she would use the information against him.

Still, protecting her baby was more important.

More important than protecting Mason? The little voice prodded again, making her chest tight. A headache bloomed.

She didn't want to hurt Mason. But given a choice between saving Mason or her unborn child, the child would come first.

She just hoped Mason would understand her actions, eventually.

THIRTEEN

Mason had been sitting as Second Chair or playing adviser to others in the last decade. Although he was a Yadili captain and led his own team, he still preferred to stay behind the scenes. There were days when he'd rather be a strategist than a managing director. Because being MD meant being the business's public face, which meant interacting with people. But Mason was not a people person.

He'd worked alongside Duke on the Maximo project since its inception. So, it had been logical to hand him the reins when his friend moved aside. Still, Duke was always a phone call and a one-hour flight away if Mason needed him.

He liked representing clients, negotiating deals on their behalf or arguing legal cases in court. Right now, he would give anything to be the adviser rather than the client.

Today he'd travelled to Bakili on an assignment personally handed to him by his godfather, Chief Odili.

No matter how much he stalled, he couldn't have avoided this meeting forever. It was inevitable.

"I must say. I'm glad you were the one chosen for this role rather than your brother," Zoe Himba said. She sat across the table from him. Members of her team sat at other tables behind her.

"What do you mean?" Mason pretended not to understand. Their interaction was a negotiation, a game of strategy. He was assessing and analysing, looking for opportunities to exploit as much as she was doing the same to him.

"I suppose your principal, Chief Odili, didn't have a wide pool to dip into." She dropped her cutlery, picked a napkin and dabbed her mouth delicately like the well-bred mafia princess she was. She'd barely eaten and was nibbling more than anything.

Mason remembered the last time he sat in a restaurant with a woman. With Sophie. She'd eaten so heartily. So sexily. His spine tingled from the memory, and he quashed the smile threatening to burst through his expressionless face. Instead, he mentally restrained himself and refocused on Zoe's words.

"Out of the Fierce Four as you all are known, Duke is by far the most eligible," she continued, "But alas, he is taken already. Maddox is a little too rugged to be my cup of tea. So that leaves you and your brother. Rocha is too damned chauvinistic for my liking. We have enough of those in the Himba family. I would have probably shot him by now if he was the one sitting in your place."

Mason chuckled. "Speak your mind. Why don't you?"

She'd analysed F4 brilliantly. She had an exceptional mind.

She laughed too, eyes sparkly. "You see, this is why I like you. You appreciate directness and honesty. Other men would sit there posturing, wanting me to stroke their egos. I don't have time for that shit."

"I can see that." He smiled and then became serious again. "Talking about honesty. Do you like me enough to marry me? And should we get married anyway?"

She tilted her head. "I like you enough to seriously consider you as my future husband. But as you are aware, the decision about whether to get married is not wholly in our hands. My father thinks securing a marriage with an influential family will protect me and his legacy. His position was weakened when Nobert died."

Nobert had been the Himba clan enforcer. What she didn't say was that the Odili family had a hand in Nobert's death. Mason had been there when they'd gone to rescue Xandra, the assassin abducted by the Himba crew. Xandra's partner, Ebuka, then killed Nobert in the shootout.

Sure, a peace deal was brokered between their clans. Still, unease prickled through Mason as he considered her words as containing a veiled threat. He didn't think any member of the Odili would be safe in the Himba clan. They would be able to protect themselves but wouldn't be able to sleep easily. What kind of marriage would that be?

"I appreciate your situation. My godfather thinks our family can provide you with the protection you need. But if you need an enforcer, Maddox is your best bet without the chauvinism."

"Yes. I could do without the chauvinism," she said but didn't smile. "You're quite right about Nobert. He'd fancied himself as my future husband. If my father had ever caved in and given his blessings for us to marry, I would have killed Nobert within days of our marriage. So, your man did us all a favour. However, as I said, Maddox is not my cup of tea."

"And I am?"

"Relatively speaking, yes. You are miles better than the rest. And I think it's because I know you. We have history."

They did have history, but not as lovers. They'd been in Law School together and got called to the Bar at the same time.

"But two lawyers in a marriage. Is that a good thing?"

"It is. It means we're matched intellectually."

"But surely you want more than an intellectual match. Surely you want *more* ... a deep connection ... an intense longing ..." he trailed off, his mind going to the one person for whom he felt those things.

Did Sophie share those feelings? Did she want more with him?

"Ah, love," Zoe said wistfully, drawing his attention again. She sounded like she'd experienced it. Like she'd once been in love. "Love is a grand concept but a tad fanciful considering our statuses."

"Are you saying people like us don't marry for love?" Mason asked.

Duke married Carla because he loved her. He'd fought Carla's father and brother to secure that love.

"No. I'm not saying it's impossible. I'm just saying that life gets in the way of affection most of the time. So, we must make the best of whatever situation we find ourselves in. But I never considered you as a sentimental person. Have you ever been in love, Mason?"

"In love? I'm not sure I know what that means." Mason laughed. Unless being in love was this feeling of intense longing that followed him around every time he thought about Sophie. But he couldn't mention Sophie to Zoe. Not until he figured out Zoe's intentions. Although she talked about honesty and directness, she still withheld things from him. "What about you, Zoe? Have you ever been in love?"

Smiling, she shook her head at him. "Maybe I'll answer your question next time if I agree to another date."

He chuckled. "So, this was a date? I thought it was just a meeting."

"Meeting. Date. Same difference."

"Fair enough."

The rest of the meeting went smoothly, and they chatted easily. But it wasn't the same as when he'd taken Sophie out to lunch the other day. He liked Zoe but wasn't fond of her. For one, he didn't consider finding a private corner to fuck her like he'd wished with Sophie. More to the point, he didn't think about filling Zoe's belly with his babies.

By the time Mason headed back to Opal City, dusk was fast approaching.

He hoped Zoe would find another suitor and he didn't have to do the meeting again. He didn't want to think of it as a date. Whilst it was a one-to-one encounter, there was nothing personal about it if he discounted their entourages. He'd gone to it because he was obligated to obey his godfather.

However, if he married Zoe, it would be purely a business transaction to provide his name and protection to her.

Come to think of it, if his godfather ordered him to marry Sophie, he would do it without hesitation. He would drag Sophie to the altar. They would have an argument while saying their vows, and he would have to shut her up by kicking everyone out and fucking her right there at the altar. Theirs would not be a typical wedding.

He chuckled as he sat in the vehicle's back seat and pulled his phone out of his pocket. He had several messages. One from Duke asking about his meeting with Zoe.

He sent a reply: *It's early days, but it went well.*

He opened another note from one of the guys in the security suite. He'd appointed a crew to shadow and watch over Sophie. He'd tried to protect her by not making their relationship public. But nothing stayed private for long around here. And he didn't want her getting hurt by someone who wanted to target him.

Madame Sophie left Maximo. She was picked up at the front entrance by Ziga and taken to Haven at 14:10.

Huh? Why did Sophie leave the hotel? He'd instructed her to wait for him. Maybe something happened at Haven.

He scrolled through his messages to see if there were any from her. Nothing new.

He returned to the rest of the notifications from the security suite.

Madame Sophie is back at Maximo. Arrived approximately 18:15 and went straight to the bar. Currently sitting with a guest.

What was Sophie doing? Going to Maximo Bar by herself was a bad idea. But sitting with a guest?

Who is the guest? He typed a reply to the security team.

Mr Osemeka Godfrey. They pinged back.

The name didn't ring any bell. But the hotel had hundreds of guests weekly, and Mason didn't know them all. He glanced at his gold watch. It was seven minutes past seven, and they were in the Niru neighbourhood. So, they would be at Maximo soon.

Let me know if anything changes; he sent back.

"Benji," he said to his second sitting in the back seat with him. "We might have a situation at Maximo."

"What's happened?" Benji asked, turning to him.

"I'm not sure. It might be nothing. But stay alert."

"Okay." Benji pulled his phone out and tapped the screen before speaking into it. "We have an amber situation. Stay alert as we enter Maximo. Cover all exits.

Report any suspicious behaviour and wait for my command."

When he put the phone down, he spoke to the two guys in front, "You two, stay with Mason and me."

"Yes, sir," they chorused.

The car pulled up under the Maximo Hotel and Casino portico two minutes later. Benji and the other security jumped out immediately. Mason and the driver waited a beat. Then the bodyguard opened his back door.

Mason stepped out and headed straight for the front entrance.

The uniformed concierge held the swinging panel open. "Welcome back, boss."

"Thank you," he responded and entered the busy lobby. He walked to the reception desk. "Any messages for me?"

"Good evening, sir," the female receptionist replied. "Nothing for you, sir."

He nodded and headed to the bar. As soon as he entered the dimly lit lounge, he spotted Sophie immediately with a man he assumed was Osemeka Godfrey. They sat next to each other on the sofa, and the man held her hand. She didn't look like she was trying to get away from him. There were empty glasses and an almost empty bottle of red wine on the table.

Was she drinking? They avoided alcohol because they were trying to make a baby. And yet...

A burning sensation started in Mason's chest as his stomach hardened. He shoved his hands into his pockets to hide the fists.

There were about ten other people in the lounge. The place wasn't too busy at this time. Most of their guests were in the restaurant on the other side of the front lobby. The guests here were usually waiting for a table to become available so they could have their evening meal.

"What do you want to do?" Benji said in a low voice beside him.

"Clear the place discretely," Mason said. This was still a legit business. Unlike the incident at the private party the other day, full of middle-aged men, this was a public space with younger folks. Any drama and people pulled out their mobile phones to record.

Benji instructed the other two men, who spoke quietly to the guests. A couple tried to make a fuss until weapons were flashed, and they quickly exited.

Mason stood rooted on the spot, fighting not to approach Sophie until the place was clear because he didn't trust that he wouldn't sink the blade into the man's heart in full view of everyone.

Motion on the corner of his left eye caught his attention. He noticed Ziga, Sophie's second, sitting in a corner. It looked like she refused to move.

Mason shook his head at the bodyguard, indicating for him to leave Ziga alone. At least Sophie had the sense to bring security to the bar.

By now, Sophie knew he was here. She must have noticed the lounge being cleared. Even the bartender and the waiters were gone. Mason's security stood at the doors, preventing anyone from entering.

When the place was cleared, Mason pulled his knife out of the sheath and finally moved slowly and deliberately.

FOURTEEN

Sophie knew the moment Mason walked into the bar, and his demanding gaze fell on her. Hyperaware of her surroundings, the skin on her nape prickled, and her heart crashed into her chest.

She'd expected him. Yet adrenaline surged through her.

She refused to look directly at him, only spatially aware of the dark figure standing near the lobby entrance.

She'd chosen the time of this encounter, so the place was quiet as it wasn't peak period. People were sitting there watching the sizeable widescreen TV or just drinking with the soft background music.

Osei had been sitting on a barstool when she'd arrived, and after their initial pleasantries, she'd suggested they move to one of the low leather sofas. She'd chosen one in the middle of the lounge with a direct view of the entrance.

Sophie had stiffened each time someone entered the lounge. Osei had noticed and asked why she was edgy.

She'd made an excuse about not sleeping well. He requested a bottle of wine, and she'd drunk less than half a glass to help her relax.

Ziga sat in an armchair by the wall to her right. She could watch Sophie and the rest of the lounge from there. She wasn't happy about Sophie's plan, yet she had come to back Sophie up and record any incident as planned.

Sophie was grateful for her presence because she couldn't pull this off otherwise. There was no one else she could trust.

But now that Mason was here, looming at the entrance like The Punisher, John Wick, or some other dark antihero about to spill blood, doubt sat heavily in Sophie's stomach.

She'd brought Ziga into a potentially dangerous situation. Not just Ziga but Osei, an innocent victim she was using to get at Mason. What kind of person had she become when she could drag innocent people into life-threatening schemes without their knowledge?

"…I will kill every person you fuck from now on."

Mason's words replayed in her mind. Hopefully, he wouldn't kill Osei because she didn't have sex with him.

All she expected was Mason to approach them and threaten Osei in full view of the other guests like he'd done at Reginald's party.

However, seconds ticked into minutes, and Mason didn't move from the spot by the door.

Sophie still didn't look directly at him. But her palms got sweaty, and her heart was racing.

What was he waiting for? Surely he could see that Osei was holding her hand. She'd purposely not pulled away because she was hoping for a reaction from Mason.

He hadn't liked it when Reginald touched her the other night, so she expected him to feel the same way now and jump in to warn the man. Yet nothing.

Instead, the bar lounge seemed to turn into a graveyard as conversations died and the place suddenly seemed emptier. Goosebumps skittered over her skin, and she glanced around.

The place was abandoned, barring Mason, Ziga, Benji and two men standing at the front and back exits. Mason's men.

No barman. No waiters.

Shit. *Shit!*

This wasn't good. This was catastrophic.

She had no audience to back up her story. To provide protection for her. She'd relied on Mason not doing anything too drastic in front of an audience. She'd calculated that he would threaten Osei, and Ziga would video it. Then someone would intervene and calm him down. Finally, he and Sophie would go somewhere else to argue like the last time. She would show him the video and threaten to use it against him if he didn't leave her alone.

Such a simple plan.

Damn it, why was Mason so unpredictable? Why didn't he follow the script of what he'd done before?

She hadn't made allowance for Mason clearing the bar of people. It was a public space! Why hadn't she considered him kicking people out of it?

The men in here were Mason's closest security personnel, handpicked for their loyalty to him. None of them would go against him.

She was definitely outnumbered.

But hopefully, not outmanoeuvred.

She had Ziga, and the woman had nerves of steel. Hopefully, she could still capture video evidence of a menacing Mason.

A quick glance at Ziga showed that she had the phone in her hand, slightly hidden between her body and the arm of the chair. Sophie prayed it was recording and no one would notice it.

Glinting metal caught the light. Sophie jerked towards it, and blood drained from her head, making her dizzy.

Mason held his knife in his hand as he approached.

Oh, God. Panic flooded her. She sharply nudged her companion, who was watching the football on the big screen above them. "Osei."

"What's going on?" he asked, speech slurring as he lifted his head from the backrest.

"Don't make any sudden movements," she warned in a low voice, hoping he would adhere.

"What?" he frowned, looking confused as he sat upright. He'd drunk most of the bottle of wine by himself, so he was tipsy, if not full-blown intoxicated.

Before she could reply, Mason pushed an armchair forward, and she froze, watching him in horrific fascination. He appeared so calm, his face expressionless.

This was how she knew he would do something terrible. It was the way he appeared before he struck people unawares. The look of a predator.

He lowered his body gracefully into the chair, the knife dangling between his thighs as he leaned his elbows on his knees.

"Who are you? What do you want?" Osei asked, suddenly looking more alert. Perhaps he noticed the gleaming knife clutched in Mason's hands.

"Mr Godfrey, who I am is not important. However, what I want is. You are trespassing on my property." His full lips hardened in a tight line. The same lips had kissed her softly, tenderly this morning.

"Trespassing. How? I'm a hotel guest. I'm staying here." Osei sounded befuddled.

Sophie wasn't looking at him, her gaze riveted on Mason, her pulse rate accelerating.

"I don't mean the hotel. I mean the woman beside you. Sophie." Mason said in a matter-of-fact tone.

Sophie's heart jolted. Mason was behaving so rationally. Not at all what she'd expected. Where was the violent behaviour she'd witnessed before?

"Sophie? I booked her for the night," Osei replied.

Mason flinched like he'd been slapped. The first outward show of emotion tonight. However, he didn't look at Sophie, and his disappointment spoke volumes.

Sophie cringed. Osei had mentioned her going to his room, but she told him she just wanted to sit here for now. She hadn't agreed to go to his room.

She opened her mouth to tell Mason she didn't want to sleep with Osei and closed it. If she said that, it would negate the purpose of this setup. She wanted Mason to think she intended to sleep with the man to get a rise out of him.

"You booked her for the night. Yet I booked her for life ten years ago, and she keeps fucking other people," Mason said in a quiet voice, and guilt pelted Sophie.

What was he saying? That he'd wanted her all those years? Did he have feelings for her?

"What?" Osei laughed derisively. "You're talking like she's your girlfriend. She's just a hooker."

Mason stabbed the knife into the low table in front of Osei so quickly. No one saw it move until it was embedded in the wood.

Osei and Sophie jerked back. Her heart nearly exploded in her chest.

"She is just a hooker to you," Mason's voice deepened with menace. "But she is mine. My hooker. My girlfriend. My woman. My …" he trailed off and stood, yanking the knife from the table.

Osei sank back into the sofa, moving away from Sophie as if she was suddenly leprous. "Look, man—"

"Shut up, Osei!" Sophie shouted, suddenly annoyed by the man's snivelling. Still, she didn't want Mason to hurt him on her account. "Mason, just let him go."

"Why should I?" Mason snapped, his back turned to her as if he couldn't stand the sight of her.

Swallowing, she glanced in Ziga's direction, and a dizzy spell overtook her.

Ziga's phone was flat on the table as Benji held a gun to her head. Shit. He must have discovered her recording the situation.

She didn't know when Ziga stopped recording or how much she'd recorded. This situation had spiralled out of her control.

Damn. She was in deep trouble.

FIFTEEN

"**A** lesson needs to be taught," Mason said as he leaned against the bar, knife still in his hand to his side, eyes hard and cold. His chiselled jaw tightened.

Shit. That meant one thing. Someone was about to endure pain. Osei probably.

Heart racing and limbs trembling, Sophie's gaze flicked around the lounge. The men stood at attention, awaiting their boss's next crucial order.

Her gaze landed on Ziga. Benji still pointed his gun at her assistant, but the woman didn't look afraid. Instead, she met Sophie's gaze and nodded as if agreeing with Mason's words.

Sophie understood. Although she wasn't a Yadili member because she hadn't taken the oath of allegiance to Chief Odili, she was an asset and a member of the Odili family. She recognized some of the rules at play here.

Respect, loyalty and honour were essential tenets of their clan. Every member of the family was expected to adhere to them.

However, respect was most crucial, especially for those in leadership positions like captains or bosses. These people demanded obedience constantly. Any disrespect was punished brutally.

Sophie swallowed as she reached a decision.

"Yes, I agree," Sophie said. Her actions had brought disrespect to Mason and herself in front of his men. She had to rectify it publicly so they wouldn't start misbehaving. She had to come clean. "But Osei is not the one who needs the lesson."

"Then who does?" Mason asked harshly.

"I do." Sophie swallowed again and stood, straightening her spine. This was not the time for fear, although her hands shook, and she clutched them in front of her. "I am the one responsible. Osei was just a mugu I—"

"I'm not a mugu. I booked you for the night," the man cut in, looking like she'd offended him.

Sophie's anger flared. Not only was the man lying, but he also was a fool.

"Shut your dirty mouth, Osei. Not only are you a mugu, but you're a mumu as well. Can't you see that I'm trying to save your miserable life? For the record, I booked you for the evening. When we met in the lobby this afternoon, and you stopped and greeted me, I was the one who invited you to the lounge at 6pm. Is that true or false?"

"Yes, it's true," Osemeka said. "But—"

"No buts. Just answer my questions. When I arrived in the lounge about quarter past six and saw you, I invited you to sit on this sofa—" she pointed at the sofa "—is that true or false?"

"Yes."

"Yes, what?"

"Yes, it's true."

"And when we sat on the sofa, and you spoke about me going to your room later, what was my response. Tell the truth, or you will lose a finger."

"What?" Osei's eyes widened.

"I said tell the truth, or Mason will claim your fingers one by one until you do. Trust me, he will do it."

Mason straightened as if about to come closer.

Osei jerked. "Okay. I'll tell the truth. What was the question?"

Sophie hid her laughter. "What did I tell you when you invited me to your bedroom this evening?"

"You said you just wanted to stay in the lounge," Osei grumbled.

"Did I ask you for any money?"

"No. But I offered."

"And I refused it. Also, who paid for the bottle of wine you drank?" Sophie asked.

"I wanted to pay for it," Osei argued.

"Yes, you wanted. But who actually gave the barman the money?"

"You did. Look—"

"Now, shut up and sit quietly. I need to speak to my man." She turned to face Mason. No, this wasn't her lover, Mason. This was the Yadili captain, Mace. The one who would punish wrongdoings brutally. "Mace, as you heard, I'm responsible for this setup. I used Osei as bait, and I ordered Ziga to assist me. Neither of them should be punished."

Mason scrutinised her, his gaze hardening. "Someone needs to be punished."

He wasn't letting her off even though she'd confessed. Instead, he would make her take full responsibility.

She sucked in a heavy breath. "I should be punished."

"So be it," Mason said in a calm voice. "Mr Godfrey, you are no longer welcome at Maximo Hotel and Casino. You will go to your room, clear your personal items and check out immediately."

"What? I paid for two more nights," Osei argued, standing.

"Your money will be refunded in full, even for the night you stayed," Mason said. "Leave within one hour and never return. If I see you on this premises again, you will lose more than your fingers. Chibuike, follow him and make sure he leaves."

"Yes, sir." The guard at the staff entrance stepped forward.

"Don't touch me," Osei barked, walking towards the lobby doors. "You people can't get away with this."

"Mr Godfrey, if you're thinking of calling the police or posting a nasty online review, you are really the mumu she called you."

Osei huffed and glared at them before stomping out, shadowed by Chibuike.

Momentary peace settled on the lounge with his departure.

Sophie sighed with relief that no blood had been shed. Now she could get to the root of those photos.

"Benji, get me a first aid kit," Mason ordered.

Benji holstered his weapon and headed towards the staff-only door.

"A first aid kit? Why?" Sophie glanced around the room. No one was injured, surprisingly, considering the number of weapons on display.

"It's time for your punishment."

Her gaze clashed with Mason's. The penny dropped as her mouth gaped.

He would need the first aid kit because he was going to cut her.

SIXTEEN

Sophie recovered from her initial shock of figuring out her punishment. After today's events, nothing Mason did should shock her. He had proven to be unpredictable yet consistent.

Because how else could she describe what was unfolding this evening.

For any other man, her plans would have worked. She'd based them on what she'd assumed to be a pattern of behaviour that would repeat given similar circumstances.

Why did she think she could foresee and therefore control Mason's behaviour? She couldn't ten years ago when they'd first met. And it seemed some things hadn't changed.

He stood quietly, watching her with dark, challenging eyes as if expecting her to dispute his pronouncement.

Oh, she wanted to dispute it. To say, "Hell, no! You're not touching me with that knife."

Even after a decade, she still had an unhealthy fear of sharp objects against her skin.

The sound of her pumping blood drummed loudly in her ears, and her palms became clammy. She gulped down her breaths, trying to quell the onset of panic. This was not the place to panic or let her fight-or-flight mode kick in.

She couldn't run. The guard stood at the lobby doors, and Benji would walk through the staff entrance any minute.

She couldn't fight. If she resisted, it meant Ziga would have to fight. Her assistant could get injured. It would be unfair on the woman who had warned her about the futility of the plan to entrap and video Mason being violent and threatening.

The staff-only door swung open, making Sophie flinch as Benji returned with the green first aid box. He placed it on the counter next to Mason and returned to stand before the door he'd just exited.

Without saying a word, Mason placed his blade on the bar, slid his suit jacket off his shoulders, folded it and placed it on the counter. Then he removed his cufflinks, and they tinkled as he put them on the granite top. Finally, he rolled the sleeves of his white dress shirt up to his elbows.

Swivelling, he faced her, legs apart. He flexed his fingers and wrists before shoving his hands into his trouser pockets and staring at her. The pose was not relaxed. It was intimidating. It was the pose of a man ready to dish out some discipline.

Her breath quickened as desire mixed with dread, her nipples hardening.

How could she find him attractive when he was about to cut her open, to make her bleed? In front of witnesses too.

What was wrong with her?

"Take your jacket off and bring it to me," Mason said in a clipped tone, jarring her from the mild sexual fog.

This was actually going to happen.

She resisted the urge to glance at the knife on the counter and looked down at her hands instead. Her long nails had been digging into her palms and created crescent indents.

Thank Goodness she'd changed the print dress she'd worn earlier. Mason's punishment would be more severe if he'd found her in the lounge full of people, looking like she was on sale.

With trembling hands, she reached for her jacket and unbuttoned it. She shrugged it off her shoulders and walked towards him, handing it over.

He took it and placed it beside his on the bar before looking her over. "Take your shoes off as well."

She lowered her body to the sofa, unclipped the straps and slid her feet out of the high-heeled sandals. Then she placed them beside the couch.

She straightened, and their height difference became evident as he towered over her.

He stepped up to her, and although her first instinct was to step away, she didn't.

She froze as his hands went to the buttons on her top. She wore a mustard-yellow twist-front asymmetrical hem blouse with a collar and three tiny buttons below the V-neck.

He undid all three, slowly and methodically, taking his time. As if he didn't care that he'd closed the usually busy lounge to guests and was losing money by the second. As if this was the most critical thing in the world. As if *she* was the most essential thing in the world.

Life bustled just outside the lounge doors—laughter, conversations, people coming and going. But here, the quietness and calmness stayed spiritual.

Momentarily mesmerised by the reverence in his actions, she forgot why he was doing it. She yearned to lean into his powerful chest, wishing he would wrap his strong arms around her. To make love to her. Right here and now.

Instead, he pushed the blouse down her shoulders until it hung around her upper arms. Low enough to reveal her lace bra straps and cleavage. Then he moved her bra straps halfway down her arms too. His touch left a trail of heat on her skin as he lifted the mass of hair and swept it over her right shoulder. Then he stepped behind her and gently kissed her bare left shoulder.

"You have always been perfect to me, right from that first night I met you," his voice was deep and calm as he made a statement of fact and meaning. "You were mine from that day. Were always mine. Would always be mine until I die."

Damn. Why hadn't she trusted him?

A lump formed in her throat, tears rushing to the back of her eyes. She turned her head, wanting to reach for him, to kiss him.

The trimmed beard scratched her skin. But his palm gripped her nape, keeping her head straight.

He moved away, leaving her bereft of his touch as he went behind the bar and fiddled under the counter. Loud music thumped through the speakers.

Shit. He wanted to mask the sound of her screams.

Adrenaline surged through her as he came around, grabbing the knife from the counter.

Instinctively she stumbled back, limbs trembling. "Mace, listen. I've learnt my lesson."

"I know," he said quietly that she almost didn't hear him above the music.

Hope flared inside her. Perhaps he would let her off. "So, you don't have to punish me."

"Oh, I do." He carried on coming forward as she stepped back. "If you fight me, I will restrain you."

Shit. Would he get the men to hold her down? From experience, Mason could do it all by himself.

He pushed the low table away from the sofa, creating space on the hard floor.

"Sophie, kneel here." He pointed at the spot in front of him and stood waiting.

She hesitated, glancing around. Everyone was watching her, including Ziga.

Sophie was responsible for this mess. She should have known that it would come down to this. That Mason would demand his pound of flesh. Her flesh.

Marking her meant so much on different levels.

Sure, it was punishment because he knew she didn't like the knife one bit.

Yet, it was more. A reaffirmation of their relationship and connection. A reset of the clock and a fresh start.

More than anything else, she wanted the new beginning. A do-over. With him.

So, she stepped forward boldly, although her limbs felt like jelly and knelt like he wanted.

***

Mason's dick went hard as a rock the moment Sophie stepped close and knelt before him. He'd sported a semi when she'd taken that buffoon Mr Godfrey down a peg or two. Knowing she hadn't wanted to fuck the man, that she'd been playing some ill-thought-out game, had greatly relieved him.

But why did she engineer the whole thing? He'd spotted Ziga's awkward posture in the armchair, raising his suspicions. He'd met Benji's gaze as he'd approached Sophie and Mr Godfrey and had nodded in Ziga's direction, knowing his second would root out any treachery. And it seemed the woman had been recording the scene. Ziga would not dare something so disloyal without Sophie's approval or order. Something so devious meriting a severe penalty.

Smacked of something his brother and mother would do. But he'd never expected it from Sophie. Begging the question, why would Sophie do it? He needed to understand her motives. They should talk.

First, he would dish out the punishment and then fuck her. Oh, he would bend her over and fuck her as she bled from his blade. Over that sofa where she'd dared to sit and let another man touch her. He would fuck her, make her scream, make her take his punishing thrusts. Then when he was done. When she was limp and exhausted, and thoroughly claimed. When he was satisfied, then they would talk.

His gaze swept over her. She was perfect, kneeling before him, waiting for her penance.

She was still covered, dressed in a pair of skinny jeans and a blouse. Perfection.

While he wanted to punish her, others were still in the lounge. His men and her assistant. She wouldn't be entertaining them. They were only here to witness his actions as he re-established control over his woman. Over his establishment.

Unlike his brother, Mason had never liked sharing, not his toys as a child or his women as an adult. Not that he'd had women except for the ones he bought at a nightly rate.

This one. Sophie. She was his woman.

The bottoms of her tiny feet were bare and exposed, showing her vulnerability. Yet her shoulders were straight and chin high. This was no meek, submissive woman. The rebellious woman he'd met ten years ago was still there, and he loved it. Loved the wild and defiant person she'd always been.

Yes, he would use the word 'love' instead of 'like' because his earlier conversation with Zoe gave him the correct phrase to describe his intense need for Sophie.

He loved Sophie.

There. He allowed the thought to crystalise in his mind, and as he stared at her, it became a tangible energy rippling through him and making him more determined.

The exposed brown skin of her shoulders, upper back and decolletage was flawless. Even now, his fingers tingled from the smoothness of touching her while he'd partially undressed her.

He wanted to mark her unblemished skin. Wanted to brand his name into her flesh. Not just as a punishment. Not just as a temporary thing.

No, he wanted her to wear his mark forever.

He wanted the world to know that she belonged to him.

"Nkem," he said in a low voice, speaking directly to her. The others wouldn't hear it because of the loud music. He didn't care. He wasn't talking to them.

A tear rolled down her cheek and dropped onto the floor. She understood the significance of the word and looked up at him, nodding.

"Eleniyan," she said in acceptance.

Warmth filled his chest as his dick throbbed. The urge to sink into and claim her skittered over his flesh.

He sucked in a deep breath to centre himself and focus.

"Lower your body onto the sofa," he ordered.

He almost missed the sharp intake of her breath as she obeyed his instruction and lay on the settee.

He moved closer, placed one knee on the sofa and the other on her back, holding her in place. He knew she feared the blade and would try to fight the moment it neared her skin. So, he didn't want to injure her.

Her muscles tensed, and she twisted her head, eyes widened, trying to watch what he did.

"Stay still, Sophie. The blade is sharp," he said close to her ear.

A good thing he had the music volume up because she screamed as he made the incision into her skin, marking her with precision until his full initials MEM were written in blood on her flesh.

It was more than he'd done the last time. But they meant more to each other now.

And while this was temporary and would heal, he would put permanent ink on the same spot as soon as it was safe.

He shifted from her, took her hand and gently raised her to stand. Her eyes were red from crying, and she didn't meet his gaze. He held her head to his chest, arm around her waist, displaying her back to his men, so they would see his bloodied mark on her skin. This was for them as much as it was for Mason and Sophie.

Benji stepped forward and grinned. "Mace, it's beautiful. Congratulations."

"Congrats to both of you," Ziga said, smiling.

Sophie lifted her head, a frown marring her face. "Why are they congratulating us?"

Mason looked down at her, his lips curling upwards. "You still don't get it? I just put my mark on you in front of witnesses. It means you're mine for life."

"What?" she jerked back, eyeing him balefully. "Like we're married?"

"The exact thing. Our bond is written in blood." He winked at her.

"So, you mark me, and I don't get to mark you? The hell with that—" She reached for the knife in his hand. He moved it away from her, but she slammed into his arm, making the blade slice into his skin.

Fuck. Pain ripped through him as a red stain soaked the side of his shirt.

Hot damn. She'd just marked him too. Claimed him.

He became breathless as warmth flooded his body, and his need for her flared like an inferno.

He would never let her go.

SEVENTEEN

Sophie screamed as Mason carved into her shoulders with his blade, the pain intense at first and then dulling as she slid into a foggy headspace.

His weight on her back anchored her, berthed her to the moment. Ensured she couldn't run, couldn't escape. Like she always did. Like she'd been trying to do today.

Run again.

She'd always been a runner. She'd run from her madam when she was a teenager. Ran from Bomba, her ex-pimp. Even ran from Mason. Sure, he'd kicked her out of his home. But she'd run first by rejecting the offer to have his baby.

Just like she'd tried to run today, just because she'd seen photos of him meeting with Zoe Himba.

The man currently on top of her, carving his initials into her skin, wouldn't marry another woman. She knew it for certain as much as she knew he was branding her right now. Yes, he hadn't explicitly said he would carve his initials into her skin. But that's what he was doing.

This was them. Their relationship wasn't conventional but was as valid as anyone else's.

His words from earlier replayed in her mind. *"You were mine from that day. Were always mine. Would always be mine until I die."*

She should have trusted him a decade ago. But perhaps she'd needed time to grow up and gain enough confidence to match his energy.

Because he was a force of nature, and he was hers now and would remain hers until she died.

She became briefly disorientated when he climbed off her back as his grounding strength disappeared. Then she felt his palm on her arm as he helped her stand, and a calming force flowed through her as he pulled her into his arm. She placed her head on his chest, grateful for the comfort of his embrace chasing away the pain on her shoulder. She loved this aspect of their relationship. This relief and freedom she felt in his arms. It didn't mean the pain vanished. It just became less severe as she focused on his strength and protection.

The strength and protection that no one else had ever offered her.

Being in his arms felt like being at home. Like safety. Something she experienced with him alone.

She heard Benji and Ziga congratulating them, and it took a few seconds to rouse herself from the foggy headspace.

Confused, she looked up at Mason, met his amused expression, and asked about the compliments.

He explained they were now bonded because he'd marked her. The urge to claim him as hers flared within her. Why should she be the only one to be branded?

She reacted instinctively and reached for the knife in his hand without much thought.

She caught him unawares, and he reacted too late. The extra sharp blade grazed him.

A gasp escaped Sophie, her horrified gaze on the crimson spreading across Mason's left side, staining his shirt.

"I cut you!" She snatched her hands back. What had she done? She didn't want to hurt him.

"You branded me," Mason bragged, giving her a cocky smile. He seemed ecstatic about it.

"You don't mind?" she asked, watching him warily as she repositioned her blouse so the sleeve and bra strap was up on the right shoulder. Unfortunately, she couldn't cover the bleeding left shoulder.

"Mind? I love it." He adjusted his crotch, and her gaze followed his motion. An enormous bulge strained the fabric of his trousers.

"You're hard," she gasped in a low voice. He'd once told her that he liked seeing her bloodied. Perhaps he got aroused from her cutting him too.

"I am, for you." He stepped into her space and leaned close to her ear. "Are you wet for me?"

"Wouldn't you like to know?" She stepped to the side. "Let me see the wound."

He tugged his shirt apart, ripping the buttons out in the process. Then he pulled it off his broad chest, wiping the blade before sheathing it in the leather pouch attached to his belt. His muscles rippled, his skin glistening with sweat. He lifted his arm, and she saw the straight-line gash oozing blood.

"Oh, Mace. I—" she started.

"Don't apologise," he cut in. "It's the best thing you've done for me this evening. The next thing you should do is fuck me."

"No. We can't fuck while you're bleeding." Not to mention that she was also bleeding. Although she couldn't feel as much blood oozing down her back as he had on his side. Hers felt more like a trickle and was probably already clotting.

"Yes, we can. I will burn this sofa because you sat with that mugu and let him touch you on it. But first, I want to stain it with our blood as I fuck you so that when you think of the sofa, you will only remember us on it."

Her mouth dropped open. "You're crazy!"

His reply was a devious smile before he spoke in a loud voice. "Benji, all of you, step outside. Now."

They likely thought he was crazy too. But without saying anything, his men and Ziga turned to leave.

Mason really wasn't about sharing her, like his brother tried to do. Or about her entertaining other people on his behalf, like Bomba. He wanted her all to himself.

Butterflies fluttered in her stomach, and her knees weakened.

How could she not love him for revering her? For valuing and respecting her. For elevating her.

She gasped as she realised what she was thinking.

She loved him. Loved Mason.

And because she loved him, she needed to feel him deep inside her, hard, fast and life-affirming.

Locking her gaze to his, she reached down, unzipping her jeans.

He stepped close, slid one hand between her legs into her panties and rubbed her slick pussy as he lowered his mouth onto hers. "Oh, you're soaking wet."

"For you." She rose on her tiptoes, meeting him halfway as they kissed frenziedly, his fingers playing with her swollen clit. She gasped and breathed heavily as she shoved her jeans down, breaking the kiss to step out of them and her panties. She lowered her body onto the sofa, even as her back hurt from the movement. She didn't care, just stayed focused on him, opening her legs in invitation.

Then he shoved his trousers down, freeing his stiff dick, his gaze fiercely focused on her. He lowered his body on top of hers, grabbed her hips and impaled her body on his dick.

"Mace," she cried out as pain and pleasure merged, her pussy tightening against him.

"Nkem." He cupped her ass, pulling out and thrusting in again. Repeating the action, pounding into her in a fast and furious motion. They wouldn't last long as her orgasm raced towards fruition.

He pulled out and flipped her over, so she knelt on the floor, her face on the sofa.

"I love looking at my mark on you, all bloody and messy," he said as he knelt behind her. "Reach down and rub your clit."

She didn't hesitate, pushing her bare ass up, and she lowered her hand to her soaking pussy. She ached for him all over.

He held her hips apart and slammed into her, and they both panted heavily as he fucked her, holding her down by the nape, driving into her. She caressed her clit, rubbing harder as he pounded faster.

The intensity of the branding and lovemaking sent her hurtling towards the edge.

Soon she was coming, thrashing, fever rushing over her, her pussy greedy for him, squeezing and rippling around him. Finally, it triggered his climax, and he pumped his seed into her, filling her up.

Exhaustion left her struggling for breath.

Spent, he lay on top of her, bracing his weight through his arms on the cushions.

She loved this post-coital bliss of having his warmth and weight on her, their breathing heavy and calming together.

He pressed kisses to her sweaty skin, her cheek, making her tear up. This was his way of telling her he loved her. He'd shown her from the first time they'd made love. Not everything had to be vocalised.

It was the reason someone sent her those photos. They hoped to drive a wedge between her and Mason. She had to mention those messages. He needed to know. There could be something sinister at play.

"There's a problem," she said quietly.

Mason shifted and sat on the sofa, meeting her gaze with a frown. "What is it?"

"I'll show you." She reached for her pants and jeans, pulling them back on. Then she walked to where her jacket lay on the bar and dug into the pocket for the phone.

Mason righted his trousers and walked behind the counter. He lowered the volume of the music so it was back to a background sound.

She unlocked the gadget and found the anonymous message. "I received these this afternoon."

She showed Mason the photos.

"Who sent these?" He narrowed his eyes.

"I don't know," she replied. "No number showed."

"Is this the reason you tried to set me up? You were trying to video me?"

Guilt pelted her skin about what she'd tried to do to him. "Yes, the note said you would marry her. I felt betrayed and had to do something. I thought you would take my baby away."

He jerked back, looking affronted. "You think I would take *our* baby away from you? That I would use our baby against you?"

He shook his head, looking disappointed. "Have you asked yourself why I never had a baby with another woman if I wanted one so much?"

She knew the answer to that. "You wanted one with me."

"Yes!"

She leaned into him, gently wrapping her arms around him to avoid hurting him. "I won't ever doubt you again."

"Good." He puffed out a sigh. "I went to see Zoe because Chief ordered me to send her a marriage proposal. I will withdraw my bid because I won't marry her even if she agrees."

Her eyes widened. "You're going to defy Chief's order. Is that a good idea?"

"Probably not. But I just married my wife tonight. So, I don't need a second wife."

"Oh, Mace." Her heart swelled blissfully. He considered her his one and only wife. She should freak out because she was now a wife. Mason's wife. Who knew it was possible in her life?

She wrapped her arms around his neck and kissed him hungrily.

But her mind couldn't settle. This was a big deal. Defying the godfather was a lethal offence which could cost Mason his life.

When they broke apart, she held onto his arms for anchor. "What are we going to do about Chief? About whoever took those photos?"

Her fingers tingled as her throat clogged. She couldn't resist touching him as she reached for the stained, tattered white clothes. "Give me the shirt."

He handed it over. "Don't worry. I will get my investigators working on the photos and who sent them. And I will handle Chief when the time comes. In the meantime, though, we're going home."

She looped the shirt around his torso. "Home? You mean your apartment?"

"No." Grinning, he stood still as she secured the tourniquet to stop the bleeding. "I mean my hometown. We're going to see Ma Bagu."

EIGHTEEN

Mason tingled with anticipation as the car neared their destination, his family residence in Umudike, their hometown. The bright sunlight coming through the windscreen reflected his disposition. Inside the car, the AC blasted freezing air as he liked it,

Sophie sat beside him in the back of the SUV, their hands linked. She stared out the window, but he doubted she saw much through the blacked-out glass, possibly reminiscing.

She'd seemed excited yesterday as they'd made travel arrangements. But, because of the impromptu nature, they'd taken a day to ensure their respective businesses were in capable hands.

Maximo Hotel had an operations manager who handled the day-to-day business. And no pressing matters required Mason's attention. Likewise, Sophie indicated she could take a few days' break.

He'd called Zoe yesterday evening. She'd seemed surprised to hear from him so soon after their meeting.

He'd explained that his situation had changed. But she started talking before he could tell her of his intentions to formally withdraw his marriage proposal.

"It was great seeing you again in pleasant circumstances yesterday," Zoe said. "But I'm afraid I can't accept your marriage proposal."

"Why?" he asked, a little shell-shocked. Perhaps his pride was hurt.

"I'll be honest, Mason. I'm a very possessive lover. I need someone who will give their undivided attention. I'm sure you understand."

He understood clearly. Zoe found out about Sophie. How?

"Did you receive anonymous photographs of me?" he asked.

"I did. She is beautiful." She sighed. "Would you have married me and kept her as a mistress?"

"No, Zoe." He scrubbed a hand over his head. "I called you to withdraw my proposal."

"You're in love with her? Madame Sophie?" she asked in a wistful tone.

"I am. I love Sophie. She fills the broken places in my heart and plasters over the cracks. She makes me whole."

"Oh. She turned you into a poet." Giggles filled his office from the phone's loudspeaker. "She's a lucky woman to have you."

He laughed. "No. I'm the lucky one to have her. I really hope you find what you're looking for in a partner."

"Thank you," she replied. "And I wish you and Sophie a happy life together. But you must watch your back. Someone in your camp is not happy about your union."

Mason agreed with Zoe's assessment. Someone close to him was trying to mess up his relationship with Sophie. Two people were at the top of that list—Mother and Rocha.

Mason had already put Benji in charge of identifying who had taken the photographs of Mason and Zoe. He'd been at the meeting with a team of four people excluding Benji, so they should be able to identify the photographer.

The person had known about Mason and Sophie, although they hadn't made their relationship public. Instinct told him it could be a member of her team or his. But why would they want to break up his relationship with Sophie? It didn't make sense.

Still, he had bigger fish to fry. Chief Odili.

Choosing Sophie meant defying a direct command from his godfather, something he'd never done before. Something he shouldn't do.

He sighed, shoving the thought away. He needed to concentrate on what he had, Sophie and their future together.

He remembered the first time he'd taken her to his hometown a decade ago, the night he'd met her. It had felt right then.

She'd been sitting in the backseat like today, with Benji as the driver. Mason had forced orgasms out of her as she'd fought him. Afterwards, she'd been exhausted, and he'd held her in his arms.

That night they'd formed an unbreakable bond. Remarkable, considering he hadn't taken any woman seriously before her. Hadn't even taken a woman to his house in the city, let alone his hometown.

Today, he was doing it again. Taking the same woman home. Taking her home as his life partner. He'd never been interested in anyone before Sophie. She was his future. The mother of his babies, hopefully.

He'd accepted a long time ago he couldn't control if or when she got pregnant.

Sure, she'd offered to have his baby. However, at the time, he'd been sceptical about her promise and just happy to have her back in his life.

Now he appreciated she genuinely wanted a baby, considering how far she'd been willing to go to protect her unborn child.

He loved her, regardless of whether she had his baby.

"Nkem, are you okay?" he asked, squeezing her hand when she turned, looking slightly distracted.

"I'm okay," she looked up and smiled. "I remembered the first night I met you. That was quite a night."

"It was an amazing night. You don't know it, but meeting you changed my life and gave me purpose."

"Really? How?"

"Well, I was lost for a long time after my father died. I didn't quite know what to do with myself or my life. My mother's and brother's behaviours hadn't helped. My father meant the world to me. So, the grief was sometimes overwhelming and suffocating. I'd gone to the brothel that night for relief. I needed sex to release the ball of emotion that was crushing me. Yet, even fucking the hooker didn't help me. So, when I stepped outside and found you fighting with your pimp, I knew what to do. Smashing into that man was a huge release."

He squeezed her hand again as she watched him.

"And then we got chased, and you ran into the car with me. I could see the adrenaline rush through you. See your excitement. Your bravery for standing up to a bully. And I wanted a piece of you, if not all of you. You brought me release. Despite what happened with my brother, spending time with you that night was exhilarating. So, when you chose to go with me instead of with him, I knew I had to protect you by any means necessary. Taking you to my hometown was a spontaneous decision. However, once we got there and I saw how you got on with Ma Bagu, I wanted to keep you for more than a few days."

"Indeed." Sophie giggled. "You wanted me to have your baby. That was so unexpected, so crazy. 'Til today, I still don't understand why."

Mason chuckled, shaking his head. "Now, I can see how crazy it might have seemed, considering we'd only known each other for a few days. But in my mind, I'd decided you would be my baby mama. Plus, Ma Bagu had a vision of your carrying my baby."

"What? Really?" Her eyes widened. "Ma Bagu had a vision?"

"Yes. She said if we had sex, you would get pregnant. And I didn't want to impregnate you without your permission. That's why I had to ask you to have my baby before we had sex."

"But I was on contraceptives, and I would have made you use a condom."

"I know you said that, but I truly believed none of that would work. I believed once we had sex, you would get pregnant. In fact, I still do."

"Wow." Her forehead furrowed in thought. "So, when you asked me to have your baby, you were trying to get my consent because you thought I would get pregnant regardless of precautions."

"Yes. I couldn't think of any other way around it."

"Oh, Mace. You were being sweet and considerate, and protective. Meanwhile, I'd thought you'd lost your mind for asking a prostitute to have your baby." She reached across and stroked the stubble on his chin.

"I was possibly out of my mind because of everything else going on. But I didn't see you as a prostitute then or now, except when you offered your services to others. That always crushed me."

"Oh. I was just trying to survive the only way I knew. I didn't think you were serious about the baby at the time. I really thought you were crazy. I'd never even thought about having a baby, and I didn't think I was good enough to be anyone's parent then."

He shifted, concerned about her uncertainty. "Is that how you feel now?"

"No. I believe I would be a good parent," she sounded vehement. "I would love him or her and give them the best of me."

"I think you're so full of love and would make a great parent," he clarified so she would know he truly believed in her.

Her eyes glistened with tears as her breath hitched. "Do you really think so?"

"Of course." He unclipped his seatbelt and moved over, pulling her into his arms. "What's the matter?"

Tears fell from her long dark lashes as she squeezed them shut and sobbed. His heart broke because he wasn't sure why she was crying. He undid her seatbelt so he could pull her closer. "Nkem, talk to me. Please. If you don't want a baby, that's okay."

Sure, he would feel an immense loss if she chose not to have his baby. But it wouldn't be the end of the world.

"No. That's not it," she said, taking a shuddering breath. "It's about my family. They don't think I'm good enough to have a baby or a family."

"Excuse me, what did you say?" He leaned back, searching her face to process what he'd just heard.

She sniffled, wiping her cheeks with a tissue. "I was so excited when my sister had her baby. They didn't invite me to the naming ceremony, and I thought it was probably because they'd wanted an intimate ceremony. But when I visited my sister, she and her husband refused to let me see the baby. The husband said I was no longer welcome in their house, and my sister backed it up. Apparently, my job isn't good enough for her in-laws."

"Your sister did what?" Mason stared at her in disbelief. "I can understand your brother-in-law, maybe, but your sister? The same one you paid to raise with your sweat and money?"

"How did you know?" She appeared shocked.

"I knew you paid her tuition and maintenance through university because you asked Duke for a loan to pay her fees. Duke was over-extended at the time because that was when we'd been throwing all our money into the Maximo construction. I had to take a loan from the law chambers accounts to give Duke so he could give it to you."

"Oh, my God! That was your money?" She got teary again. "You don't know how you saved me. Saved her. I was so stressed out then. I thought she would drop out of school or become a runs girl. I didn't want her to do what I did. And I didn't have any money. Haven didn't exist, and I was just doing odd jobs for Duke then. I had to borrow the money and felt ashamed to ask Duke for it. I had no clue it was your money."

"It wasn't my money. It belonged to the law firm. Duke mentioned that you needed money for your sister's school fees, and I had to scramble to get it somewhere. We had cash flow problems because Maximo was sucking all our cash. I was earning from the law firm, but it wasn't a huge amount because I wasn't a partner then. I spoke to my father's former partner, and he agreed to lend me the money from the account, and I had to pay it back."

"Thank you so much. You were protecting me, and I didn't even know it." She cupped his face, and he leaned into her palm.

"You were mine, and it was my job to protect you however I could. That's what my father taught me. But I can't understand why your sister is so ungrateful after what you did for her."

"It broke my heart. But what can I do since she kicked me out of her life? And my mother is not calling her out on it," She sounded dejected.

His anger only flared. He didn't forgive or forget so readily. Anyone who hurt his lover was in for a world of pain. "Mark my words. Your sister will come to beg you one day."

NINETEEN

For the first time since her father died, Sophie felt like she was going home. But the strange thing was that home was in the most unlikely place—Mason's family residence in his hometown.

This was the place she'd first felt free.

The place she'd stood her ground and defended Mason when his brother wanted to use her against him. Sure, she'd been punished for siding with Mason—the caning by Mrs Maduka and Rocha hitting her. But Mason had gone berserk and had threatened to kill his entire family if they hurt her again.

This was the first place that she felt she truly belonged. Because sitting at the kitchen table eating okra soup with Mason, laughing and joking with Ma Bagu had been the best experience of her life. She'd almost forgotten what family felt like until that night.

Sophie's heart raced as their vehicle pulled into the compound and parked in front of the portico. Someone opened Mason's door, and he decanted, coming around to help her down. She stepped out into the sunshine, holding his hand and sucked in a deep breath.

The place seemed busy as Mason's men unloaded the car boots. They'd arrived in a convoy of three vehicles and ten security personnel, including Ziga.

Sophie had requested for Ziga to come along for the trip. She trusted Mason's team. However, she'd thought there might be places she needed to go that the men couldn't enter. This was a rural area with traditional cultural practices.

"Why did we come with so many people?" she asked.

Mason's alert gaze bounced around the premises. "The last time I brought you here, I made the foolish mistake of thinking I could protect you alone, and I couldn't. I swore never to make that mistake again."

Her heart clenched at his determination to keep her safe.

"Oh, Mace, but you brought an army." She kissed their joined hands.

"Exactly. Better to be safe than sorry." His eyes sparkled with amusement.

Just then, Ma Bagu came around the corner, dressed in an Ankara blouse and skirt set. Her excitement and joy in her body posture and bright eyes. "Ehe. Ụmụ m alọtala." *My children have come home.*

Sophie understood her words. After living in the Southeast region for a decade, she'd learned the Igbo language.

"Ada, kedu? How are you?" Ma Bagu opened her arms, and Sophie stepped into her comforting embrace with a huge smile. It was as if the intervening ten years hadn't happened. As if Sophie was indeed her child returning home.

It had been so long since anyone welcomed her so warmly, joyful tears pricked her eyes. "Mma, àdị m mma. Daalụ." *Mama, I'm well. Thank you.*

"Ah!" Ma Bagu leaned back, her smile spreading wider. "Ị na-asụ Ìgbò ugbu a." *You now speak Igbo.*

"Nke ọma," *Very well.* Sophie said with a cheeky giggle.

"Ọ bụkwa eziokwu." *It is very true.* Ma Bagu laughed. Then she turned to Mason, who watched their interaction with a grin. She opened her arms again. "Ezigbo nwa. Ị kpọlatara nwa m nwanyị." *Good child. You brought my daughter home.*

"Ama m na obi ga-adị gị ụtọ ịhụ ya." *I knew you'd be happy to see her.*

Mason hugged the woman, winked at Sophie over her shoulder and mouthed, "I told you so."

Indeed. He'd mentioned that Ma Bagu had been asking about Sophie for years. She'd thought he'd said it to keep her sweet. She realised Mason never lied. His words might be painful, but they would be the truth.

"Obi dị m ụtọ nke ukwuu. Bata n'ime ụlọ." *My heart is so pleased. Come inside the house.*

Ma Bagu held Sophie's hand as she walked down the passage into the side door.

Sophie's heart expanded with warmth. She couldn't express the joy filling her with the old woman's welcome. She'd thought the woman would dislike her because of her job or the abrupt way she'd left Mason's house the last time.

But her job didn't seem to matter to Ma Bagu or Mason. It had never bothered them.

A young woman dressed in a servant's uniform and hair in cornrows curtseyed. "Welcome, ma, uncle."

"Thank you," Sophie replied. The servant must be new because she wasn't the same one who had served Sophie the last time.

People went past them, taking the luggage upstairs.

As Ma Bagu ushered her into the kitchen just like the first night, comprehension dawned. These two people—Mason and Ma Bagu—were her new family. Her old one discarded her. Nevertheless, she was valuable to Mason and Ma Bagu, and they wouldn't abandon her.

Tears clogged her eyes as she went to sit at the small table.

Like a hawk, Mason noticed and lowered his body beside hers. "Nkem, o ginị? What's wrong."

"Nothing." She chuckled as she took a tissue from her purse and dabbed the corners of her eyes. "These are tears of joy. The welcome is a little overwhelming. Thank you, Ma Bagu."

"Ah." The woman waved her off. "When my son brings home his new wife, she is supposed to be welcomed warmly."

Surprised, Sophie turned to Mason. "You told her we're married?"

Mason was serious about this marriage, and Sophie couldn't be happier.

They'd stopped over at the Local Government Secretariat on the way here because, to her shock, Mason had registered their marriage intent, ten years ago. And since there had been no objections, they could sign the marriage certificate and make it official.

However, the registrar had told them to return tomorrow because it was short notice, and he'd needed to prepare paperwork.

Mason had told Sophie he'd thought the man wanted to inform Mrs Maduka first that her son was getting married. He didn't mind if they called his mother as long as they didn't come up with another excuse to refuse their marriage registration.

Now he grinned. "Of course. I had to tell her so she would prepare for your arrival. Marriage is a big deal. I have to tell my family."

"It is a wonderful thing, a celebration. I have been praying for it for so long." Ma Bagu turned to the girl. "Nkechi, get them something to drink."

"Yes, ma." The girl came over. "What can I offer you?"

"Just water for now," Sophie said and glanced at Mason.

"Same for me," he said.

"Yes, sir." Nkechi walked to the tall fridge freezer, opened it and took out a water bottle. She returned with two tall glasses and placed them on the table. After pouring the drinks, she went to help Ma Bagu, who was dishing out food.

Sophie took a sip of the chilled water and sighed happily. Then a thought occurred to her. "This is not where your family eat their meals, right?"

She assumed there would be a separate dining area in such a mansion. The last time she'd been in this house, she hadn't seen much beyond the kitchen, the stairs and Mason's bedroom. They'd arrived at night, so she hadn't seen the rest of the house, and she'd spent the two days in Mason's room.

"No. We have a separate dining room for the family. I'll take you on a tour after Ma Bagu feeds us because she won't let us out of here before we've eaten." He chuckled.

"Yes, I know." She laughed, too, remembering the first time she'd been here when the older woman had hijacked her and taken her straight into the kitchen despite Mason wanting to take her upstairs. "But do you always eat your meals here?"

She loved the intimacy of eating at the kitchen table instead of the formal dining room.

"These days, yes. When I was younger, and my father was alive, I ate meals with the family. But after Ma Bagu came to live with us, I started sitting here and eating with her. My mother didn't like it. She said the kitchen table was for servants. But I would sneak in here occasionally and sit with Ma Bagu, especially at night when Mother was in bed or not around." He grinned, and then his face clouded over. "After my father died, I stopped eating meals with my family. The last meal I ate with them was the morning after you arrived here ten years ago. I was in such a good mood that I sat and ate with them for the first time in months. I was foolish to not see them for the venomous creatures they are."

His voice sounded croaky, and she reached out and covered his hand with hers, squeezing it. That he still remembered the events of that day with such emotions showed how much he cared for her, even back then.

"That was the last time I ate with them. So, I eat here or upstairs," he continued.

"Upstairs? In your bedroom?" she asked, recalling he had the ensuite bedroom with a wardrobe, an armchair and a bed.

"Yes, that whole wing belongs to me now and is a self-contained two-bed suite. I converted the old rooms next to mine. So, we have an open-plan living room and diner, a small kitchen and a spare bedroom with an ensuite. It's our space."

"Oh, that's wonderful." She sighed in relief. She wouldn't have to stay in the same living room as his mother. Although the woman was currently in the Federal Capital Territory because she was a senator representing the district.

Nkechi brought dishes of food over and set the table.

Sophie's face lit up as she saw the bowl of Okra Soup. "Ma Bagu, you don't know how happy you just made me. I've wanted to eat your soup for so long."

"Thank you, my child. Enjoy the meal." Ma Bagu smiled and carried on dishing out food and sending Nkechi to give to the security personnel who'd arrived with Mason.

Ziga sat in a chair just outside the kitchen door to eat hers.

Sophie washed her hands quickly and started eating, mewling in pleasure with every mouth full as Mason watched her with a heated gaze.

He chuckled, leaning into her to whisper. "If you keep making that sound, I will send them out and fuck you here."

"You are so naughty." The imagery sent her nipples hardening, and she giggled, shifting in her seat. But she also believed he would carry out his threat, and she wanted to enjoy the food first. So, she stopped teasing him and focused on the meal.

After eating, Mason walked her through the house with the large kitchen, three ensuite bedrooms on the ground floor, two large reception rooms and a dining room. Upstairs was split into two wings. Each wing contained a large reception room, a family bathroom and three bedrooms with ensuite bathrooms.

Mason had commandeered a wing and turned it into his apartment. His mother and brother lived in the other wing. Although Rocha also had an apartment in the block behind the main house, which he used for partying and entertaining.

As soon as Sophie walked into Mason's old bedroom, the memories came rushing back and overwhelmed her—the good with the bad. Gasping, she turned into Mason, and he wrapped his arms around her.

"Nkem, are you okay?" he asked gently.

"Just give me a moment." She sucked in deep breaths.

"If you don't like this suite, we can stay in one of the flats in the BQ," he said.

"And kick your security team out. I'm sure it's cramped in there already."

He leaned back. "I'm sure they won't mind. There are six apartments in there."

"But you mentioned that some of the apartments were rented out. So, there's limited space. Look, I'll be fine in here. I just need to associate this space with you loving me and not me being tortured by your mother."

"I know." He sighed, and then he tilted his head. "Well, there is something we never did in this room."

"What?" She frowned, trying to picture something else, when her mind played back images of being chained and the cane setting fire to her skin.

"I never fucked you in the bed." He winked and stepped into her space.

Her heart thumped as she inhaled his musk.

"That's true," she said in a breathy voice. "Is the chain still under the bed?"

"The chain?" His eyes narrowed. "Yes. Why?"

She walked to the bed and sat on it. "What's the deal with the chain? Ten years ago, it seemed like a crazy thing to have in your room. I know you much better now. But I still don't get it. Is it a sex tool? You've never tied me up during sex, so I can't quite make the connection."

He nodded and sat beside her on the mattress. "The chain is not a sex tool. You were the first and the only woman I'd ever brought home, let alone into this room."

"Really?" That information shocked her, but she didn't think he was lying. "Your brother said you shared women in the past."

"Yes, he shared *his* women with me. I never brought home any woman, so I couldn't share any of mine. That was why he was shocked when he saw you because it was the first time he met a woman with me. He assumed I would share you. But that was never going to happen."

"Wow. I never knew." She took a moment to process that. She really had been unique, and she hadn't known it. "But the chain. Why do you have it in your room? Was it there in case you brought someone home eventually?"

He shook his head again. "The chain wasn't for anyone else because it was for me."

"For you?" Her eyes went wide as she shook her head. Why would he need it?

"Yes, my mother had the chain installed because of me. She used it to restrain me."

TWENTY

Sophie's breath hitched, and she gripped Mason's arm. "She did what?"

Mason just shrugged as if it was a regular thing. Hell, this was not normal behaviour.

She shook her head, her eyes widening with the horror of the situation. "Wait, o. Your mother used to cane you too? She used to have you chained so she could cane you?"

He nodded and sighed as if he'd accepted it as part of life. Part of his life.

"But … why?" She couldn't accept a human would treat a child who came out of their womb so horribly. "Are you adopted? Is that why there's rivalry between you and your brother?"

He barked a laugh, but it was without humour. "I asked my parents if I was adopted once, and they said no. When I turned eighteen, I requested a DNA test as a birthday present. Lo and behold, I am the son of the Late SAN Alfred Maduka and Senator Mabel Maduka. Same as Rocha. We are full-blood siblings."

"But…"

"I know," he said. "Mother does not treat my brother and I equally. She labelled me a difficult child. My father said she had postnatal depression and struggled to bond with me when I was born. He got help for her, and I think she might have had therapy. But honestly, I'm not sure how much it helped. I had nannies, but then again, so did my brother. So, I don't think that was the problem."

He lowered his head to his hands and scrubbed his face. Then he smiled wryly. "Do you know my brother tried to drown me in the bath?"

She jerked upright. "What?"

"Oh, I was little. I must have been around four, and he was ten. Somehow I was in the kitchen covered in flour. Then he took me to the bathroom and put me in a bath full of cold water. I was crying because the water was cold, and he held me under the water until one of the servants rushed in and pulled me out. I ended up in hospital. The servant was caned and sacked. But, my brother did that on purpose. Over the years, he did other things where other people got the blame, me most of the time, and he never got punished. I was always being caned by my mother. To be fair, I think my brother hated when I was born because he was the only child for a long time, six years, and then I came along and took the attention away from him."

Sophie nodded. "That makes perfect sense. Rocha thinks he is better than everybody."

"Absolutely. As I was growing up, he ensured everyone thought something was wrong with me. And to be fair, I started acting like something was wrong with me. And perhaps there was something wrong with me. How could there not be when I was surrounded by people who hated me."

"Don't say that. Your father loved you. You've said that often."

"Yes, he did. But he wasn't around all the time. That's why my mother could get away with caning people. Caning me. There was no one to stop her. For me, it was easier to deal with the things happening to me by behaving crazily. It meant that people left me alone. So, I was rebelling, misbehaving, and breaking the rules. If I was going to be punished, I should be punished for a good reason. And I gave her the reasons."

He shook his head.

"One day, Mother tried to cane me. I think I was fourteen then. I snatched the cane from her and flogged her with it. I was mad with rage that day. Enough was enough. She lay on the floor, and people tried to stop me, but I flogged everyone who came near me. Until my father came home that night. He was the one who talked me down. He listened to me, and I gave him the cane. He didn't touch me because he understood my rage. He'd warned my mother previously not to cane me anymore, but she was obviously still doing it in his absence. After that day, she didn't cane me again. I was sent to boarding school because my mother didn't want to see my face after that incident."

"So, how did the chain get under your bed?"

"That came later. One day I'd skipped school on a jolly trip when I met a mob whipping this half-naked woman. The woman wasn't fighting back. She was just walking along while everyone was jeering and taunting her. I guess it reminded me of how people sometimes treated me. I exited the cab and started fighting people, smashing bodies, and everybody scattered."

He laughed.

"Anyway, the taxi driver helped to cover the woman up, and I took her to a hotel where I called my father. He came and picked us up and took us home to the house in the city. That woman was Ma Bagu."

"So, I wasn't the first. I said it. I said you were a hero," she exclaimed, her heart filled with love for him.

"Yeah. I didn't think of myself as a hero. I just saw someone being mistreated for no good reason. I mean, calling someone a witch and claiming she ate her unborn children and killed her husband. How ridiculous is that? That's how some people claimed I was possessed as a child. That is why my mother started caning me. So, I wasn't going to watch someone else suffer a similar fate. Anyway, my mother didn't want Ma Bagu to stay with us. So, I made a deal with her. She could start caning me again when I misbehaved, but she would let Ma Bagu stay."

"You did what?"

"I had no other choice. Mother was going to kick Ma Bagu out. It was the only way I could get her to agree for Ma Bagu to stay. Finally, she agreed but insisted she would install the metal chains in my bedrooms. There's one in the city house, and there's one here. After they were installed, she made the men chain me onto the bed with my shirt off, and she caned me and left me there overnight."

"Oh no!" Sophie wrapped her arms around him and hugged him tight, tears slipping from her eyes. "Your mother is cruel."

"I know. But it was the price I was willing to pay to let Ma Bagu stay. My mother allowed her to live in this house, and my father permitted her to farm on our land. She was also included in his Will. She has a hundred-year lease of the room in this house and the land. So, no one can ever kick her out of this house."

"That's wonderful. But doesn't Ma Bagu have a family?"

"No. We are her family, you and me. She treats me more like a son than my mother does. And I've sworn to take care of her. She had a husband but never had children. The husband's relatives conspired to kill her husband and blamed it on her so they could take his property. It was her husband's brothers. One wanted to sleep with her, and she refused. The other was nasty and didn't want her to have land or property because she had no children. So, they left her a destitute widow and still labelled her a witch to be stripped naked in public."

"Goodness. Why are people so horrible?" she gasped.

"I don't know. But when I investigated and found out the truth, I went to war on her behalf and with her permission."

She leaned back, staring at him. "What did you do?"

He made a cutting motion across his throat with his thumb, and she understood him. "I dispatched them to meet their ancestors and account for their actions."

TWENTY-ONE

"**A**re we doing the right thing?" Sophie asked in a low voice, worry wrinkling her brow and making her fidget with her dress.

She wore the most beautiful dress Mason had seen her in, a teal, strapless, embroidered, lace and satin dress with a fitted bodice and a fully flared skirt. It was designed by Binyerem, whose mother had made some clothes for Sophie a decade ago when they'd first met.

Ma Bagu was friends with Mama Binye and had spoken to the woman yesterday about Sophie needing a wedding dress. The woman had called her son, who worked in the city, and Binyerem had arrived yesterday evening with this outfit.

He'd made it for a client's red-carpet event, but the client hadn't completed the payment and had gone to the event in a different dress. So, he was happy to give it to Sophie instead. Of course, he'd spent the night adjusting it to fit Sophie's fuller figure.

But this morning, when Mason had seen Sophie in the attire, she'd taken his breath away. He'd thought she would wear a skirt suit for the simple event he'd planned. Seeing how gorgeous she looked in the unconventional bridal gown, he wished he had time to organise a larger celebration.

And, of course, Binyerem had insisted on dressing Mason too, fitting a three-piece suit on him.

Still, the most important thing right now was to get this done. To have their union recognised by civil law.

When he'd called Ma Bagu to tell her to prepare for their arrival days ago, Ma Bagu had mentioned that she'd seen a vision of a shadow following Sophie. That the shadow had been hanging around Sophie for years. When he'd asked if the shadow had been there ten years ago when he'd met Sophie, she'd said no. She hadn't seen a shadow that first time. However, the shadow had been around Sophie for many years. She felt the shadow was human, someone who held malice against Sophie.

When Sophie had told him about her family rejecting her, he'd thought the shadow could be them. However, he'd awoken this morning with a sense of foreboding he couldn't shake.

He took Sophie's hand, pulling it gently away from where she fiddled with the embroidery on the skirt.

"Yes, we are," he said sincerely, meeting her gaze and holding it, hoping she understood why everything was being rushed.

They'd had a long talk yesterday. Bringing her back to his hometown was cathartic for both. There had been many unresolved issues that they'd carried for a decade. Just being back in the house and reliving some of it had been helpful for him and, by the sounds of it, for her too.

But there were still matters hanging over them.

One was the legitimacy of their union.

Sure, in terms of the Yadili Brotherhood, every member would recognise his claim on Sophie and their union because it was made in blood and witnessed by other members.

However, outside of the Brotherhood, it had little legitimacy. They were nothing more than common-law partners, which would give Sophie little protection if something happened to him.

He hoped to live a long life with her and their children. He wanted to make a loving family, the family he'd found in Sophie and Ma Bagu.

Still, he was a lawyer. He'd seen too many accounts of women deprived of their rights and properties because their relationships with their partners were disputed or not recognised by family members.

Ma Bagu was a prime example. He didn't want Sophie to suffer what the other woman did. And in Sophie's case, it would be a lot worse because he had no doubt that Rocha and Mother would rip everything away from Sophie if they could.

So, getting their wedding registered as soon as possible was insurance in case something happened to him. He'd already made a will and named Sophie and Ma Bagu his beneficiaries. But he needed iron-clad evidence that he and Sophie were partners, and the only way to do it was through the legal system.

Hence they stood in front of the registrar at the LGA secretariat. The hall was surprisingly full.

Aside from the team of ten men he'd brought from Opal City as security because he knew trouble would find him one way or the other, there were other people here.

Ma Bagu had invited some of her friends, including Mama Binye. Binyerem was here too and had brought a friend who had done Sophie's makeup. Ziga, who'd arrived with them yesterday and Benji, who'd arrived this morning. Benji had brought Chiamaka and another woman, Sophie's colleagues from Haven. There were people from the village.

More people than Mason expected. He wasn't a people person, too obstinate to have many friends. Sure, he had brothers, as defined by the Yadili network and the Odili family.

Top of his hierarchy of trust was Duke.

Duke was the brother he should've had and his childhood friend. When they were younger, Rocha liked to behave like he was sharing his 'friends' with Mason. But Rocha was the same one taunting him and telling his friends to avoid Mason. Just like he would invite girls to party at their house and ask them to 'pity-fuck' Mason because he was crazy and didn't have any friends.

Duke was always there during that period when no one else wanted to hang with Mason. And over time, they'd become best friends. Mason had never needed more than one friend he could trust totally. He wasn't like Rocha, who liked to be the centre of attention and liked having people around him eating off his palm.

Next in his hierarchy of trust came Benji, whom he trusted with his life daily. The man had been part of the family's security team when Mason's father was alive. When Mason took the Yadili oath about ten years ago, he asked Benji to work with him as his second, and the man agreed. It was one of the best decisions he'd ever made because the man hadn't let him down. In Mason's absence, he trusted that the man would protect his interests.

Then there were his close protection team, who he trusted to varying degrees.

There were also his brothers in the Fierce Four.

Maddox, he trusted because they had worked together for years before Maddox moved to Lori Osa to support Duke as Enforcer. Maddox was a no-nonsense guy, and if anything, he disliked Rocha. So, there was a reason to like Maddox.

He stifled a smile as footsteps approached, making him turn.

"Duke!" Sophie said in a loud whisper.

Mason stared in shock as his best friend walked into the small hall with his wife, Carla, holding his hand.

"Duke, what are you doing here?" Mason asked when his friend reached him.

"Really, you're going to ask me that?" His friend pulled him into a shoulder-tap embrace, grinning. "Did you really think you could get married without me by your side?"

"You did," Mason said, reminding him that Duke's first marriage ceremony had been a closed-door affair involving the couple and the Ani priestess.

Duke chuckled. "Maybe you should have tried the same technique because half the brotherhood knows you're getting married."

What the hell.

"Talk about the worst-kept secret in the history of secret-keeping." Mason had to chuckle. He knew that anything involving his family never stayed hidden for too long. His mother had too many spies.

"Exactly. Someone called your mother, who called Chief, complaining, and Chief called me. So here I am."

Mason stiffened. "So, are you here to stop me?"

While he trusted Duke, his best friend was still their godfather's nephew and heir, and his loyalty to the old man was undeniable.

"No. But if you don't get on with it, someone else might. I hear your brother is on his way here. And he is not very happy." Duke turned to the registrar. "I am Duke Odili, Chief Odili's nephew. I want you to speed this up immediately. They need to sign the document in the next ten minutes."

"Yes, sir." Of course, mentioning Chief Odili got the man standing up and getting to business immediately.

Duke stepped back and joined his wife on one of the benches.

Mason turned back to Sophie and smiled as they made their declarations. His heart was whole because everyone who mattered to him was here, witnessing him declare his commitment and devotion to Sophie as she did the same.

He refused to think about what was coming because dread knotted his gut. Instead, he focused on the here and now, on the smile on Sophie's face as she signed on the dotted line.

The rest of it almost turned into a blur as people surrounded them, congratulating them as they took photographs in the halls. Mason held onto Sophie's hand and smiled at the cameras.

Suddenly commotion erupted as they stepped outside the building.

Rocha had arrived and was shouting. "Where is it done? That my younger brother will get married and not invite me. Not invite any member of his family. What nonsense is this!"

Duke broke away from the group and approached his capo. "Rocha, this is not the place to do this. Calm down."

"I should calm down? Me? Kpa rịkwa onwe gị nge àhụ," *Insult yourself there.* Rocha said insolently. "If it is you, will you calm down?" He turned his attention in Mason's direction. "Bia, Mason. Who do you think you are? You think you can get married, not even in the city where you could have gotten away with it. But you had to come back to your father's land and hometown to get married, and you didn't tell your mother who is alive. Who the fuck do you think you are!"

Mason ignored his brother and ushered Sophie towards the vehicle. The security team had formed a barrier between him and his brother, and as long as Rocha didn't get in his face, they would be fine.

Rocha was just ranting his frustrations, which Mason understood to a certain extent.

Mason had snubbed him and Mother by getting wedded without their prior knowledge or invitation to the event. Then again, they had snubbed him by excluding him when his father had been dying. Tit for tat and all that.

"You're ignoring me, o kwa ya?" Rocha continued pacing the forecourt. "Ever since you were born, I've always tried to be a good brother to you. I took care of you, shared my toys, and introduced you to my friends. And what do I get in return? You're constantly undermining me. This time around, you do it for this thing—" Rocha waved at Sophie derisively "—this subhuman. This prostitute."

Sophie's breath hitched, and she stiffened.

"What did you say?" Mason released Sophie's hand as his temper flared. He would accept all the insults in the world directed at him. But when it was directed at Sophie, at someone he loved, he couldn't ignore it.

"Ihe a ị lụrụ o bụ mmadụ?" *This thing you married, is it human?* Rocha taunted.

"Go back into the building," Mason said to Sophie. Next to her were Ziga and Chiamaka. He nodded at Ziga, indicating for the woman to go with Sophie.

He reached for the sheathed knife, pulled it out, and walked towards his brother. "Rocha, you wanted my attention. Now you have it."

"Yes, come on. Let's see if your knife is faster than a bullet." Rocha pulled a gun out of his jacket.

"Stop it!" Duke stepped between the brothers before Mason could reach Rocha.

A gunshot ripped through the air, and pain sliced Mason's left shoulder. He stumbled back.

"Ndị ntọ! Kidnappers!" someone shouted.

Pandemonium broke out as more gunshots ricocheted through the secretariat premises, and guests ran in different directions.

Ignoring the blood dripping down his arm, Mason swivelled towards where Sophie was standing, but she wasn't there. He assumed she'd obeyed his instructions to return to the hall and made eye contact with Benji, indicating where he was headed. Then, keeping low, he ran across the forecourt and entered the reception area. His heart jolted.

Ziga lay on the floor out cold, a metal chair beside her. It seemed someone had surprised her and knocked her out with the chair.

No Sophie or the other woman she'd been with, Chiamaka.

Benji ran in a few seconds later and saw the same thing. "What happened?"

"I don't know. Sophie is missing. She was in here with Ziga," Mason said, hurrying further into the building, looking into every room they passed.

"Do you think someone took her? She didn't go out the front because I would have seen her. The people who fired the shot drove away in an SUV. I sent the boys after them."

"Then search every room in this place. Burn this town down if you have to but find her!" Mason shouted as a weight constricted his chest.

He couldn't lose her. Not now. Not when she was finally his legally.

TWENTY-TWO

I'm married to Mason!

One moment Sophie was buzzing with euphoria as she was surrounded by well-wishers hugging and congratulating them after they said their vows and signed on the dotted line of the marriage certificate.

Mason looked stunningly handsome in the stylish and embroidered three-piece suit that Binyerem had dressed him. He'd wanted to wear one of his black court suits which would have looked like a funeral suit against the beautiful unconventional bridal gown Ma Bagu had gifted her. So, she'd asked Binyerem to find something suitable for the groom to match her outfit. The stylist outdid himself.

She'd been surprised to see many people at the event. Benji had brought Chiamaka, who'd found out about the wedding and had insisted on attending. Sophie didn't mind. Seeing some of her colleagues and friends here was good since her mother and sister were not. She had no regrets about not inviting them. She didn't need their bad energy, just like Mason didn't need his mother's and brother's destructive vibes.

Still, the negative feelings arrived with Rocha, who ranted about being excluded from the wedding ceremony. Duke tried to intervene, but Rocha was having none of it, determined to disrupt the proceedings. Thankfully they'd already signed and received their marriage certificate. Mason and Sophie were legally married, and nothing would separate them.

Except death.

Sophie's heart dropped as the atmosphere, which had been previously joyful, became tense and grim. Dread wrapped its claws into her. This was supposed to be a new beginning with Mason. She didn't want anything terrible to happen to her husband.

Thankfully, Mason ignored his brother's provocations and directed her towards the car park while his security team kept Rocha at bay.

Then, Rocha openly called Sophie a prostitute, and nausea rolled through her as her throat constricted.

Why did the man hate her so much? What did she do to him except reject his advances a decade ago? Chief had adjudicated the quarrel between brothers involving her, and the matter had been settled as far as she was concerned. In the intervening years, she'd worked with him as he was one of Duke's capos, and they occasionally interacted.

Then again, he'd shown similar vitriol for Duke's wife before they married. He'd insisted that Carla be punished when she'd been Duke's hostage and her father's thugs had targeted Odili family businesses. Sophie had been there and had been assigned as Carla's punisher, which Rocha had thoroughly enjoyed watching.

So, this was a Rocha thing. He was determined to undermine other members of the F4 just so he could feel superior and look better to their godfather.

Still, Mason noticed Sophie's discomfort immediately and sent her back into the registrar's office before facing off with his brother.

Her heart raced. She'd known he would go to her defence. It was a matter of his honour as well as hers. His men and other members of the Yadili brotherhood were there to witness Rocha insult his new bride. Something he should never be allowed to get away with.

She tried not to worry and gathered her long skirt in her hands, walking back to the building with Ziga and Chiamaka. This was the life she'd signed up for. She'd married Mason with her eyes wide open, knowing about the tension within his family. Knowing that he would occasionally bloody his knuckles on her account and others.

Still, before the brothers could sort out their differences, a gun battle ensued, and people scattered.

Ziga pushed her through the door immediately, seeking cover, while Sophie turned towards the exit to see if Mason was alright.

Someone in a balaclava stepped out of the corner and whacked Ziga from behind with a metal object, knocking her off balance, and she collapsed.

"Chiamaka, run!" she shouted at her colleague, her heart nearly exploding. Instinct and adrenaline kicking in, she ran further into the building. But she wasn't fast enough because she had to hold her clothes and the heels were too high.

The man caught her in the corridor and shoved her against the wall, hitting her head and giving her a splitting headache that made her dizzy.

"Shut your dirty mouth," his voice was muffled through the mask with only two holes around his eyes. He pointed a gun at her face.

Yeah. Like she would listen to that. She wouldn't keep quiet and let him get away with her. She opened her mouth to scream, but someone else appeared on the other side and stuffed a cloth around her mouth, tying it at the back.

Sophie tried not to panic as she felt claustrophobic and queasy. Instead, she struggled, kicking and clawing. Her vision blurred, but the flash of colourful outfit seemed familiar, and the last thing she felt was a bag over her head as she passed out.

***

Mason was going nuts. The clock was ticking, and Sophie was still missing.

He paced the reception area of the secretariat building as his men roamed the premises, gathering everyone in the vicinity.

Local police had arrived, but Duke was handling them. They milled in the far corner where some had gathered, lending their help with the search. Abductions were rare in this community. So, people were shocked that a jubilant occasion like a wedding ceremony would degenerate into jeopardy for the new bride.

Mason found Ma Bagu in a cluster of her friends. Seeing his injured arm, her worry for him spiked. He'd discarded his jacket, and a tourniquet had been tied around the injury where a bullet had torn through his outer upper arm. Another few inches, and it could have been embedded in his chest or his heart.

He reassured Ma Bagu that he was okay. Not the truth because he wouldn't be okay until he found Sophie alive and well. Still, he asked the older lady to return to the house with her friends. He would contact her as soon as he had an update. The woman was reluctant to leave, but Carla, Duke's wife, intervened and volunteered to go with the older women and stay with them. Binyerem would also go with them.

Mason exhaled in relief when Ma Bagu agreed. He didn't want to worry about her welfare, too, especially in the current fragile and changeable situation. He wasn't sure someone else didn't have a weapon aimed at him. Things could get seriously nasty around here. He couldn't afford to lose Ma Bagu too.

Duke spoke to Jide, his head of security, about sending his crew with the women so that Mason's team could focus on finding Sophie. As they loaded the women into the vehicles, Rocha approached Duke.

"Duke, you don't want to send the women home by themselves," Rocha said. He seemed a lot calmer since the news spread that Sophie was missing. "Let me go with them and make sure they're safe."

"You're not going anywhere," Mason snapped as he swivelled to face his brother. He didn't trust his brother as far as he could throw him.

"What? You can't be serious." Rocha's gaze bounced around as he laughed uncomfortably. But no one else joined in his laughter, everyone watching him. He must've realised most people thought he was involved in the kidnapping. "Guys, I'm trying to help."

"Ha. You, trying to help?" Mason's voice boomed with his rage. "The only person you try to help is yourself. Sophie went missing after you arrived. You know what happened to her."

Rocha laughed. "You see what I mean. You really are crazy. I try to help my brother, and I still get accused." He strutted around the forecourt in his usual showman pose, a smirk on his face. "How exactly did I kidnap her? Is she in my pocket?"

Mason fought the urge to pull out the knife he'd re-sheathed, throw it and embed it into his brother's treacherous heart. Because every instinct in him screamed, Rocha had a hand in Sophie's disappearance. But he had no proof, and killing his brother without proof would only make him seem like the crazy person Rocha had labelled him. Also, he needed to find Sophie before he could dish out retribution.

Still, the necessity to take his smug brother down a peg made his fingers itch. He glanced around the forecourt. The people surrounding him were his and Duke's teams. All Yadili.

He bent down, scooped sand from the ground into his hand, and lifted it in a cupped, opened palm.

"As the earth and the sun bear me witness, as my brothers bear me witness. If anything happens to Sophie, my wife, and she dies because of this incident or any unnatural causes, the first head to roll will be yours, Rocha Maduka."

"What!" Rocha jerked back, his widened gaze darting over the place as if he expected someone to stop Mason.

Instead, the men formed a circle around them because this was a Brotherhood ritual.

Mason ignored his outburst and continued, letting the sand slip off his fingers as he made the oath. He had to beat his brother at his own game. "Likewise, if anything happens to me and I die in an untimely fashion, Rocha, your head will be the next to roll."

The smug smile slipped off Rocha's face, and he looked visibly shaken. Sweat beads appeared on his hairline and his Adam's apple bobbed repeatedly as he swallowed several times. He knew the significance of his brother's oath. Even if Mason could not accomplish the action himself, his team would do it on his behalf. "Are you people listening to this and keeping quiet? This is proof my brother has gone mad. He should be locked up and sectioned. He is threatening to kill me."

"Lock me up. Section me if you think it will help you." Mason said in a cool voice. He had to stay calm. Otherwise, he would give his brother the ammunition he needed. "But if she dies, you are next. The contract is already out, and they know what to do when the time comes."

"Duke, you're here. Are you not going to say anything?" Rocha sounded angry.

Good. If he got angry, perhaps he would reveal something useful.

"What do you want me to say?" Duke sounded annoyed. "When I asked you to stay calm, you insulted me. Now you want me to intervene. The truth is that whether you are innocent or guilty, right now, you look guilty. So, if you truly want to help your brother and save his wife's life, tell him anything you know. If you know nothing, keep out of the way and stop all your nonsense posturing. It's just wasting our time."

Rocha opened his mouth. Duke glared at him, and he shut it.

"Mace, over here!" Benji called out.

Mason hurried to where his second stood with a woman wearing a lanyard. She was one of the civil servants who worked here. There were other workers there too.

"What is it?" Mason asked.

Benji pulled the woman inside the building and said. "I questioned all of them, and she was the most willing to talk." He turned to the woman. "Tell him what you told me."

"I'm Mason Maduka. What's your name?" Mason asked, keeping his voice as calm as possible. He could read her lanyard but wanted to watch her expression and body language to see if she told the truth.

The woman was middle-aged, in her late forties or early fifties. She frowned and lowered her voice.

"My name is Mrs Onyema. I've lived in this community most of my life, and I married a local man, although he works in the city. I knew your father. He was a kind man, and the scholarship he set up for the community, which your family is still funding, is what is helping me send my children to university."

Mason knew about the scholarship. He'd ringfenced the fund and fought Rocha, who wanted to dissolve it and make it smaller so it could go to fewer students rather than the current ten per year that their father had stipulated in his will. Sure, it meant that Mason was practically funding the scholarship. But he was about to get some good karma out of it.

"I'm glad the Alfred Maduka Scholarships Fund is helping your family. But what do you know about my wife's disappearance?"

"I know that I'm not happy about it, cha-cha. This is not the way that newlyweds should start their married life." She glanced behind her and leaned closer. "Yesterday, after you came with your wife to check for objections to the Bann notice, I overheard my direct oga calling someone on the phone. He was talking about you and your wife. From the sound coming from the phone, it sounded like he was speaking to a man. Today again, when you arrived, I think he was speaking to the same man on the phone."

Mason's heart raced. This could be the break they needed. "Where is your boss? Is he outside with the rest?"

"No. I didn't see him after the shooting. I'm sorry, but I think he left when your wife went missing. Maybe he's with the people that took her."

"Where does your boss live?" Benji asked.

"He lived in local government staff quarters close to the expressway. But he has another place where he's building a new house on Old Road just as you head to Iyi Nta. It's on the left and not finished yet. But it is fenced, and the first level has a ceiling, so it's possible that they might keep your wife there if she was kidnapped."

"That's it. Get the men ready to go." Mason met Benji's gaze, who nodded and went outside. He turned back to Mrs Onyema. "Thank you for your help. Do you have somewhere safe you can stay? I'm worried other people may be involved, and they may target you if they know you spoke to us."

"Don't worry about me. I know some of the police officers outside. They will look after me and make sure I get home safely. I just hope you find your wife unharmed."

"Thanks again." He hurried outside and hopped into the vehicle with Benji as the driver.

Duke joined him in the back seat as the car raced out of the premises and headed in the direction the woman described.

"Do you think this is it?" his friend asked.

"I hope so. It's the best information we've had all afternoon." Things had moved fast, and it had been about thirty minutes since the commotion. He hoped they were on the right track.

The car ahead swerved off the main road into an unpaved side road which was little more than a dirt track because there were no houses on it except one which was uncompleted. The one that Mrs Onyema had described. The speeding SUV ahead with the reinforced grill and bull bars smashed through the metal gates, mangling and ripping it open. It crashed into another car that was parked there.

"That's the car used to fire at us this afternoon," Benji said as they drove in behind the first SUV.

"No prisoners," Mason ordered, which was code to kill every enemy combatant.

"Absolutely, Mace," Benji replied and passed the message to the rest of the team via their comms and phones.

Someone ran out of the building and raised a weapon, but Benji hit him with a shot. Gunfire opened around them as Mason's men joined the melee. His men worked in units of two, taking down the bandits and clearing the building one room at a time.

Although he had basic military training, his expertise was in law. Benji and Co were the actual soldiers, and he let them do what they were good at. He didn't want to jeopardise Sophie's life further by going in gung-ho.

Mason and Duke stayed back, working together, sweeping up any leftovers. Thankfully there were no doors to break through. Instead, they followed the trail of blood his men left behind. He counted five dead bandits before someone called out. "In here!"

And before he reached the room with the door, he could hear a woman shouting. His heart filled as he recognised the beautiful sound of his wife's rage. A huge grin broke on his face because it meant one thing.

She was alive, and that was all that mattered.

"Bitch, I helped you. I was good to you, and this is how you repay me?" A heavy slap resounded as Mason stepped through the door.

Sophie slapped an angry Chiamaka and shoved her onto the floor, where two men knelt. One was a middle-aged man and looked oddly familiar. Was that Sophie's former pimp? Bomba? The second he recognised immediately. But he ignored them for now.

"Nkem," Mason spoke the endearment with such feeling at the sight of his enraged wife.

She swivelled as soon as she heard it, eyes widening and filling with tears as she ran into his arms and hugged him tightly. "I knew you would come."

"I will always come for you," he whispered into her hair, then leaned back and kissed her forehead. "I want you to go with Duke—"

A gunshot exploded, and Mason ducked, covering Sophie's body with his. When he looked up, the middle-aged man had collapsed onto the concrete floor with a bullet hole in his head. Chiamaka screamed.

"What the hell did you do?" Duke shouted, shoving Rocha, who stood by the doorway.

"What else? I killed the person who kidnapped Mason's wife. I said I wanted to help," Mason's brother shrugged nonchalantly.

"It wasn't your shot to take. Give me your gun," Duke demanded.

Rocha glared but handed the weapon over before walking away. "Whatever."

"What the fuck!" Mason swore as he met Duke's apologetic gaze.

Now Mason might never know if Rocha was involved in the kidnapping.

TWENTY-THREE

Bomba was dead.

Holding onto Mason's hand, Sophie stared at the prone body with a hole in his head sprawled on the cold concrete floor. The body of her former pimp. The man who claimed her virginity when she was still underage. Who groomed her to become a sex worker when all she'd wanted was to be his woman. The one who stole and withheld her money so he could keep her subjugated and beholden to him.

She didn't feel any remorse or regret at his death. Only anger that he'd dared to disrupt her wedding day. Her life.

She remembered the day she'd seen someone who looked like him in Opal City. The day she'd been in court with Mason, and the case against her was dismissed. She'd seen him outside the restaurant.

It turned out to be Bomba. He'd been there. He'd been at the court premises too.

Because he'd been the reason she was in court in the first place. Bomba and Chiamaka.

She clenched her jaw as her anger returned, glaring at the woman kneeling and sniffling on the floor.

She remembered when the girl had come to her a couple of years ago, asking for work and a place to stay. She'd said she was a student at the state university but was struggling to pay for tuition fees because she didn't have a family.

Sophie had listened to her sob story and had taken her in, giving her accommodation in Haven. Over time, Chiamaka worked well, and the comments from clients were positive. However, lately, the feedback from the other girls about her became negative. They said Chiamaka undermined them just to boost her own profile with the clients. At first, Sophie thought Chiamaka was being competitive against the cooperation Sophie advocated for amongst the hookers. However, she noticed something more sinister was at play when she saw how Chiamaka had run Haven, resulting in the warrant out for Sophie's arrest.

Now Sophie realised Chiamaka had conspired with Bomba to undermine Haven and get Sophie arrested and locked up. When that failed due to Mason's intervention, they resorted to kidnapping as their last resort.

When they'd grabbed her, she'd passed out briefly because someone had stuffed a cloth in her mouth and covered her head. She'd felt claustrophobic and dizzy and had woken in this room when they'd dumped her on the cold floor.

She'd looked up at the people standing over her—Bomba, Chiamaka and Osei.

They'd recruited Osemeka Godfrey as their accomplice. The man would have abducted her the other night if she'd gone to his bedroom as he'd wanted. She should have allowed Mason to slit his throat that night in the lounge.

She'd fumed as all the pieces clicked into place, and she cursed them all.

Before they could even settle into anything, a loud crash made everyone duck for cover. Then the gunfight started, and she knew Mason was here.

"You are all dead!" Sophie shouted. "Mason is going to kill you all."

"Shut up," Bomba snapped and sent men out to check things out while he stayed with Osei and Chiamaka here with Sophie. They barricaded the door. Chiamaka stared daggers at her.

Sophie just laughed. "How foolish are you? You thought you could go against me, go against Mason and survive? I hope you have an army out there because Mason brought an army. All of you are Dead Men Walking. Mtcheew."

Chiamaka blocked her ears and cowered in the corner as the gunshots drew closer.

"If you don't shut up, I'm going to kill you, o." Bomba waved his weapon at her.

She hissed and chuckled some more. But she didn't speak again. She'd already figured out he only had one handgun with limited bullets.

Mason's men had brought ammunition boxes for semi-automatic weapons to his hometown. She wasn't joking when she'd said he had an army. It was as if he'd foreseen something like this happening.

A scuffing sound drew their attention, and Bomba started firing at the door, putting holes in it. They all held their breaths when he stopped, and an eerie silence descended. Suddenly the door smashed in. Bomba clicked his weapon, but nothing happened. The cartridge was empty.

"Hands up, or you die!" Two men with weapons walked in.

Sophie raised her hands as she recognised Benji with another of Mason's team, and relief flooded her. The men disarmed Bomba and tied him up along with Osemeka.

Angry, Sophie jumped up and grabbed Chiamaka by the hair. She cursed and slapped and shoved her.

Then she heard Mason's voice, and she swivelled so fast she almost made herself dizzy.

Her husband stepped into the room. He was alive and well, except for the bandage on his arm.

She'd never been so happy to see someone in her life. Emotions clogged her throat, and tears clouded her eyes as she ran into his open arms. He embraced her tightly.

She sucked in a deep breath inhaling the scent of him. It couldn't have been that long since she saw him, but she'd missed him.

Then there was a loud bang. Mason pushed her down, covering her body with his to protect her in a crouch. A few seconds later, she looked up.

Bomba was dead, shot by Rocha.

Good riddance as far as she was concerned.

But Mason didn't seem happy about it. Instead, his rage vibrated through him as he held her.

She reached up and cupped his hairy chin. "Eleniyan, do what you must do. Let the world know that we are not to be crossed."

A precedent needed to be set. This was them. Cross them and pay with your blood.

It would deter anyone who thought they could chance it.

Mason nodded. "Do you want to stay?"

"Yes," she said. "They conspired to ruin my life. To ruin our lives. To take me away from you. On our wedding day. I want to see them pay for their actions in blood."

She didn't particularly want to see blood, but she had to stay because this was about her. About Mason. About them. They had to be united in the decision. His men had to see she wasn't afraid.

He kissed her forehead again and stepped away, swivelling to face the two accomplices.

"Mr Godfrey, I warned you that if I saw you again, you would lose more than your fingers." He holstered his handgun and reached for the sheathed blade, pulling it out.

Chiamaka gasped, and Osei shifted.

Sophie smiled. That knife inspired terror like no other weapon she'd seen anyone else wield. The jagged edge looked like it would badly mess up someone's insides.

"You—you said I—I shouldn't go to Maximo. I—I haven't been there." The man stammered.

"You really are a mumu." Mason sneered, and he said to the man behind Osei. "Yank him up."

The bodyguard obeyed, pulling Osei to his feet.

Mason stepped closer to him, knife in his hand to the side. "So, what was the plan the night you came to the hotel and tried to seduce my wife? You were planning to kidnap her that night, right?"

"It—It was Bomba's plan. Not me. I was just helping him because he was my friend."

"Well, you can join your friend in Hell."

Mason sank the blade into Osei's belly, and both hands held the knife as he yanked upwards.

Fighting her gag reflexes, Sophie looked away as Osei grunted. She could imagine the knife splitting the man's chest in two.

Mason stepped back, and the man collapsed in a heap. His death would be agonisingly painful and slow.

"Sophie, please. I'm sorry. It was the devil," Chiamaka started crying, shuffling away as Mason approached her.

"Then go and meet him wherever he is," Sophie said.

Mason glanced at her, and she nodded. He stepped behind Chiamaka, grabbed her by the head as she froze and drove the knife across her neck, severing the jugular veins and carotid arteries. He let her go as blood spurted out. Then he came towards Sophie. His hands were covered in blood, and some splashed on the waistcoat.

She unbuttoned the waistcoat, and he shrugged it off. He used it to wipe his hands and the blade. "Burn this place down."

Benji gave the instructions as Mason and Sophie headed out. The men standing outside cheered and clapped when Sophie exited the building with Mason.

She smiled, almost getting teary because she knew most of these people. She hadn't known they had this respect for her. For Mason.

She got into the backseat with Mason, and Duke sat in front with the driver. Benji stayed back with the clean-up crew. As they left, the house was already on fire.

Osei was really a mumu. Not only did he lose his life, but if he had a family, they wouldn't benefit from the house he'd started building.

It didn't take long to arrive at the Maduka residence. The old women sang and danced as soon as they arrived, celebrating their well-being and safe return. Ma Bagu gave them the tightest of hugs. Everyone seemed pleased to see them. Even Rocha was mellow when he appeared briefly and disappeared again.

The locals stayed under the canopy, partied and ate while Sophie and Mason went upstairs to their self-contained suite with their closest friends—Duke, Carla, Benji and Ziga, who sported a bandage around her head.

While their friends sat in the lounge, the newlyweds went into the bedroom to clean up and change their clothes. Afterwards, they joined them in the living room. They laughed and chatted, ate and drank. The mood had lifted, and everyone was merry.

Suddenly the music from the loudspeakers downstairs stopped. At first, Sophie thought the locals wanted to return to their beds because of the late hour.

However, Jide walked into the living room and whispered something to Mason, who sat beside her. He stiffened.

"What is it?" she asked, sitting up.

He scrubbed a hand over his face. "I've been summoned to face the masquerade."

"What?" Duke sat up, too, as the other men stiffened, the mood changing.

"What does that mean?" Sophie asked as a cold finger travelled down her spine.

"It means that I've been accused of violating Brotherhood laws, and I have to answer for my crimes," Mason replied, looking worried. "The masquerade is the spirit enforcer. The Brotherhood enforcer."

"Is this because of me? Because you married me instead of Zoe Himba?"

"No. How can following my heart be a crime?"

"Then it must be because of the people you killed today."

Mason shook his head. "There is no man here who wouldn't have done what I did today."

"That's true," Duke said, reaching for his wife's hand. "Those people deserved what happened to them. Listen, Sophie. Don't worry about this. I'm going to be there with Mason."

"You're going?" Carla sounded shocked.

"I must go with him. I can't let him face the masquerade alone."

"Neither can I." Benji stood. "This is Brotherhood matter. Whoever accused Mace accused him falsely, and we'll be there to undergo the trial with him."

"Oh God," Sophie muttered as her hands shook.

"Don't be afraid." Mason reached for her, cupped her cheeks and kissed her deeply.

He stood and left with the other men.

Carla and Ziga stayed with her. Ma Bagu joined her for a while, reassuring her that Mason had done nothing wrong and that he would be okay. The women tried to find ways to distract her.

Sophie still couldn't relax. She paced and fidgeted and worried.

Seconds turned to minutes, and minutes turned to hours.

Everyone crashed. She shared the bed with Carla while Ziga slept on the sofa.

Sophie had a fitful sleep. When she sat up in bed, daylight was coming through the window. She felt queasy and ran to the bathroom to throw up into the WC bowl.

"Are you okay?"

Sophie straightened when she heard Carla's soft voice and went over to the sink to brush her teeth.

"I think so." And then a thought occurred to her. "Oh, my God. I think I'm pregnant!"

She held her tummy as excitement raced through her.

"You think?" Carla came closer.

"Yes, I think. I know. I need a pregnancy test kit. But I can't go out. I have to wait for Mason." She'd missed her period by a few weeks, and nausea had been happening for a few days. She was confident a baby grew inside her.

"I'll go and get one for you."

"Are you sure? You're waiting for Duke too."

"Yes, but you went missing yesterday. I don't think anyone will be happy if you went out today." Carla smiled.

"That's true." Sophie chuckled. She was right. If she wasn't here when Mason came home, she would be punished. She still had the mark from the last punishment on her shoulder.

"Can I use the shower? I have my overnight bag, so I can change." Carla left the bathroom.

"Sure." Sophie finished brushing her teeth and found some towels for Carla to use when she returned to the bathroom.

Sophie went into the living room and found Ziga awake and dressed.

"Mrs Maduka is back," Ziga said.

"When? This morning?"

"No. Late last night. I didn't want to tell you last night because you were wound up already. I didn't want to add to your stress."

"Thank you. I better go and greet her. Is she still in bed?"

"No. She is having breakfast right now in the dining room."

"She's eating? How is she keeping food down when her sons haven't been home since last night?" She'd found out that Rocha had gone with the other men to the midnight meeting. "That woman get liver."

"I swear, I fear am," Ziga said.

Sophie shook her head and headed downstairs to see Mason's mother, Ziga right behind her.

True enough, the woman sat in the dining room eating her breakfast like she had no worries in the world. There were dishes of food spread on the table.

Sophie's anger rose as she sashayed into the dining room. How dare this woman eat like a fucking queen when Sophie didn't know if Mason was still alive.

"Good morning, Mother," She greeted in the sarcastic tone Mason used sometimes.

"Who is your mother? Kitikpa racha gị onu nge ahụ!" the woman swore at her.

Sophie smiled and pulled out a chair, happy she'd riled Mrs Maduka, who wasn't as unfeeling or composed as she projected.

"Did I say you could sit down?" The woman glared at her.

"Why not? I want to join you. Since you think it's a good idea to sit and eat like a pig while your children have been summoned to the masquerade."

"E—hee." The woman dropped her cutlery. "It seems you didn't learn your lesson the last time. You came back for more."

"More of what? Of you having your boys chain me so you can whip me." She turned her shoulder so the woman could see her son's initials branded into her skin. This time the seal was a waterproof spray leaving the mark visible to everyone when she wore tiny straps or off-shoulder sleeves like this dress.

"Have you met your son, Mason? You know what he can do. Try any nonsense, and you will meet an early grave."

"Are you threatening me? Have you gone mad?" The woman pushed her chair back, standing up.

"Yes, I decided to join you in the madness since you think you are the only one who can be mad." Sophie swept the plates off the table. Glass and food smashed onto the marble floor. "You're sitting here, eating while my husband is who knows where. He could be injured. He could be dead. He is your son, for goodness' sake. Don't you care?"

"Of course, I care about my sons. But Mason defied his godfather. He chose to marry you. He must face the consequences of his actions."

"So, you pestered Chief into punishing him, and he sent the masquerade after Mason. What if Mason dies? Is that how far you're willing to go?"

The woman said nothing, giving her a hard stare.

Sophie swallowed and shook her head. "You know I was willing to give you the benefit of the doubt. I was willing to forgive what you did to me ten years ago. I thought you were just a mother trying to protect her sons. But I've since found out that you are something else. What you've done to Mason is pure wickedness. And for that, I cannot forgive you. So, if you want fire, you will get fire. I will match the energy you give and raise it. And let me tell you something, if my husband dies because of your nonsense, I will come for you. I swear—"

A sound behind her made her turn.

Mason stood at the door. He was dirty and bloody, but he was alive. His eyes were intense and fixed on her. Was he angry at her for threatening his mother?

"Mason, did you hear what your wife said? Did you hear her threaten me!" his mother screeched.

"Yes, I did, Mother. And I love her for it." He swaggered into the room, his gaze never leaving Sophie's as her heart raced.

"What? You must punish her. You can't let her get away with it. Do something!"

"I will. I'm about to fuck my wife. So, get out!" he ordered.

His mother jerked in shock and hurried out of the room.

"I love you," he said again, and her heart filled with joy.

"I love you too." She reached up for his shoulders.

Then he was cupping her face, and they were kissing passionately, frenzied. His hands slipped into her dress, pinching her nipples, making them taut as electricity sizzled through her nerve endings. She clutched his shoulders and moaned his name.

She didn't care who heard, didn't care that he was caked in mud. Only cared that he'd come home alive and well. That he'd survived the trial by masquerade.

No one could point an accusing finger at him any longer. Not his brother. Not Chief Odili. He'd fulfilled all righteousness.

And he was hers. He loved her. Just like she loved him.

He showed her by the way he loved her body, lowering his head to bite her nipples when he pulled down the dress. Then going even further and burying his face between her legs, finding her slippery and warm. He sucked her clit and prodded her opening with his tongue, sending her flying into heaven in no time. Then he spread her on the dining table, on a bed of silk and satin. His hardness slammed into her repeatedly until they were both sated and panting for breath.

"We're having a baby," she said afterwards as he rested his head on her chest, and she stroked her fingers over his face.

He jerked upright, a smile spreading on his face. "We are?"

"Yes. I missed my period. Carla is going to buy a test kit for me."

"Wow." Then he paused. "But you've seen my family history and what I have as parents. That's not what I want for my children. So, honestly, do you want to be a parent?"

"Of course, I want to be a parent with all my heart. I want to be a parent with you. I want to love our baby, our children, with the same love I have for you. So, one hundred percent yes."

"I love you so much," he pulled her into his arms and kissed her again.

And she knew they would be fantastic parents and formidable partners for life.

Thank you for reading the Rough Diamond duology. If you enjoyed this story, please rate it on the site of purchase and leave a brief review if you can.

Mason, Sophie, and the rest of the Odili clan will return in the next Yadili Series book, Tough Alliance. kirutaye.com/yadili-series

Want more? Scan the QR code to receive bonus content.

For news about upcoming books in the Yadili series, sign up to receive Kiru's Newsletter on the website: www.kirutaye.com

YADILI SERIES

<u>Duke: Prince of Hearts</u>
<u>Xandra: Killer of Kings</u>
<u>Osagie: Bad Santa</u>
<u>Rough Diamond</u>
<u>Tough Alliance</u>
Honour in <u>Love and the Lawless</u> **anthology**